Why America's Top
Pundits Are Wrong

CALIFORNIA SERIES IN PUBLIC ANTHROPOLOGY

The California Series in Public Anthropology emphasizes the anthropologist's role as an engaged intellectual. It continues anthropology's commitment to being an ethnographic witness, to describing, in human terms, how life is lived beyond the borders of many readers' experiences. But it also adds a commitment, through ethnography, to reframing the terms of public debate—transforming received, accepted understandings of social issues with new insights, new framings.

Series Editor: Robert Borofsky (Hawaii Pacific University)

Contributing Editors: Philippe Bourgois (UC San Francisco), Paul Farmer (Partners in Health), Rayna Rapp (New York University), and Nancy Scheper-Hughes (UC Berkeley)

University of California Press Editor: Naomi Schneider

Why America's Top Pundits Are Wrong

ANTHROPOLOGISTS TALK BACK

EDITED BY
CATHERINE BESTEMAN AND
HUGH GUSTERSON

UNIVERSITY OF CALIFORNIA PRESS
Berkeley   Los Angeles   London

University of California Press
Berkeley and Los Angeles, California

University of California Press, Ltd.
London, England

Library of Congress Cataloging-in-Publication Data

Why America's top pundits are wrong : anthropologists talk back /
edited by Catherine Besteman and Hugh Gusterson.
    p.   cm.—(California series in public anthropology ; 13)
  Includes bibliographical references and index.
  ISBN 978-0-520-24356-9 (pbk. : alk. paper)
    1. Mass media and anthropology.   2. Communication and society.
3. Communication in anthropology.   4. Communication—Political
aspects.   5. Specialists.   4. Errors, Popular.   I. Besteman, Catherine
Lowe.   II. Gusterson, Hugh.   III. Series.

P96.A56W49   2005
302.23—dc22   2004014201

Manufactured in the United States of America

15   14   13   12   11   10   09   08   07
11   10   9 8 7 6 5 4 3 2

To Franz Boas and Margaret Mead,
pioneers of public anthropology

Contents

ONE Introduction

Hugh Gusterson and Catherine Besteman

This book confronts some of the most controversial and divisive issues of the day. Why does poverty persist in the United States? Do the poor, through laziness or lack of initiative, somehow deserve their plight? Why do African Americans continue to get left behind in the American race for success? Are feminists right about violence against women in our society? How much of our behavior is genetically programmed? Why do some countries do better than others in the global economy? Why has the U.S. military found itself fighting Muslims so much of late? Will globalization and U.S. intervention abroad create a more peaceful or a more polarized world? Should the United States have intervened in the former Yugoslavia in the 1990s, or is that part of the world doomed to bloody and irremediable ancient hatreds?

In Congress, in coffee shops, in classrooms, in dorm rooms, on talk shows, and over the dinner table, these have been some of the most debated questions in American public life in recent years. Some of these questions—about race, gender, and class—are hardy perennials of American disputation; others, such as those about globalization and the apparent conflict with Islam, are particular to our times. In our national debate about such questions, some of the loudest voices belong to pundits: men (and, yes, they do almost all seem to be men) such as Thomas Friedman of the *New York Times,* Robert Kaplan of the *Atlantic Monthly,* Samuel Huntington of Harvard University, and Dinesh D'Souza of Stanford University's Hoover Institute. Some of these pundits are based in universities, others are not, but they share an ability to reduce controversial issues to sound bites and, consequently, to harness the full power of the media to project their opinions. Some are self-identified liberals, while others are conservatives; some focus their attention on international relations, while others write about domestic politics within the United States. Although they do not all come from the same side of the political map, they draw on and embellish a loosely coherent set of myths about human nature and culture that have a strange staying power in American public discourse: that conflict between people of different cultures, races, or genders is inevitable; that biology is destiny; that culture is immutable; that terrible poverty, inequality, and suffering are natural; and that people in other societies who do not want to live just like Americans are afraid of "modernity." We have put together a book subjecting these pundits to cold, hard scrutiny because of our concern that, while their voices are often the loudest, they are not necessarily the wisest. Although they may be glibly persuasive writers with strong points of view, their writing is also dangerously simplistic and ideologically distorted.

Pundit comes from the old Hindi word *pandit,* used to refer to a teacher of Indian religion and law.[1] The *Oxford English Dictionary* defines a pundit as "an authority on a subject." *Merriam-Webster's* gives two definitions. The first—"a learned man; teacher"—echoes the *Oxford English Dictionary.* The second—"one who gives opinions in an authoritative manner"—is more to the point here. The pundits we discuss here are not particularly learned and are only superficially authorities on the subjects about which they write. Their skill lies not in detailed knowledge about their subject but in their ability, in an age of mass media and short attention spans, to learn quickly about the broad contours of a wide range of subjects and to project confidence and authority in talking about them. Indeed, their skill often lies not in authoritative knowledge of their subject but in their ability to hide their lack of authoritative knowledge. Pundits are people who, like the *New York Times* columnist Thomas Friedman, speak to a general audience rather than to specialists, often on many different issues. To win and keep a wide audience, they have to hurl out bold ideas, make big generalizations, and speak colorfully. While they are expected to pepper their arguments with facts and information, they know that their audiences will not—and usually cannot— judge them on their detailed knowledge of the subject at hand and will, instead, judge them on their ability to appear knowledgeable and be entertaining. This means that the pundits who thrive the most are those who cater to their audiences' existing prejudices, rather than those who upend their easy assumptions about the world and challenge them to see the world from a new angle. As the cultural critic Edward Said puts it, in reference to the appeal of Samuel Huntington's *Clash of Civilizations,* one of the works we discuss in this book, "What has made it strike so responsive a chord among post–cold war policy makers, is this sense of cutting through large amounts of unnecessary detail, of masses of scholarship and huge amounts of experience, and boiling all of them down to a couple of catchy, easy-to-quote-and-remember ideas, which are then passed off as pragmatic, practical, sensible, and clear."[2]

Pundits, then, are modern-day mythmakers. All societies have mythmakers—people who provide a comforting explanation of why things are the way they are. Mythmakers provide a way to make sense of complexity, to reconcile contradictory realities, and to justify a particular course of action or worldview. They help a society imagine itself and its role in the world. Mythmakers in "primitive" societies explained why children died, why crops failed, and why chiefs were chiefs and the rest were not. They found design and purpose in pain and suffering. Mythmakers in contemporary America provide just-so stories to explain, for example, why many foreigners are angry at the United States, why the poor are poor, and why racial inequality persists.

The pundits we review here are American mythmakers with authority.[3] They have captured our attention because of their book sales, their high profiles in public discourse, and their ability to influence the highest policy makers in the land. They are not the most extreme of America's contemporary commentators—the Ann Coulters and Bill O'Reillys. Rather, they hold positions at famous universities, publish in mainstream news magazines and newspapers, and are read by American presidents. While they successfully present themselves as globally knowledgeable and reasonable commentators, the myths they promote exert a reactionary force in public life. Often based on stereotypes of other people, these myths hobble our ability to think critically or to empathize with different kinds of people, and they have the effect of legitimating the status quo. They are also based on wrongheaded assumptions about human nature that we are determined to debunk.

All the contributors to this volume are distinguished and experienced anthropologists who can no longer watch America's pundits at work without speaking up. As anthropologists, we specialize in studying human nature, cultural interaction, ethnic conflict, social stratification, and the workings of race and gender—all the issues the pundits write about. In the following chapters we demonstrate over and over that the myths of the punditocracy, whether overtly liberal or conservative, are based on loudly voiced rhetorical and not scientific claims, and on the cultural assumptions of the privileged. Uncorrected, their assumptions about human nature and culture are not just wrong but also, given the pundits' influence in American public life, dangerous. Although most of the contributors to this book are to the left of political center, we do not have a shared political agenda. We are less concerned with speaking as exponents of a particular political philosophy than as anthropologists. We see America's pundits, in turn, not as sectarian partisans but as joint contributors to a set of "myths we live by." Anthropology's traditional charge is to understand myths as charters for worldviews and ways of life. We evaluate myths that societies tell about themselves and others, and we try to understand where these stories came from, why they endure, and most important for our purposes here, how they might be dangerous. After all, some myths justify unnecessary human suffering while breeding fear, xenophobia, and ignorance about other ways of life.

As anthropologists who have all done fieldwork, we get our knowledge by deeply engaged, intense, face-to-face research, often in settings where disease and violence pose a real threat. Along with reading all the learned books and professional journals related to our subjects, we spend years in local communities, listening, observing, interviewing. Wanting all sides of the story, we talk with everyone from government officials and executives to peasants, activists, workers, and criminals. We are experts in the history, the politics, and the economics of the places we study, but we also understand these places in terms of the human interactions we have had with the people who live there. Significantly, our methodology encourages in-depth relationships with people generally ignored by pundits—those on the margins of society, rather than just the elite. Anthropology has a historical commitment to take seriously the perspectives of non-Western societies and non-elites. Such perspectives are front and center in our analyses, and they undergird anthropology's distinctive view of the world. Ours is the discipline whose best-sellers include the biography of a !Kung bushwoman in South Africa and the story of Ishi, "the last of his tribe" of Native Americans.[4] Now, in the era of globalization and cyberspace, we are reporting on conversations with war refugees in the Congo, Islamic militants in the slums of Egypt, illegal immigrants who clean your local Wal-Mart and can barely make the rent, and young women who lose their eyesight assembling computers in sweatshops in Malaysia and the Philippines. We bring into the global conversation the voices that would otherwise be lost. Good anthropology, like good literature, challenges readers to see the world from inside someone else's skin and to rethink taken-for-granted assumptions.

The arguments we challenge here were published in articles and books that received widespread media attention in the 1990s, but our decision to write this book took on particular force with the renewed power and prominence of these writings following the September 11, 2001, tragedy and the American invasion of Iraq. The need to define the contours of the post–cold war world has taken on a new urgency for Americans reeling from the shock of a devastating terrorist attack on American soil and mired in the chaos of a post-Saddam Iraq. When we discovered that books by some of the pundits we target—Robert Kaplan, Samuel Huntington, and Thomas Friedman—were being promoted by a major national bookstore chain as useful roadmaps to our global reality in the era of the war on terrorism, we realized that our task—to draw on our anthropological knowledge to tell more accurate stories about the post–cold war world—was more important than ever. There was a time before the Vietnam War when anthropologists were themselves pundits playing a vital role in public debate. Franz Boas, the founder of modern American anthropology, championed Native Americans and was an outspoken public critic of eugenics and of racially biased intelligence testing in the early twentieth century. Margaret Mead, the most famous anthropologist of the twentieth century, used knowledge she gained from her research on adolescence and gender among Pacific Islanders to intervene in public debates about American sex roles and education. With less happy consequences, Margaret Mead also intervened in public policy debates about American foreign policy, including the Vietnam War. The debates of the Vietnam era, which left the American Anthropological Association deeply divided over the ethics of military research and over the propriety of the Vietnam War itself, scarred anthropology and left many anthropologists feeling that it was safer to avoid participation in national policy debates. We came together to write this book out of the conviction that it is time for anthropologists to reclaim Margaret Mead's legacy and find our voice as public intellectuals once more.

THE PUNDITS LOOK ABROAD

Let's begin with Robert Kaplan. Described by the *New York Times* as combining "the attributes of the journalist and the visionary,"[5] he is the author of the influential books *Balkan Ghosts* and *The Coming Anarchy.* *Balkan Ghosts* was published in 1993 just as the former Yugoslavia was beginning to come apart at the seams and the newly elected U.S. president, Bill Clinton, was deciding whether or not to reverse the policy, inherited from his predecessor, of nonintervention in the Bosnian conflict. In *Balkan Ghosts* Kaplan sketched a picture of the Balkans as a region

doomed to perpetual strife because of ancient feuds and grievances dat-
ing back to the Middle Ages that set Orthodox, Catholic, and Muslim citizens at each others' throats. Although Kaplan was not an expert in
Balkan history or culture, the commonsense appeal of his "ancient
hatreds" argument combined with a muscular and vivid writing style
won his book a wide audience at a time when newspaper and television
screens were full of searing images of atrocities from the Bosnian war. Bill
Clinton read the book during his first term as president, and it is said that
Kaplan helped persuade him for a long time that people in this corner of
the world had always hated one another and probably always would,
and that the United States should stay out of their conflicts. *Balkan Ghosts*
is a discomfiting reminder of the terrible damage that can be done by an
author with a persuasive writing style and a good publicist, even if the
account is largely a mishmash of myth, superficial impressions, and recy-
cled stereotypes.

In the present volume, Tone Bringa sets the record straight on Bosnia.
Unlike Kaplan, Bringa did not simply pass through the Balkans between
book tours. Bringa is an anthropologist who won her knowledge the hard
way—by living in a Bosnian village before and during the Yugoslav wars
of the 1990s, getting to know its Bosnian Muslim and Croat Catholic
inhabitants intimately. She was there when the villagers turned on one
another. While Kaplan would have us believe that people in this part of
the world were just itching for a chance to revisit old grievances, Bringa
points out that, until the ethnic cleansing of the 1990s, Muslim and
Catholic villagers had strong neighborly friendships. These interethnic
friendships had been the rule rather than the exception in this part of the
world and were blown apart only under the pressure of a war begun by
Serb separatists in Belgrade. Far from being eager to attack one another,
villagers finally turned against one another only after hard work by
nationalist politicians. Bringa suggests that Kaplan's question—can these
people ever be expected to get over their differences?—is the wrong
question to ask. The right question, and the question Bringa addresses, is,
How were people who had lived quietly together as neighbors for forty-
five years manipulated into killing one another and burning each other's
houses down?

Kaplan's subsequent book, *The Coming Anarchy,* was no less influential and, unfortunately, no less misguided. The book was preceded by an *Atlantic Monthly* article of the same name that was, remarkably, faxed by the U.S. State Department to every U.S. embassy in Africa. In it, Kaplan argues that the world is increasingly divided between the orderly, affluent societies of the West and anarchic, crime-ridden, overpopulated Third World societies headed for environmental degradation, outbreaks of disease, downward spirals of poverty, and civil strife. He likens the citizens of the West to passengers in a stretch limo, saying, "Outside the stretch limo would be a rundown, crowded planet of skinhead Cossacks and juju warriors, influenced by the worst refuse of Western pop culture and ancient tribal hatreds, and battling over scraps of overused earth."[6] Warning about "places where the Enlightenment has not penetrated," and predicting that "distinctions between war and crime will break down,"[7] he fears that globalization will make it harder and harder for the people in the stretch limo to avoid "the coming anarchy." Telling us that democracy is culturally unnatural in many parts of the globe, and that some cultures are too weak or pathological to cope with the stresses of globalization, he predicts that anarchic waves of crime and violence will wash across various regions of the globe, particularly Africa.

In chapter 5 below, Catherine Besteman takes issue with this dystopic vision of the present and the future. An anthropologist who has worked in Africa for many years, particularly in Somalia and South Africa, Besteman points out that the impression Kaplan gives of the African continent as an imploding zone of chaos and crime is empirically selective— that while Africans may be poor, in many parts of the continent their societies are peaceful and orderly. Echoing Bringa on the Balkans, she excoriates Kaplan for his attribution of "ancient tribal hatreds" to Africans, pointing out that colonial powers in Africa practiced a form of divide and rule that created and exacerbated tribal identifications, and that these "hatreds," far from being "ancient," are recent inventions. She also points out that, while Kaplan gives the impression that Third World societies are being eaten away by their own internal weaknesses (tribal hatreds, a congenital inability to create strong states, and an inability to control population), they are actually being undermined and deformed by exploitive relationships with the West. Western nations have made them a source of cheap raw materials and underpaid labor, and agencies such as the International Monetary Fund (IMF) have forced them to cut social programs in order to demonstrate fiscal discipline. It is not that their unique cultural weaknesses are creating a wave of anarchy that may spread like a tidal wave from the Third World and drown us all, but that our relationships with them are generating suffering and exploitation that may blow back on us in the West.

The deformities in Kaplan's writing are, sadly, not unique to him. They form part of a broader pattern of distorted vision on the part of contemporary commentators that lends a coherence to the work of the pundits discussed in this book—even though they address quite disparate topics and would not see themselves as a unified group. Look at some of Kaplan's major themes—the inertia of ancient cultures and conflicts, the alleged inability of much of the Third World to deal with modernity, and the innocence of elites in the suffering of others—and you will find ideas that recur in different forms in the work of all the pundits we discuss in this book, like viruses that keep mutating and coming back. Thus, for example, if Kaplan presents human beings as captives of timeless, frozen cultural imperatives, a similar assumption mars Thomas Friedman's writing on "olive tree" cultures that cannot deal with modernity, Samuel Huntington's work on a supposedly predetermined "clash of civilizations," and Thornhill and Palmer's argument that contemporary men are compelled by ancient evolutionary imperatives to behave like sexual cavemen. In Kaplan's writing about the Balkans and about a rising tide of violence in the Third World, we see a penchant for blaming the victims. Similarly, Dinesh D'Souza blames poverty on the indolence and incapacity of the poor, Herrnstein and Murray say that intellectual inadequacy has held back African Americans, and Thornhill and Palmer tell us that women who do not want to be raped should not wear short skirts.

These are more than superficial resemblances. The pundits discussed here were all writing at a moment in time—on the brow of the new millennium—when the social and intellectual order of the late twentieth century, both at home and abroad, was suddenly up for grabs following the end of the cold war. This was a moment characterized in the international system by an intensification of globalization and civil conflict and, within the United States, by fierce debate about the domestic legacies of the 1960s, especially the civil rights and women's movements. At a moment when progressives, responding to the end of the cold war and the election of a democratic president and Congress, hoped that the 1990s would see a substantial demilitarization of global society, greater equality within and between societies, and further progress in civil and human rights, the pundits discussed in this book argued against them on many fronts. They argued that the world after the cold war was destined to be a violent one full of new threats to the West; they attacked the naïveté of those who argued for democratic forms of globalization that would ameliorate social conflict and inequality; and they disputed insights from the 1960s that the plight of women, the poor, and people of color was the product of an entire social system—a system that could be changed. Taken together, in other words, the pundits we discuss here have been engaged in a collective assault on the legacies of the Great Society era in American history. In the works discussed here, they are attempting to replace an established recognition—that we are all connected and that it is within our power to collectively change and improve our world—with a sort of neo-Darwinist ideology reminiscent of the ugly and mean-spirited ideas ascendant in the period of high capitalism and colonialism at the turn of the nineteenth century. The new social Darwinists preach the inescapability of conflict and competition, the unreformability of those who are not like "us," and the responsibility of the poor, the weak, and the oppressed for their own suffering. In writings on international affairs, expressions of this ideology range from Friedman's strident neoliberalism to Huntington's smug cultural separatism; in discussions of domestic politics, we see a revivification of old Dickensian ideas that everyone gets what they deserve.

These arguments offend us not only because of the callous politics that underlie them but also because they are sustained through a willful ignorance of a huge swathe of human experience and academic knowledge that we, as professional anthropologists, claim as our professional domain. For example D'Souza's arguments about the poor, Herrnstein and Murray's arguments about the low intelligence of African Americans, and Thornhill and Palmer's arguments about an alleged male propensity for rape fly in the face of decades of painstaking research by social scientists. Similarly, the assumptions about frozen traditions, conflicts, and cultures that one finds in the work of Friedman, Kaplan, and Huntington are premised on a stunning ignorance of the professional literature on culture and tradition — a literature that emphasizes the fluidity and malleability of culture and argues that ethnic conflict in such places as Rwanda and Bosnia has been the product of recent pressures, not ancient hatreds. The anthropologists in this book critique these ideas and the pundits who propound them in the fresh, vigorous prose of the punditocracy itself, but they do this without compromising their learning or simplifying the issues at stake.

Samuel Huntington, another pundit who writes on international affairs, is a Harvard professor who first became notorious as one of the architects of the "strategic hamlet" policy of counterinsurgency in the Vietnam War. In the 1990s, setting his jaw against Clintonist internationalism, he moved into the public eye once more with his predictions of an impending "clash of civilizations," which made him a cause célèbre, especially among those who hoped that the end of the cold war would not mean the end of cold-war levels of military spending. According to Huntington, the world contains seven civilizations: Western, orthodox, Chinese, Japanese, Hindu, Islamic, and Latin American. (If you are wondering where Africa went, Huntington is not sure that it qualifies as a civilization). Of these civilizations, Huntington sees the West as uniquely compatible with democracy, human rights, and secular reason. He has a special animus against Islam, which he presents as incompatible with modernity, saying that "Muslim bellicosity and violence are late twentieth century facts" and that "Muslims have problems living peacefully with their neighbors."[8] Claiming that wars tend to occur on the "fault lines" between civilizations rather than within them, Huntington argues that globalization will probably intensify global conflict. This is because globalization makes it harder for countries to stay within their own civilizational backyards and because globalization is creating multicultural societies that, according to Huntington, suffer from "cultural schizophrenia" and are therefore unsustainable. He says, for example, in an argument that echoes Kaplan's warnings about the perils of multiculturalism, that the influx of Mexican immigrants into the United States creates a sort of Latin American fifth column within the United States that may eventually cause the loss of territory the United States once took from Mexico.

Hugh Gusterson, an anthropologist who writes on international security issues, attacks Huntington for the incoherence of his basic categories and for his cartoonish caricatures of complex cultural traditions. He points out, for example, that Huntington's separation of "Western" and "Orthodox" civilizations (the latter including both Russia and Greece) is odd, since so many cultural conservatives in the United States trace Western civilization and its democratic traditions back to the ancient Greeks. Gusterson also suggests that Huntington's characterizations of different cultures are often based on egregious stereotypes (Muslims are violent fundamentalists, the Chinese are authoritarian) that blur the diversity of opinion and belief within a society and deny the ability of societies to change over time. Taking issue with Huntington's representation of civilizations as enacting a timeless essence, Gusterson argues that if Europe "could evolve from a period when there was . . . no schism between Protestantism and Catholicism, and an assumption that kings ruled by divine right, to today's secular and pluralistic democracies," then surely the other civilizations of the world can also change in substantial and unpredictable ways.

Keith Brown's critique of Huntington is based on a fascinating close reading of his use of the notion of "kinship" within civilizations as a force in international relations. Kinship has traditionally been one of the central topics in anthropology, which has documented an astonishing variety of kinship practices around the world. By shining a light into the gap between Huntington's simplistic assumptions about kinship and anthropologists' rich knowledge of kinship as it is actually lived in all its diversity, Brown illuminates the simplifications and false assumptions that mar Huntington's work more generally. Huntington's argument depends upon a crude determinism that assumes civilizational "kin" will always tend to take one another's side against outsiders—like the Orthodox Russians tilting toward the Serbs in Yugoslavia in the 1990s. Brown points out that, in the Balkans, this generalization seems highly dubious once one takes more than a superficial look. Thus, for example, the predominantly Christian United States was willing to take military action on behalf of the Bosnian Muslims and Muslim Kosovars in the 1990s, and, on the ground, other alliances in the region turned out to be more complex and counterintuitive than a theory of civilizational affinity would predict. Brown points out that marital ties can be as important as blood ties, and that, in the Balkans as in many other parts of the world, there are relations of "fictive kinship"—as exemplified by godparents—that enable people to turn allies and friends unrelated by blood into kin. Using as his starting point a Kosovar who named his daughter Kfor (after NATO forces) and who wanted a NATO general to be her godfather, Brown argues that new nations and oppressed peoples in eastern Europe in the 1990s used the idioms of fictive kinship to make real a powerful sense of lived solidarity with the United States, and that, more broadly, Huntington's flat and impoverished use of kinship as a way of understanding international alliances rests on a grave misunderstanding of the pliability of actual kinship relations and an underestimation of the human capacity to imagine relations of solidarity with others.

Our third foreign affairs pundit, Thomas Friedman, chides Kaplan and Huntington for their negativity and suggests that globalization and international trade can counteract tendencies toward anarchy or civilizational clashes. Best known for his biweekly opinion column in the *New York Times* and an earlier book on the politics of the Middle East, Friedman is also the author of *The Lexus and the Olive Tree*, a book that is, by nonfiction standards, a best-seller. Five years after its initial publication, it is still among the few hundred top sellers on Amazon.com. The Lexus in Friedman's title, a luxury automobile, represents the promise of affluence in globalization; the olive tree, the pull of the traditions that often inhibit countries from embracing market capitalism and its promise of progress and modernity. Friedman writes that a world without barriers to the flow of goods, ideas, and capital—a globalized system based on neoliberal economic policies—is the best hope for economic growth, political progress, and a world at peace. (Friedman claims that no two countries with McDonald's franchises have ever gone to war with one another.)

Countries that refuse to embrace globalization, according to Friedman, are often inhibited by a fear of modernity and an irrational attachment to cultural tradition. Such countries will be left behind economically. The only hope for them is to open themselves to the market rationality of the "electronic herd" of banking experts and investors and to "globalution"—democratic revolution through globalization; the big danger is that they will allow themselves to be led astray by the "backlashers" and ignorant "turtles" who "just don't have the skills sets or the energy to make it into the Fast World."[9]

In this book, chapters by Angelique Haugerud, by Carolyn Nordstrom, and by Ellen Hertz and Laura Nader reveal the shallowness of Friedman's arguments. Angelique Haugerud, an anthropologist who spent fieldwork time in Africa over a period of two decades, and who is currently studying globalization activists, suggests that Friedman "misses the main story" about globalization. She argues that Friedman is so blinded by his perception of a global clash between modernity and tradition, and that his knowledge of the countries he jets into is so superficial, he cannot see that what he calls tradition is far from traditional. Friedman, Haugerud tells us, perceives a "dichotomy . . . between two rigidly separate worlds: that of the constantly ringing cell phones in his train car full of forward-looking middle- and upper-class Egyptians, and that of the 'barefoot Egyptian villagers . . . tilling their fields with the same tools and water buffalo that their ancestors used in Pharoah's day.'" This latter image, Haugerud notes, is visually arresting, but it is also "utterly false," given "Egypt's long history of agricultural innovation." Moreover, Haugerud points out, these villages with their water buffalo are actually at the center of a globalization from below, which Friedman fails to see. Many villagers have left the village to try their luck as migrant laborers in Egypt and beyond, and their relatives depend on the money they send and on the knowledge of labor and commodity markets they embody.

In the end, Haugerud concludes, Friedman's dichotomy between modernity and tradition is a phony distraction from the reality that resistance to globalization is "rejection not of modernity per se, but of the social injustices, environmental destruction, and brutal economic inequality that can accompany industrialization and economic neoliberalism." Observing that "globalizers" include migrant workers, protesters against the World Trade Organization, and rural farmers—rather than merely the banking and political elite so favored by Friedman— Haugerud explains that "what villagers, migrants, shantytown dwellers, and protesters seek is global and local social justice, not isolated olive groves of tradition." The globalizers from below who interest Haugerud are concerned with the neoliberal policies that shape how people must participate in the current global economy. Thus Haugerud concludes her chapter by offering ideas for reforming globalization and enhancing its possibilities. Activists in the West and Third World villagers, whom Friedman so deprecates, do not insist on living in the past, but instead ask what alternative forms of globalization we might pursue in the future. While Friedman presents an up-or-down choice—globalization or no globalization?—they ask, "Globalization for whom?"

Where Friedman suggests that poor countries will be the countries unable or unwilling to participate in the global market, Carolyn Nordstrom, drawing on many years of field research in such desperately poor countries as Mozambique and Angola, shows that in reality this is not true. Nordstrom argues that, while poor African countries may appear to be left out of globalization according to official IMF or World Bank indices, they actually have huge black market sectors that bring everything from weapons to cigarettes into the country while extracting diamonds (known to the locals as "conflict diamonds") and other precious materials for sale on terms highly favorable to the West and highly exploitive of the bulk of the local population. If Friedman thinks such countries have been left out of globalization, or that globalization will produce stable and balanced economic growth for their peoples, it is because he cannot tell the difference between the UN or IMF statistics he reads in the limousine from the airport and the world of the people his limousine whizzes past. (As Hertz and Nader observe, Friedman "has not talked to very many different kinds of people on his jaunts across the four-star-hotel-dotted globe.")

Pointing out that experts estimate that the black market represents 50 percent of Mozambique's economy and a staggering 90 percent of Angola's, Nordstrom warns of the danger of relying on formal economic statistics as a measure of such countries' participation in the global economy. Against Friedman's talk of Lexuses and olive trees, Nordstrom's icon of globalization is Marra, an African war refugee who survives where others drop from hunger and exhaustion by smuggling out from the war zone a diamond, for which she is paid the pitifully small sum of twenty dollars. Far from being an olive tree clinger, Marra is resourceful, adaptive—and exploited. Marra could not escape from globalization if she wanted to, since it is the warp and weft of her life: the impetus for the war that made her a refugee, and the source of the twenty dollars that may enable her children to live rather than die. Marra is the human face on the sharp end of globalization that Friedman, busy talking to World Bank economists and secretaries of the treasury, cannot see. Nordstrom's painstaking local research on globalized black market economies in southern Africa gives the lie to Friedman's claim that democratization and affluence are the universal benefits of plugging into the global market.

Struck by Friedman's manic authorial voice and his "globally proportioned ego," Ellen Hertz and Laura Nader write their critique in a parody of his style, which they describe as "breezy, sarcastic, anecdotal, accessible, and optimistic—the kind of not-too-serious writing that people might choose to read at the end of an all-too-serious workday." Since his understanding of the societies about which he writes is so superficial, and his arguments about globalization so simplistic, Hertz and Nader conclude that Friedman's style rather than his message attracts readers. Highlighting the dangers of a journalist who "relies so heavily on advertising copy for insights into worldwide phenomena," their chapter focuses on how Friedman's ad-copy writing style allows him to make gross generalizations and appalling simplifications and to avoid any kind of engagement with serious questions. Such questions, suggest Hertz and Nader, include: What kind of globalization do we want? What do we mean by free market capitalism? How is free market capitalism carried out? Does democracy mean nothing more than the freedom to consume? Do financial markets democratize society, as Friedman insists? Hertz and Nader conclude by offering anthropological studies of globalization that counterbalance Friedman's "political-economic propaganda."

THE PUNDITS AT HOME: THE GENETIC BASIS
FOR WEALTH, RAPE, AND IQ

The last three chapters of the book focus on *The Virtue of Prosperity* by Dinesh D'Souza, *A Natural History of Rape* by Randy Thornhill and Craig Palmer, and *The Bell Curve* by Richard Herrnstein and Charles Murray. Whereas the three pundits discussed above seek to define the strengths of and challenges to American society in the global arena, these three books focus on American domestic issues. Taken together, they argue that we should accept the inequalities of class, gender, and race hierarchies in our society as inevitable, natural, and unalterable by social programs designed to promote equality. They offer a feel-good set of myths to gloss the fact that American society is growing more polarized and stratified every year.

D'Souza made his reputation in the early 1990s with his book *Illiberal Education*, a controversial attack on political correctness on campus. His subsequent books include *Letters to a Young Conservative*, *What's So Great about America*, and *The End of Racism*. In *The Virtue of Prosperity*, the book we focus on here, D'Souza writes about the distribution of wealth in contemporary America. Portraying himself as an "anthropologist in a strange land" in the opening chapter, he says that "you don't have to go anywhere" to understand the socioeconomic system emerging today. "Just turn on your computer and get on the internet."[10] In a book where he quotes liberally from conversations with dot.com millionaires and writers for *Forbes* magazine, D'Souza argues that the poor have never had it so good: "Poverty . . . is no longer a significant problem in America," he tells us.[11] Citing statistics showing that 98 percent of those below the official poverty line in America have refrigerators, 93 percent have televisions, and 72 percent have washing machines, he asks what they are complaining about, given that the poor in the Third World—the "real" poor as against the coddled American poor—could only dream of owning such commodities. More generally, arguing that "capitalism civilizes greed just as marriage civilizes lust," he says that American capitalism is a finely tuned piece of social machinery that converts talent and industry into wealth and status so that everyone ends up more or less where they deserve to be.[12] "The prime culprit in causing contemporary social inequality seems to be merit," he says. "The guy who is worth little has probably produced little of value."[13] As evidence that the American poor lack the virtues of those above them, he points to their higher incarceration rates.

Kath Weston is an anthropologist who has studied poverty by spending time with the poor rather than by opportunistically gathering the sorts of statistics and anecdotes about them that give comfort to the rich. Criticizing D'Souza's "commodity-based conception of class" and his "shopping-cart conception of capitalism," she points out that, when the federal government developed measures for the "poverty line" in the 1960s, it focused on consumer items and food but left out such expenses as child care and health care, which are much more important now than they were then. We live, she points out, in "a topsy-turvy economy in which it becomes possible to scrape together the money for household appliances that look like luxuries, yet inconceivable to cover the basic necessities that sustain life." While D'Souza says that the poor in India would envy the American poor their microwaves and televisions, Weston reminds us of the recent experiment by the best-selling Barbara Ehrenreich in which she abandoned her comfortable middle-class life and tried to live on the minimum wage she could earn as a waitress or hotel maid. Although eighty dollars per day might sound like a lot, Ehrenreich found that it was hard for many to live anywhere nicer than their cars or transient hotel rooms once confronted with the need for rental deposits, health care costs, transportation costs to work, and so on.[14] Weston drives home the lived meaning of poverty (which cannot be measured by commodity indices) and dramatizes how little progress we have made in fighting it, despite decades of a rising gross national product, when she quotes James Baldwin's recollection of growing up poor and black in Harlem in the middle years of the twentieth century: "a cousin, mother of six, suddenly gone mad, the children parceled out here and there; an indestructible aunt rewarded for years of hard labor by a slow, agonizing death in a terrible small room; someone's bright son blown into eternity by his own hand; another turned robber and carried off to jail."[15]

If we were forced to pick the most offensive and intellectually shoddy of the books discussed here, it would be Randy Thornhill and Craig Palmer's *Natural History of Rape*, a book that surely would have had Margaret Mead reaching angrily for her pen. Sadly, this is the one book in our hall of shame that was published by a university press—MIT Press, which doubled the initial print run to twenty thousand to capitalize on the controversy the book generated as its authors embarked on a media blitz against feminist accounts of rape. The authors—a biologist and a biological anthropologist who identify with evolutionary psychology— argue that rape is not about power, as many feminists, rape victims, and reformed rapists have argued, but is instead an evolutionary product best understood through processes of natural selection. Thornhill and Palmer argue that men are genetically predisposed to spread their sperm as widely as possible, while women are naturally monogamous. They offer proof of the male genetic propensity to rape in the form of examples of forced copulation throughout the animal world. Thus a special "rape organ" in male scorpionflies—a clamp that restrains a female scorpionfly so she cannot escape copulation—is offered as an analogue to the human male psychological imperative to rape. Concluding with a policy recom- mendation that takes us back to the '50s (arguably the 1650s rather than the 1950s), they suggest that, if we want to reduce the incidence of rape, then teenage boys should be taught about their natural urge to rape, and the importance of trying to restrain it, when they get their driver's licenses, while teenage girls should be taught not to dress provocatively.

Stefan Helmreich and Heather Paxson attack *A Natural History of Rape* as "conjectural biology" and a collection of "just-so" stories. They point out the shoddiness of the three-step argument favored by evolutionary psychologists (or as they used to be known, sociobiologists): "First, describe some aspect of universal 'human nature'—here, that men have a tendency to rape women—and offer analogies from animals to suggest that these traits are seated in shared nature. Second, claim that what is universal must be so because it emanates from biology. Third, since the evidence is not available, claim that traits in question arose through nat- ural or sexual selection, and construct a logical tale for how whatever is universal was favored by evolution." The problems with this method are that the behavior is not universal, categories are confused by applying human cultural words such as *rape* and *marriage* to animal behaviors, and the case that rape was favored by evolution is assumed rather than proved. The result is a fairy tale dressed up in the language of science.

Helmreich and Paxson dramatize the lunacy of Thornhill and Palmer's argument particularly effectively in their discussion of recent organized rape campaigns in the Rwandan and Bosnian wars. In Rwanda, Tutsi women were raped, then killed—difficult to link to an evolutionary tale of reproductive fitness, one would think. In Bosnia the Serb rape camps were clearly an attempt not at individual genetic reproduction but, as in the Rwandan case, a nationalist and genocidal assault on another ethnic group through the bodies of its women. Helmreich and Paxson, referring to Thornhill and Palmer's advice that women who do not want to be raped should dress modestly, point out that the Bosnian and Tutsi rape victims were not raped for wearing bikinis and miniskirts. "Could tragedy in Rwanda have been averted if Tutsi women had paid closer attention to their attire?" they ask ironically. No example could more vividly demonstrate both the social causes of rape and the almost surreal irrelevance of Thornhill and Palmer's prescriptions for avoiding it.

The Bell Curve by Richard Herrnstein and Charles Murray also uses the rhetorical trappings of science to mask a selective use of evidence and a malodorous political agenda. Herrnstein and Murray's agenda is to show that social programs such as affirmative action and Head Start are a waste of resources given that intelligence—and hence achievement—is largely inherited, and inherited in a way skewed by race. Herrnstein and Murray believe that raw, context-free intelligence exists, that it can be measured by IQ tests, and that these tests show, among other things, that whites have more of it than blacks do.

Jonathan Marks, a biological anthropologist, points out first of all that Alfred Binet, the inventor of IQ tests, always saw these tests as a device for assessing how roughly comparable children were doing in school, not as ways of measuring a questionable metaphysical abstraction called intelligence. Noting that "it is hard to imagine that the ability to participate successfully in a buffalo hunt, say, is in any way measured by pencil-and-paper tests," Marks points out that intelligence is always specific to a particular context and that, besides, different cultures value different approaches to problem solving: in Samoa, for example, it is thought that the best route from A to B is the prettiest, not the quickest—an answer unlikely to earn high marks on an American IQ test. IQ tests measure only "what they were originally designed to measure," Marks argues: "performance in school."

Marks also points out that Herrnstein and Murray mishandle the statistics they use to make their case. The two compare IQ scores of blacks and whites without making much effort to ensure that the blacks and whites they stack against one another are comparable. According to Marks, when black children are compared with white children from families with comparable incomes, numbers of children, educational backgrounds, and access to good schools, then the statistical difference is negligible.

As Marks points out, we have seen these arguments before. In the early twentieth century, American anthropology was born out of the intellectual struggle between its founder, Franz Boas, and the social Darwinists of the time who argued that Irish, Mediterranean, and eastern European immigrants, as well as blacks, were poor because they were intellectually inferior. For some, these arguments led logically to a program of eugenics to limit the reproduction of the poor. Boas and his intellectual allies won the debate with the social Darwinists, showing that what they took to be natural was cultural. In today's context it would be bizarre to argue that Poles, Italians, or the Irish are intellectually inferior to people of English or German stock. But Herrnstein and Murray seek to revive this discredited social Darwinist tradition and apply it to our new minorities, papering over the cracks with new charts and graphs. As Marks says, "It is hard to see the goal of *The Bell Curve* as other than to rationalize economic inequality, to perpetuate injustice, and to justify social oppression. Such science gives the rest of the field a bad name."

All three of these books have received scalding reviews by scholars and commentators, who have subjected them to a thorough debunking. Yet the myths they promote seem to resonate deeply with American readers. It is somehow comforting to believe that biology and culture are linked, that one's outcome in life is genetically predetermined, that those who have more deserve it. Otherwise, how could we bear to live in a society characterized by such enormous inequality, such astronomical incarceration rates of African Americans, such obvious gender inequities? These myths provide a familiar set of stories that will not die—they get resurrected every few decades and trotted out to explain why our great democracy continues to produce poverty, incarcerate minorities disproportionately, and suffer violence against women.

Such myths nurture complacency in their justification of the way things are. They confirm the naturalness of a social order where white is superior to black, where women look over their shoulders in fear, where the wealthy deserve their wealth and the poor deserve their lot, and where Americans dominate the world. Anthropology, sometimes, is the voice of discomfort. By telling alternative stories about the way things are, by drawing on non-elite or marginalized knowledges and perspectives, the anthropologists in this volume seek to develop a humanistically complex, nonethnocentric, democratic understanding of the contemporary world.

The pundits critiqued in this book all share what we might call a reactionary determinism. They often call this "realism." In their essay on Friedman, Hertz and Nader call it TIS ("the inevitability syndrome"). These pundits all argue in their own way that what is must be, and that arguments to the contrary are naive and dangerous. If African Americans are disproportionately poor, it is because they are intellectually inferior, and social programs cannot change this; the rape of women is an inevitable consequence of our genes, not the result of a distorted culture; globalization is in the hands of "the electronic herd" and cannot be remade in a more humane fashion by activists, trade unionists, and environmentalists; the Serbs, Croats, and Muslims will keep on killing one another because that is the way they are; democracy will not come to Asia because it does not fit their timeless culture; and people from different cultural traditions are destined to interact antagonistically rather than constructively.

The authors of this book, believing that these ideas are based not only on bad politics but also on bad social science, promote a kind of realism different from that espoused by the pundits. Social science is neither left nor right, liberal nor conservative, but it does show quite clearly, if it shows anything at all, that cultures can change, that traditions are invented rather than indelible, that the poor carry heavier burdens than the rich, and that human beings constantly misrecognize the world they have made as the natural order of things. While the pundits whisper in our ears that nothing can be done to make the world a better place, we know that this is wrong.

TWO

The Seven Deadly Sins
of Samuel Huntington

Hugh Gusterson

> Culture is most easily conceived as a static generalization of
> collective behavior. . . . Yet it is increasingly evident that no
> civilization is ever actually static. It always flows.
>
> Alfred Kroeber, "The Delimitation of Civilization"

> In reading about the clash of civilizations we are less
> likely to assent to analysis of the clash than we are to
> ask the question, Why do you pinion civilizations into
> so unyielding an embrace, and why do you go on to
> describe their relationship as one of basic conflict, as
> if the borrowing and overlappings between them were
> not a much more interesting and significant feature?
>
> Edward Said, "Clash of Definitions"

Harvard University's Samuel Huntington is a member of America's
scholarly elite. His books are blurbed by Henry Kissinger and widely
read by professionals in the fields of international relations and compar-
ative politics. He has a knack for getting the ear of policy makers and
pundits. In the 1960s he was an important adviser to the U.S. government
and was reportedly an architect of the "strategic hamlet" policy in the
Vietnam War. In the mid-1990s, at a moment when opinion makers were

debating what would replace the cold war, his ideas burst onto the scene with, first, a widely discussed article in *Foreign Affairs* called "The Clash of Civilizations?" and then, three years later, a book by the same title.[1] While Huntington's political science colleagues picked holes in his argument in the professional journals, in the wider world *The Clash of Civilizations* was—for a book by an academic with thirty pages of densely packed endnotes—a stunning success. It was translated into several foreign languages, and its ideas were widely discussed by the foreign policy establishment and media elites.

Remarkably, Samuel Huntington has written a three-hundred-page, heavily footnoted book about all the cultural civilizations of the world without citing any foreign language sources and with scarcely any reference to the anthropologists who study them for a living. The result is a book that should make any intelligent reader wince, but it will have a particularly jarring effect on anthropologists because it stereotypes entire cultures while denying the reality of change and diversity within cultures and the possibility of solidarity between them. If only Samuel Huntington had taken one or two good classes in anthropology, he could have avoided the seven deadly sins he commits in this book. I detail them below, but first let's look at his argument in *The Clash of Civilizations*.

THE CLASH

In his book, Huntington argues that seven civilizational blocs are emerging from the ruins of the old cold war global order. "Peoples and countries with similar cultures are coming together," he says. "Peoples and countries with different cultures are coming apart. Alignments defined by ideology and superpower relations are giving way to alignments defined by culture and civilization" (p. 125). These emerging civilizational blocs "are the ultimate human tribes, and the clash of civilizations is tribal conflict on a global scale" (p. 207). He identifies these seven civilizations as Sinic (Chinese), Japanese, Hindu, Islamic, Orthodox, Western, and Latin American (although, at times, he suggests that Latin

America may be part of Western civilization). He says Africa is "possibly" a civilization.

Using a metaphor from geology, Huntington says the flashpoints for conflict in this new world order are found at the "fault lines" where different civilizations adjoin. These fault lines are particularly dangerous if located within states, where they create what Huntington calls "cleft states," since—he says—members of different civilizations find it hard to live in peace together under a single government. Shifting to a metaphor from physics, he goes on: "In a cleft country major groups from two or more civilizations say, in effect, 'we are different peoples and we belong in different places.' The forces of repulsion drive them apart and they gravitate toward civilization magnets in other countries" (p. 138). Examples of "cleft states" include the former Yugoslavia—where Western Christians, Bosnian Muslims, and Orthodox Serbs were forced to cohabit—and India, where tensions between Hindus and Muslims often run high.

According to Huntington, except for the rather more anarchic Islamic bloc, each civilization has a "core state"—a primary power within the bloc—such as the United States for the West, and Russia for the Orthodox bloc. Adopting what one might call a mafia model of international relations, Huntington argues that these core states will coordinate assistance to members of their civilization who are attacked, and will also keep order within their bloc: "A core state can perform its ordering function because member states perceive it as cultural kin. A civilization is an extended family and, like older members of a family, core states provide their relatives with both support and discipline" (p. 156).

Asserting that "the world will be ordered on the basis of civilizations or not at all" (p. 156), Huntington argues that a relatively peaceful and stable world is one where core states are allowed to order their own civilizations without outside interference and where different core states respect one another's spheres of influence, minimizing friction along the fault lines between civilizations. He identifies several possible threats to this potentially peaceful world. One is Islam, which he sees as an absolutist and aggressive civilization lacking the inner restraint enforced by a core state. Declaring that "Muslim bellicosity and violence are late twentieth century facts" (p. 258), he worries that "wherever one looks along the perimeter of Islam, Muslims have problems living peacefully with their neighbors" (p. 256).[2]

Huntington sees China as a second threat to global stability because it is a rising power that will eventually, inevitably, challenge the United States for hegemony in Asia. Huntington argues that Asian states differ profoundly from Western states in their outlook on the world: they are unified by their emphasis on "the value of authority, hierarchy, the subordination of individual rights and interests, [and] the importance of consensus" (p. 225). Because these societies have, in his view, "little room for social or political pluralism and the division of power" (p. 234), he expects Japan and other Asian states to band together with China when it challenges the United States for dominance in Asia.

A third threat to global stability is migration, which jumbles up people from different civilizations. Like Robert Kaplan, Huntington fears that "France and Europe [sic] are destined to be overwhelmed by people from the failed societies of the South."[3] In particular, Huntington worries that Islamic migration to Europe has created, in effect, an additional (transnational) nation within the European Union (p. 200), and that Mexican migration to the United States may eventually enable Mexico to recover what the United States took by force in the nineteenth century. He fears that liberal support for multiculturalism within the United States will lead to domestic conflict and undermine Americans' sense of their own identity as a nation, hastening national decline.

The fourth threat to global stability that Huntington identifies is the Western impulse to spread democracy around the world and Westernize every country it can. Warning that "what is universalism to the West is imperialism to the rest" (p. 184), Huntington argues that democracy is a uniquely Western invention, and that attempts to spread Western values and democracy to other nations will only cause conflict. "The dangerous clashes of the future are likely to arise from the interaction of Western arrogance, Islamic intolerance, and Sinic assertiveness," he says (p. 183). He ends the book with a speculative scenario for a Third World War that begins when the United States comes to the aid of Vietnam as it is attacked by China. This triggers a global conflagration in which Japan, drawn to its Asiatic kin, allies with China against the United States, while India and Russia attack China, and the forces of Islam attack the West. Latin America sits out the conflict on the sidelines, then moves in to scavenge the pieces of a battered United States.

First Deadly Sin: Basic Definitions

Huntington's argument rests on the premise that there are distinct civilizational zones that have been relatively culturally homogeneous and stable over centuries. However, we are long past the period in anthropology described by anthropologist Ulf Hannerz as one in which "the dominant imagery was one of many small and separate worlds, in which the Nuer, the Tikopia, the Kwakiutl, and all the others seemed to exist almost as separate species."[4] Most contemporary anthropologists would find Huntington's assumption deeply problematic, as I explain below, but for the moment let it suffice to point out the terrible empirical mess it creates for Huntington when he actually has to draw the line between civilizations. Take this tendentious passage in which he demarcates the boundary between the Western world and its neighbors, alluding to "the great historical line that has existed for centuries separating Western Christian peoples from Muslim and Orthodox peoples. This line dates back to the division of the Roman Empire in the fourth century and to the creation of the Holy Roman Empire in the tenth century."[5] Huntington argues that "Europe ends where Western Christianity ends and Islam and Orthodoxy begin,"[6] and that therefore such countries as Greece, Bulgaria, and Romania are not part of the Western cultural bloc. He says that the enduring significance of this civilizational boundary is demonstrated today by the fact that the countries to the West of this line are those "that have made significant progress in divesting themselves of the Communist legacies and moving toward democratic politics and market economies."[7]

Any reader with even a smattering of classical education will be puzzled by this exclusion of Greece from Western civilization. Why are so many European and American students forced to read Plato and Aristotle, and why were conservative educators in the 1980s and 1990s so concerned to protect them as the core of "Western civilization" on college reading lists under attack by multiculturalists, if Greece was never part of Western culture anyway?[8] And how can it be that Greece is placed on the other side of the line separating the democratic West from the nondemocratic rest, when it is a democratic nation-state whose ancestral city-states originated the Western democratic tradition in so many political genealogies? The answer, of course, is that Huntington's attempt to draw this line of demarcation is arbitrary and flawed—not because the line is drawn in the wrong place but because complex webs of similarity and difference do not lend themselves to the geometry of straight lines.

I have illustrated the flimsiness of Huntington's definitional approach by highlighting his problematic "eastern boundary" for Western civilization because that part of the world is most familiar to me and will be also to many readers, but one could easily quarrel with his characterizations of other cultural zones as well. The anthropologist Aihwa Ong observes, for example, that "Indonesia, which is only nominally Muslim, is considered by Huntington to be a subdivision of Islamic civilization."[9] Perhaps most bizarre, even scandalous, is Huntington's assertion that Africa is only "possibly" a civilization. Given that he makes no argument that Africans take part in any of his other seven civilizations, one can only conclude that he considers it possible that Africans are a people without culture, which is to say that they are not people in the complete sense at all. Given the postcolonial efflorescence of African literature, the Western interest in African art at least since the time of Picasso, and the documentation of cultural norms and social practices in Africa by anthropologists at least since the 1930s, Huntington's dismissive portrayal of Africa as a civilizational blank zone is deeply perplexing.

Second Deadly Sin: Stereotyping Cultures

A corollary to Huntington's assumption that civilizations can be clearly demarcated is his description of civilizations as if they were homogeneous, with culture as a sort of computer program sitting in the heads of all people within a civilization instructing them to behave the same way. He defines civilization as "the values, norms, institutions, and modes of thinking to which successive generations in a given society have attached primary importance" (p. 41).[10] This definition leads him to stereotypes such as the following: "Asians generally pursue their goals with others in ways which are subtle, indirect, modulated, devious, nonjudgmental, nonmoralistic, and non-confrontational. Australians, in contrast, are the most direct, blunt, outspoken, some would say insensitive, people in the English-speaking world" (p. 154). Although Huntington's adjectives in this passage are as much slogans as precise terms of social description, anyone who has interacted with "Asians" or "Australians" will recognize that there is a grain of truth in these characterizations. However, they will also be able to think of exceptions among Asians and Australians they have met, and will realize that, if you watch them closely, individual Asians and Australians, like other human beings, vary their behavior in different contexts rather than robotically following a single script. That is because, even before the mass migrations of colonialism and globalization scrambled societies demographically, societies did not consist of individuals with personalities and belief systems that were mass-produced to behave identically and consistently, but of complex patterns of integrated heterogeneity. As Edward Said puts it in his own critique of Huntington, to speak of civilizations in boxes as Huntington does "is completely to ignore the literally unending debate or contest . . . about defining the culture or civilization within those civilizations, including various 'Western' ones. These debates completely undermine any idea of a fixed identity."[11]

Huntington's notions are based on an antiquated view of culture. In the period before and after World War II, a group of anthropologists who liked to speak about "national character" and "modal" or "normal" personalities within societies held sway in American anthropology. Margaret Mead and Ruth Benedict were the most prominent members of this group.[12] Later generations of anthropologists concluded that such anthropologists' empirical descriptions of cultures were often simplistic or even inaccurate, and that this was in part the consequence of theoretical blinders that led them to filter out diversity and heterogeneity, producing reductive stereotypes of complex lifeways. Today, in place of Margaret Mead's talk of "national character" and "normal personality," anthropologists tend to reach for such formulations as James Clifford's image of culture as "collage" or Renato Rosaldo's likening of culture to a "garage sale."[13]

The problems with Huntington's picture of civilizational traditions as integrated by "values, norms, institutions, and modes of thinking" become clear if we stop for a moment and think about American society. Who represents American values and modes of thinking? Would it be followers of Jerry Falwell, who reject evolution and believe in divine revelation of truth and strict biblical norms of morality? Scientists who ground their belief in evolution in appeals to the scientific method? Or devotees of, say, the rock star Madonna, who enjoys turning the transgression of Jerry Falwell's strict biblical norms into a form of entertainment? Huntington characterizes Western civilization as Christian in its origin and unfolding; he also argues that it is deeply committed to ratio nal thought. And yet the three American subcultures invoked above swirl around his characterization in ways that immediately destabilize it.

Third Deadly Sin: Ignoring Change

Ulf Hannerz has observed that Huntington "shares with other versions of cultural fundamentalism the tendency to naturalize cultural immutability and persistence."[14] Huntington speaks of his seven civilizations as if they are timeless, and he repeatedly characterizes different civilizational traditions—especially the Islamic—as impervious to change. His Westerners are always already democratic, rational, and individualistic, just as his Asians were authoritarian and hierarchical yesterday, and will be tomorrow. The Roman and Holy Roman Empires have long since risen and fallen, but the line between Western and Orthodox civilizations that they embodied remains as firm as ever. Declaring that "political leaders imbued with the hubris to think that they can fundamentally reshape the culture of their societies are doomed to fail" (p. 154), Huntington argues that countries which have sought to change their civilizational identification—Russia and Turkey by Westernizing, Australia by seeking to redefine itself as an Asian power—have all failed in their attempts and have created a fatal "schizophrenia" in their societies in the process. Concerning immigration, where others have seen the promise of new cultural mixings, Huntington warns of the danger that, as Muslims resettle in Europe and Mexicans move to the United States, "Europe and America will become cleft societies encompassing two distinct and largely separate communities from two different civilizations" (p. 204). He argues that Islam has a sort of eternal cultural essence that makes it incompatible with the modern nation-state and with democratic liberalism: "The idea of sovereign nation-states is incompatible with belief in the sovereignty of Allah and the primacy of the 'ummah' [community of believers]" (p. 175). About prospects for liberal democracy, he argues that, "in one Muslim society after another, to write of liberalism and of a national bourgeois tradition is to write obituaries of men who took on impossible odds and then failed" (p. 114).[15]

Ulf Hannerz aptly calls this "cultural fundamentalism." While no one would deny the striking cultural continuities across generations that enable us to recognize, for example, today's Chinese as, in some complex but very real ways, the descendants of yesterday's Chinese, it would be foolish to deny the equally striking changes that separate generation from generation within cultural traditions. The ethnographic and historical literature is full of examples: the Ilongot of the Philippines giving up headhunting, the Semai of Malaysia learning in recent years to make war for the first time,[16] and American Mormons (largely) giving up polygamy. On a larger scale, one thinks of Japan's extraordinarily swift and complete transition from authoritarian to democratic rule after World War II—a story beautifully told in the fine book *Embracing Defeat* by the historian John Dower.[17]

Some of the problems with Huntington's assumptions about continuity and change come into sharper focus if we consider, to take one small example, his observation that Westerners find it hard to do business in China because "in China trust and commitment depend on personal contacts, not contracts and laws" (p. 170). Quite apart from the fact that "personal contacts" are hardly unimportant in the Western business context today,[18] the problem with this formulation is that it misrepresents as immutably cultural a particular moment in the evolution of a set of bureaucratic institutions in China. Precisely because Huntington assumes that cultures are immutable, he mistakes a slice in historical time for an eternal cultural present. There was a time in the West also when "personal contacts, not contracts and laws" were the primary basis for business relations. Indeed one could narrate the history of the West as the constant expansion and refinement of contract law into spheres of human life where it formerly had no place—most recently, for example, into the licensing of corporate ownership of genetic resources (such as medicinal plants and human DNA) once thought beyond commodification. Even as Western life is being ever more colonized by the laws of market and contract, so too in China: as the current wave of market reforms remakes Chinese society, and as China is drawn further into the global trade regime through the World Trade Organization and other institutions, we will see the form of economic rationalization represented by contracts assume greater importance—just as eastern European societies have begun to assimilate the economic practices of western Europe since the end of the cold war.

One could make similar arguments in response to Huntington's claim that Islam is incompatible with liberal democracy or with the nation-state. After all, at one time the countries in western Europe that Huntington naturalizes as democratic states were neither democratic nor states and, while Huntington is right that there is a profound tension between the nation-state and a pan-Islamic sense of transnational community, there was once a time, before anything called "Germany" or "Italy" existed, when the pan-Christian community of the Holy Roman Empire seemed stronger than many states in Europe. If European nation-states could evolve from a period when there was a Holy Roman Emperor, no schism between Protestantism and Catholicism, and an assumption that kings ruled by divine right, to today's secular and pluralistic democracies, we can hardly rule out the possibility of new forms of political community and institutions in the Islamic world.

Fourth Deadly Sin: Denying Multiculturalism

Given Huntington's assumptions that cultures are homogeneous, timeless, and clearly bounded, it almost goes without saying that he is suspicious of multiculturalism and other forms of cultural hybridization. Warning that immigration threatens to undermine the coherence of societies in Europe and the United States and that globalization threatens to produce local cultural backlashes against the West, Huntington advocates a strategy of cultural apartheid, assuming—like South Africa's apartheid leaders—that cultural miscegenation is dangerous and unnatural. This is true whether he is speaking of the Westernization of other cultures or the intrusion, through multiculturalism, of non-Western cultures into the United States. In a striking passage that represents Westernization in hygienic metaphors of disease and madness, he warns that "the western virus, once it is lodged in another society, is difficult to expunge. The virus persists but is not fatal; the patient survives but is never whole. Political leaders . . . infect their country with a cultural schizophrenia which becomes its continuing and defining characteristic" (p. 154). He uses even stronger language to discuss the dangers of multiculturalism in the American context. Accusing multiculturalists of turning the United States into a "torn country" because they have "denied the existence of a common American culture, and promoted racial, ethnic and other subnational cultural identities and groupings" (p. 305), he warns that "history shows that no country so constituted can long endure as a coherent society" (p. 306):

> The clash between the multiculturalists and the defenders of Western civilization and the American creed is, in James Kurth's phrase, "the *real* clash" within the American segment of civilization. Americans cannot avoid the issue: Are we a Western people or are we something else? The futures of the United States and the West depend upon Americans reaffirming their commitment to Western civilization. Domestically this means rejecting the divisive siren calls of multiculturalism. internationally it means rejecting the elusive and illusory calls to identify the United States with Asia. Whatever economic connections may exist between them, the fundamental cultural gap between Asian and American societies precludes their joining together in a common home. Americans are culturally part of the Western family; multiculturalists may damage and even destroy that relationship but they cannot replace it. When Americans look for their cultural roots, they find them in Europe. (p. 307)

This is a remarkable passage, conveying a powerful sense that it is dangerous and polluting to mix cultural categories that should be kept pure and distinct.[19] What is most striking about this passage, however, is a startling failure of language and perception: does Huntington really believe that when African Americans, Arab Americans, Asian Americans, Latino Americans, or Native Americans "look for their cultural roots, they find them in Europe"? The extraordinary erasure of all but Euro-Americans in his declaration of "we" leaves one wondering what rock Huntington has been living under all these years. When he looks out at the students in his Harvard classes, does he see only white faces? He speaks of multiculturalism as a present and future danger without, apparently, noticing that massive immigrations from Asia, Africa, and Latin America have already transformed American national culture, and without acknowledging that the United States has, in any case, been a multicultural society since the first contact with Native Americans and the first imported slave. In other words, the society whose cultural purity and coherence he is so concerned to preserve was always already hybrid.

While I disagree with Huntington's jeremiad against multiculturalism, my point here is not so much a political one about cultural politics in the United States as an analytical one about the relationship of hybridity to culture in the United States and elsewhere. Most anthropologists would agree with Edward Said, who asks, "What culture today—whether Japanese, Arab, European, Korean, Chinese, or Indian—has not had long, intimate, and extraordinarily rich contacts with other cultures?"[20] Or with Aihwa Ong, who, in her own critique of The Clash of Civilizations, expresses "skepticism about whether any civilization can be anything but a blend of different ethnicities, cultures, and traditions."[21] Drawing on her own area of expertise, Asia, she notes that, although Huntington describes Japan and China as separate civilizations, Japan has historically been "much influenced by Chinese Confucianism and culture," while Southeast Asian culture is "a mélange of Hindu, Buddhist, Islamic, and Christian religions intermixed with animistic traditions."[22] One could make similar observations about the reciprocal influences of the Islamic, Orthodox, and Western civilizations upon one another over centuries of contact or, within civilizations, about processes of cross-fertilization such

as those between Germanic, French, and Scandinavian cultures that combined to produce what we now refer to as English culture. There is a
famous story told by the anthropologist Clifford Geertz about an informant who said that the world is carried on the back of an elephant
which, in turn, stands on the back of a turtle; when asked what the turtle
was standing on, he replied that from there it was "turtles all the way
down."[23] And so it is with cultural identity: hybridity all the way down.
Cultural syncretism is not a dangerous program of naive liberals but a
fact of cultural life. While it is true that cultural differences can become
flashpoints for conflict and that nations can fragment and disintegrate
along ethnic, religious, and cultural fault lines, as we recently saw in
Yugoslavia, it is also true that without difference there would be no culture and that interactions across cultural differences are always producing new cultural integrations and conversations. Huntington sees danger
in difference, and the danger is real, but by speaking about cultures as if
they are pure, distinct, and unchanging, he is blind to the fact that, culturally speaking, we are all mongrels, and that hybridization is not something which threatens cultures but is, rather, one of the essential cultural
processes.

Fifth Deadly Sin: Maligning Islam

The Clash of Civilizations has been popular in conservative circles largely
because it has been read as a prophetic book explaining a coming war
with either China or the states of the Islamic world (which he characterizes as, in many cases, "tribes with flags.")[24] Arguing that the West was
already, even in the mid-1990s, in a "quasi war" with Islam that had burst
into flame with the Iranian revolution, the Lockerbie bombing, and the
Gulf War (pp. 216–21), Huntington argues that "the underlying problem
for the West is not Islamic fundamentalism. It is Islam, a different civilization whose people are convinced of the superiority of their culture
and are obsessed with the inferiority of their power" (p. 217). He argues
that conflict between Islam and the West is overdetermined by the fact
that both cultural traditions are universalistic and proselytizing, by an
Islamic abhorrence for Western secularism and commercial culture, by

the lack of a "core state" to keep order in the Islamic world, and by a recent huge population surge in the Islamic world.[25] He casts Muslims as inherently violent, observing that, "wherever one looks along the perimeter of Islam, Muslims have problems living peacefully with their neighbors," and that "Islam's borders are bloody and so are its innards" (pp. 256, 258). He finds the roots of the antagonism between the West and Islam not in recent historical developments but in an essential antipathy expressed through centuries of violent antagonism, and warns that "Islam is the only civilization which has put the survival of the West in doubt" (p. 210). He suggests that "the twentieth century conflict between liberal democracy and Marxist-Leninism is only a fleeting and superficial phenomenon compared to the continuing and deeply conflictual relation between Islam and Christianity" (p. 209).

There are three major problems with this formulation. The first is that, in portraying Islam as a monolithic entity, it underestimates the profound diversity of Islamic life and of Islamic attitudes toward the West in particular. This diversity was readily apparent in divergent Islamic reactions to the September 11, 2001, attacks on the World Trade Center and the Pentagon. Even as the hijackers who undertook these attacks apparently perceived themselves as enacting God's will in a holy war against the West, and their acts met with applause by some Muslims, other Muslims in the West and the Middle East reacted with horror and saw the attacks as a perversion of Islamic teachings. While some Islamic nations remained neutral in the ensuing conflict, others—Egypt and Pakistan, for example—aligned themselves with the United States' war on terrorism.

We can make the same basic point about the diversity of Islamic culture in a more academic way with the help of Clifford Geertz's book *Islam Observed*.[26] Geertz is an anthropologist who, having conducted fieldwork in Morocco and Indonesia, the two geographical extremes of the Islamic world, sought to identify the ways in which both countries could be said to belong to a single cultural bloc, and the ways in which the distinctive cultural traditions of the two countries infused the practice of the same religion with difference. While Huntington argues that Islam is militant and aggressive because it has historically expanded its reach by military conquest, Geertz points out that Islam was brought to Morocco by the sword but to Indonesia in the baggage of traders. "To say that Morocco and Indonesia are both Islamic societies," Geertz says, "is as much to point up their differences as it is to locate their similarities" (pp. 13–14).

> Indonesian Islam has been, at least until recently, remarkably malleable, tentative, syncretistic, and, most significantly of all, multivoiced. What for so many parts of the world, and certainly for Morocco, has been a powerful, if not always triumphant, force for cultural homogenization and moral consensus, for the social standardization of fundamental beliefs and values, has been for Indonesia a no less powerful one for cultural diversification, for the crystallization of sharply variant, even incompatible, notions of what the world is really like and how to set about living in it. (p. 12)

The second major problem with Huntington's argument is that it attributes to an ancient and immoveable antagonism between cultures what might just as plausibly be seen as the consequence of particular U.S. policy decisions. Thus, instead of seeking the essential attributes of Islam that doom it to eternal confrontation with the West, we might find some of the origins of the current "quasi war" between Islam and the West in, for example, recent policies of U.S. intervention in the Middle East—policies that have led the United States to sustain unpopular regimes such as the Shah's in Iran and to throw its considerable resources behind the Israeli state's occupation of Palestinian territory. (It is, incidentally, remarkable that, in a book now best known for its prediction of a clash between Western and Islamic civilizations, Israel is barely mentioned.)

The third problem with Huntington's argument about Islam concerns the methodology through which he claims to "prove" that "Muslims have problems living peacefully with their neighbors" (p. 256). This brings us to Huntington's sixth deadly sin.

Sixth Deadly Sin: Phony Scientific Methods

Huntington does not just state that there is a "Muslim propensity toward violent conflict" (p. 258); he claims to prove it with statistics, saying, "The evidence is overwhelming" (p. 256). The "evidence" in question is three-fold: first, he cites studies that counted ethnic or civilizational conflicts in the early 1990s and says that "Muslims were engaged in more intergroup violence than were non-Muslims, and two-thirds to three-quarters of intercivilizational wars were between Muslims and non-Muslims" (pp. 257–58). Second, he counts the number of military personnel per thousand population in different countries and points out that the ratio is particularly high in the Islamic world. And, third, he divides military personnel by gross domestic product to produce something he calls "military effort indices" and argues, again, that the figure is particularly high in the Islamic world. "Quite clearly," he says, "there is a connection between Islam and militarism."[27]

While the use of numbers and measurements lends a superficial sheen of objectivity to Huntington's declamations here, he is playing with a stacked deck. With different indices, he could have shown instead that the United States is one of the most militaristic societies on earth. The United States focuses on the accumulation of advanced weaponry rather than the mobilization of mass armies as a source of military strength and, if Huntington had measured militarism as the proportion of government research and development money spent on the military, or as the proportion of physicists and engineers with doctorates working on military projects, then Islamic countries would have moved down his league table of militarism and the United States would have moved up. The same would be true if he had used as his measure the number of foreign military bases a country maintains—surely a good indicator of its "military effort." Moreover, the United States tends to intervene militarily in other countries through indirect means; instead of fighting directly, it has in recent years funded one of the parties in civil wars in Israel and Palestine, Nicaragua, El Salvador, Guatemala, Colombia, the former Yugoslavia, Afghanistan, and elsewhere. If the measure of militarism is whether or not one's own troops are directly involved in fighting those from other countries, then the particular forms that U.S. militarism often takes will be overlooked.

We might also point out that, even by his own slanted criteria, if one had gone through Huntington's counting exercise in the late nineteenth century to the mid–twentieth century, Western civilization would surely have come out listed among the most militaristic on earth. Its armies in the colonial period were everywhere engaged in conflict with other civilizations, and the military effort it expended in World Wars I and II was stupendous. Fortunately, civilizations change, and American defense intellectuals now complain that Europe—a continent whose internecine wars were greatly feared by American leaders in recent memory—is too focused on creating a prosperous free trading zone and is not devoting enough of its resources to preparation for war.

Seventh Deadly Sin: The West as the Best

Finally, Huntington assumes that the West is the only civilization capable of secular reason, liberal democracy, and true individualism. At one point, disregarding twentieth-century Western experiences with fascism, he speaks of "the dominance of individualism in the West compared to the prevalence of collectivism elsewhere" (p. 71). He also says, "The great ideologies of the twentieth century include liberalism, socialism, anarchism, corporatism, Marxism, communism, social democracy, conservatism, nationalism, fascism, and Christian democracy. They all share one thing in common: they are products of Western civilization. No other civilization has generated a significant political ideology" (pp. 53–54). This is an extraordinarily ethnocentric statement. What about Maoism, Gandhianism, and Nasserism? The first two were important not only in the Asian societies where they took shape but also, through cultural diffusion, in Western society. Martin Luther King and the civil rights activists of the 1960s, for example, were deeply influenced by Mahatma Gandhi. Maintaining that the only important political ideologies have been Western requires one to believe that only Western political ideologies have been important.

Huntington argues for the uniqueness of Western civilization: "Western civilization is valuable not because it is universal but because it *is* unique. The principal responsibility of Western leaders, consequently, is not to attempt to reshape other civilizations in the image of the West . . . but to preserve, protect and renew the unique qualities of Western civilization" (p. 311, italics in the original). While there is a superficial relativism, even liberalism, to Huntington's arguments that each civilization has its own unique values and that the West should not seek to impose its own values, including democracy, on other civilizations, the insistence that only the West can originate political ideologies seems quaintly old-fashioned—like a fedora in a sea of baseball caps—in our current post-colonial era. The argument that democracy is Western and Western alone is simply belied by the development of democratic polities (which Huntington apparently fails to recognize) in Japan, India, Taiwan, South Korea, and other non-Western nations. The rise of such democracies in different corners of the world gives hope that, instead of Huntington's prescription for a rigid system of global cultural apartheid, there are possibilities for convergence and consanguinity in the current global system that are not dreamt of in Huntington's philosophy.

CONCLUSION

I like to imagine that Samuel Huntington has a doppelgänger who is little known in the West. The doppelgänger's name is Osama bin Huntington, and he teaches at the University of Riyadh in Saudi Arabia, where his work is held in high esteem by the conservative elite. Like Samuel, Osama anticipates that globalization will produce a "clash of civilizations" at the center of which will stand a conflict between Islam and the West. Osama, like Samuel, believes that it is dangerous to mix different cultures, and he is particularly concerned that the purity and vitality of Islamic culture is threatened by Westernization. Pointing to the Crusades of the medieval period, he says that history shows that Islam and the West cannot comfortably coexist. Peaceful coexistence is made more difficult, he argues, by the West's intrinsic militarism and love of violence. Here he points to several centuries of colonial expansion by the West, two world wars that originated in the West, the fact that the United States has, since the end of World War II, fought wars in Korea, Vietnam, Grenada, Panama, the Persian Gulf, Bosnia, and Kosovo, and the relentless celebration of violence in Hollywood culture. His recent book features a table of the number of violent incidents and deaths per hour of film, showing that Hollywood films have a higher "violent incident index" than films made in other civilizations. "It is incontrovertible," he claims in a much quoted passage, "that Western culture is irremediably violent to the core."

Although he does not advocate the conquest of other civilizations by Islam, arguing that each civilization can coexist with the others if it stays within its own sphere of influence, Osama bin Huntington is read by his colleagues and followers to say that Islam is clearly the greatest of the civilizations: its religion is the most austerely monotheistic; it has not fallen prey to the decadent consumerism that besets the West; and political discipline in the Islamic world is relatively uncompromised by the divisive theatrics of democracy, and by constant regime shifts, found in Western countries. Writing about the West—here he has been attacked by French scholars for equating the West with the United States—he argues that the West is headed for an internal crisis because it is a civilization of decadent unbelievers who derive meaning in life from the pursuit of promiscuous sex and the futile accumulation of commodities while ignoring the plight of the poor in their own civilization and abroad. He argues that Western culture has been materialistic since the time of the ancient Greeks and Romans, and that its descent into arrogant consumerism and undisciplined pluralism was in a sense inevitable.

I indulge this exercise in fantasy to make a number of points. First, one can quite plausibly construct a narrative in which it is Westerners, not Muslims, who "have problems living peacefully with their neighbors." Second, we can see how simplistic and reductive are the kinds of generalizations Huntington makes when we imagine them being made by someone else about our own civilization. (What about all the churchgoers, we ask, in response to Osama's stereotyping of Americans as decadent unbelievers.) My choice of the name Osama for Samuel Huntington's Islamic twin is, of course, not accidental, and it is remarkable how much resonance there is with the ideology of that more notorious Osama when we translate Samuel Huntington's ideas into an Islamic idiom. If we reject the cultural fundamentalism of the Osamas of this world, as I believe we should, then we should give no more respect to their doppelgängers in the West, foremost among whom is Samuel Huntington.

THREE Samuel Huntington, Meet the Nuer

KINSHIP, LOCAL KNOWLEDGE,
AND THE CLASH OF CIVILIZATIONS

Keith Brown

In his influential 1993 *Foreign Affairs* article, the leading political scientist Samuel Huntington made the phrase "the clash of civilizations" his own.[1] In the article, and in his ensuing 1996 book, Huntington made a bold and straightforward central claim: Political ideologies and self-interest, although still factors in international relations, are being superseded by cultural ties between groups and countries. In Huntington's vision, the contemporary world can (and should) be understood as composed of seven (or eight) "civilizations," many of which are led by a "core state," and all of which are held together by what he calls "cultural kinship." Conflicts between countries from different civilizations, in which each side may draw on the support of "kin-countries," pose the greatest risks of escalation and potential nuclear confrontation, as core states may then be pitted against one another in "fault-line wars." World order will be preserved against cataclysmic war, he concludes, only if world leaders recognize and respect the importance of culture when they make policy.[2]

The notion that civilizations are key units of analysis in world history is hardly new, and Huntington offers a list of his intellectual forbears that includes Oswald Spengler, Arnold Toynbee, Fernand Braudel, and Immanuel Wallerstein.[3] He also identifies the influential American anthropologists Alfred Kroeber, Ruth Benedict, and Margaret Mead as sources for his model of cultures as internally coherent units, different and irreconcilable with one another.[4]

In favoring this model, though, Huntington and his culturalist colleagues ignore or dismiss a substantial shift in thinking within anthropology since the 1980s. Culture is now more often understood as being perpetually in process, shaped by human interactions and societal interconnections. The discipline still depends upon the method of extended fieldwork in a social setting, which produces what Clifford Geertz famously termed "local knowledge."[5] While some contemporary anthropologists still draw on this material to depict cultures as homogenous and distinct, a more general trend is to use the fruits of fieldwork to criticize and challenge the oversimplification, ethnocentrism, and stylization on which such representations often depend.[6]

In this chapter, I seek to show how culturally minded political scientists like Samuel Huntington might benefit from anthropology conducted since the days of Benedict, Mead, and Kroeber. My argument has two main parts. First, I examine Huntington's usage of the term *kinship* in his argument regarding relations between states in the contemporary world, and seek to identify parallels for his usage in anthropological literature. His formulation of the power of kinship draws on a model that emphasizes the importance of common descent over marriage (whether for love or interest) and owes much, wittingly or no, to the model of "segmentary lineage" made famous by Edward Evans-Pritchard in his classic 1940 work, *The Nuer*. I trace some of the nuances that later anthropologists have located in the Nuer case, and in the field of kinship studies more generally. Thinking through the issues of agency, property ownership, and gender roles that underlie the surface simplicities of ethnographic classics can also, I suggest, contribute to a better understanding of the role of identity politics in the modern world order.

In the second part of the chapter, I seek to demonstrate the utility of local knowledge for culturalist theory by suggesting that, if we insist on narrating political processes through kinship metaphors, we should be open to alternative forms of kinship reckoning. I focus on the Balkans, where I have conducted fieldwork over the last decade. In 1993, Huntington's argument that Bosnia was a "fault-line war" between "Western," "Islamic," and "Eastern Orthodox" civilizations, in which protagonists were aided by "cultural kin," was still plausible. When the United States intervened on behalf of (Muslim) Bosniaks in 1995, Huntington regarded it as an "anomaly."[7] Subsequently, though, in 1999, the North Atlantic Treaty Organization (NATO) intervened on behalf of (Muslim) Albanians in Kosovo; Libya and Iraq (both Muslim) expressed solidarity with Orthodox Serbia; and Bulgaria and Romania (both Orthodox) defied Orthodox Russia. In 2001, when (mostly Muslim) Albanian insurgents declared war on the (Orthodox majority) Macedonian state, (Muslim) Turkey, Bosnia, and Albania, and (Orthodox) Serbia, Greece, and Bulgaria remained rooted on the sidelines, and a peace agreement was brokered by the (Western) European Union and United States.

If one anomaly is unfortunate, such a profusion smacks of carelessness. It is hard to know which would be more galling for a devotee of Huntington's doctrine that kin-countries rally, and that states should not act outside their civilizational limits: the extracivilizational hyperactivity of the United States; the apparent treachery of Libya, Iraq, Bulgaria and Romania; or the "kin-indifference" of Macedonia's near-neighbors. Perhaps, though, to recycle a phrase used by the anthropologist David Schneider to criticize doctrinaire kinship theorists in the 1960s, the problem lies in muddles in the model.[8] Whereas Huntington emphasizes the importance of kinship's primordial ties and contrasts them strongly with instrumental calculations of self-interest, Balkan societies (as well as others) do not necessarily make such neat divisions. Anthropologists working in the former Yugoslav republics of Serbia and Macedonia, and in Greece, Albania, and Bulgaria, have documented the importance of what they term *fictive kinship*, whereby people unrelated by blood nonetheless forge bonds that are enduring and sacred. One such bond is enshrined in the institution of *kumstvo*, or godfatherhood. This chapter concludes, then, by exploring how far the introduction of notions of fictive kinship in general, and *kumstvo* in particular, might help political scientists seeking to find space for culture—not just their own but also that of others—in their models of international politics.[9]

SAMUEL HUNTINGTON: KINSHIP THEORIST?

After the considerable impact of his 1993 article, in 1996 Samuel Huntington published a refined and extended version of his "clash of civilizations" theory. In the book, which shed the question mark of the article title, he explicitly deals, in particular, with the basis of ties between groups, countries, or states within his civilizations, stating early in the work his core premises that "societies sharing cultural affinities cooperate with each other," and "countries group themselves around the lead or core states of their civilizations."[10] He goes on to use a metaphor more commonly found in anthropology to further describe both of these forms of relationship. In explanation of Islamic countries providing funds and arms to Bosnia in the early 1990s, he states that their actions were guided not by ideology, power politics, or economic interest but by "cultural kinship."[11] Later he refers to the European Union countries as "cultural kin" to Austria, Finland, and Sweden.[12] He extends the same metaphor in describing the role of core states within civilizations, stating that "a core state can perform its ordering function because member states perceive it as cultural kin. A civilization is an extended family and, like older members of a family, core states provide their relatives with both support and discipline."[13] His view of intrafamily relationships is further illuminated by his use of a similar metaphor to explain "bandwagoning," or throwing in one's lot with a powerful actor. Stressing sibling ties, he writes that "a younger boy will bandwagon with his older brother when they confront other boys; he is less likely to trust his older brother when they are alone at home. Hence more frequent interactions between states of different civilizations will further encourage bandwagoning within civilizations."[14]

Although power inequalities and distrust are factors within Huntington's civilizations/families, their effects are trumped in "fault-line wars." In his account of the mechanism of escalation that such conflicts produce, he again uses the metaphor of kinship, and claims that the bonds of shared culture have effects, regardless of interest: "In the usual communal conflict, Group A is fighting Group B, and Groups C, D, and E have no reason to become involved unless A or B directly attacks the interests of C, D or E. In a fault-line war, in contrast, Group A1 is fighting Group B1 and each will attempt to expand the war and mobilize support from civilization kin groups, A2, A3 and A4, and B2, B3, and B4, and those groups will identify with their fighting kin."[15] He dubs this phenomenon the *kin-country syndrome*, crediting a Boston Globe journalist, H. D. Greenway, with the invention of the term.[16]

By treating these references to kinship as we might those of an anthropological informant, we can infer how Huntington sees cultural ties working. Clearly, his starting point is a comparison with ties of blood, rather than ties of marriage. In his "extended family," members are distinguished only by seniority in age: there seems to be no question of possible differences between sibling, spousal, or in-law relations. Additionally, we can note that the only gender-marked reference he makes is to males. Fuller details of what he means by kinship, though, are not provided explicitly, suggesting that he believes the metaphor is wholly transparent and obvious in meaning. And to the casual Western reader, this is perhaps the case: we all know, near enough, what kinship means.

DEBATING DESCENT, MULLING OVER MEANINGS

Anthropologists, though, do not take the term so lightly, and much ink has been spilt in the course of the discipline's history over the intricacies of kinship. Scholars have investigated kinship systems both near and far to ascertain the different ways in which people reckon the ties created by descent and by marriage, and weigh the obligations that they create.[17] Scholars have also waged bitter wars with one another over the relative merits of different approaches to the topic; and more recently, there has been a higher level discussion over whether there are sufficient grounds for presuming that kinship can be treated as a discrete topic of study.[18]

In anthropological debates over kinship, a key point of departure is

Edward Evans-Pritchard's seminal work on the Nuer, a Sudanese people.[19] During the 1930s, British colonial authorities trying to establish control over Sudan were perplexed by the Nuer capacity to organize relatively large forces for combat without having a clear central command
structure located in a "state." Evans-Pritchard set out to explain this phenomenon, and did so by reference to what he called the segmentary lineage system. The Nuer, according to Evans-Pritchard, were internally
divided and subdivided into social groups or segments defined by their
ties to named ancestors; these could fight one another or unite to fight a
common foe. Loyalties were thus ordered, nested within each other, limiting internal conflict and allowing Nuer to unite against an external foe.
When a man quarreled with his brother, for example, others did not join
the fighting. But when some dispute arose between members of different
descent groups, then each could rely upon fellow descent-group members
for support, and as a result, the conflict could escalate. The limit of conflict, in each case, was the point in the adversaries' genealogical history at
which they recognized a common ancestor. Brothers in dispute had the
same potential allies, and so could not call on them against one another:
first cousins in dispute could mobilize their own brothers, and their
fathers, but no one beyond that. In contrast, two men in dispute whose
first common ancestor lay six generations back could each call upon a host
of allies. And when the enemy was non-Nuer—either the Dinka (a neighboring Sudanese people) or the British colonial authorities—all Nuer
potentially could rally.

The concept of segmentation remains influential, especially in contemporary scholarship on national identity. Michael Herzfeld, for example, notes that Cretan villagers might feud with one another, but that,
when Cretan pride is at stake, they rally to the island's cause; and when
Greece is threatened from the outside, Cretans put aside their quarrels
with Athens.[20] Anthropological studies of ethnicity and nationalism, and
historical studies of the relationship between local and national identities, have reproduced Evans-Pritchard's diagrammatic representations in
their explanations.[21] Part of the enduring appeal of *The Nuer* is its unity of
affect, achieved through a stark and declarative style that invokes the
authority of good, English common sense.[22] In explaining the fluid Nuer

concept of *cieng*, for example, Evans-Pritchard employs a robust, easily comprehensible parable:

> If one meets an Englishman in Germany and asks him where his home is, he may reply that it is England. If one meets the same man in London and asks him the same question, he will tell one that his home is in Oxfordshire, whereas if one meets him in that county he will tell one the name of the town or village in which he lives. If questioned in his town or village he will mention his particular street, and if questioned in his street he will indicate his house. So it is with the Nuer. . . . The variations in the meaning of the word *cieng* are not due to the inconsistencies of language, but to the relativity of the group-values to which it refers.[23]

Samuel Huntington's model of the world as composed of seven (or eight) civilizations, in which individual member-states look to their civilizational kin for support, bears a superficial resemblance to this anthropological abstraction developed in the first half of the twentieth century. On closer examination, though, its relative thinness quickly becomes apparent. According to Evans-Pritchard, "Nuer habitually express social obligations in a kinship idiom" and go to war together because, they say, "their ancestors were sons of the same mother."[24] By contrast, the basis of the kinship that Huntington detects between states is simply "culture." Whereas, in the formal model proposed by Evans-Pritchard, tribes display a clear hierarchy of loyalties and order of allegiance determined by descent-depth and tied to feelings of home, Huntington's civilizations have no such clear social mechanism for progressive mobilization of their membership. Where Evans-Pritchard and other anthropologists see nested, "socio-spatial" loyalties at work—from hut to hamlet to village; to primary, secondary, and tertiary tribal sections; to tribe; to "Nuerland"— Huntington's model focuses on just two levels of loyalty: civilizations and states. And whereas in Evans-Pritchard's account and those of the more reflective scholars of national identity, higher levels of mobilization are inherently hard to sustain and always vulnerable to processes of internal fission, Huntington portrays a one-way path to civilizational clash, in which the "lesser" identities simply lose their significance.[25]

NO LONGER MEN ONLY

The "clash of civilizations" argument, then, seems to have less structure than a sixty-year-old classic of formalism. When viewed from the perspective of subsequent work on the Nuer material, pioneered by Evans-Pritchard himself, this argument's shortcomings as a model of reality become even clearer, and the vision of kinship it embraces more inadequate. Since Evans-Pritchard's own follow-up account of Nuer kinship and marriage, subsequent studies have stressed the fluidity and change in Nuer lives and the dangers of overrigid models.[26] Sharon Hutchinson, for example, describes social and cultural systems as "inherently unfinished, open-ended, and riddled with uncertainties." As she points out, "What earlier generations of anthropologists tended to view as 'the logic' of a particular social system has . . . often appeared, on closer inspection, to be merely the logic of some segment of it."[27] Evans-Pritchard's first book represented descent through the male line as the decisive source of loyalty, but Hutchinson elaborates the dimensions of *maar*, a Nuer word that she translates as "relationship" as well as "kinship." The bonds of *maar* can be created through the maternal line and through the binding power of cattle given by a father to an adopted son.[28] Susan McKinnon emphasizes how Evans-Pritchard's analytical distinction of descent from kinship makes it more difficult for readers to grasp how the effects and significance of marriage alliances and blood ties mingle. Evans-Pritchard's early focus on biological lineage through the male line, she suggests, conjures a world populated only by men, by and large considered interchangeable, whereas the reality is that an individual's membership in a group was more often established by the exchange of cattle between competing groups at marriage or at birth than by simple genealogical connection.[29]

In the case of the Nuer, then, work by Hutchinson and McKinnon builds on Evans-Pritchard's own work to show the significance of various kinds of exchange between people of different genders, generations, and bloodlines in creating kinship. Some people, it turns out, are far more important than they "really" should be by Evans-Pritchard's strict geometry, and many of those people turn out to be women. One response to

Samuel Huntington's model of kinship between states and cultures, then, would be to ask where gender fits in the metaphor.

What kind of older relative, for example, does Huntington imagine Orthodox Russia to be to the Eastern Orthodox states of the Balkans? Asking the question in this way might sound like dogged, misplaced literalism, but anthropologists, who as a group can claim some authority on the subject of kinship, could reasonably argue that it matters a great deal. Core states, in Huntington's description, may resemble older brothers or authority figures of an older generation—the stern uncle, perhaps, or the hard-to-please father. But Huntington also sees these core states as enjoying, or at least seeking to elicit, near-automatic loyalty from their kin. David Schneider's research in the late 1960s had already demonstrated how indistinct the lines were between kin and nonkin in North America: the only point on which his informants provided near unanimity was that one should always help one's mother when ill.[30] In Huntington's world, then, it could be argued that, for all the masculinist language and rhetoric, core states aspire not only to command grudging support but also to attract the same unconditional love that American mothers once did.

Beyond Nuerland and the nuclear family, other anthropologists have taken the study of kinship still further from its associations with blood ties. From a growing literature focusing on patterns of social relations in gay and lesbian communities, it is clear that many individuals count as kin those with whom they have relationships of care. Traces of such attitudes were apparent in David Schneider's work in Chicago mentioned above, where he identifies three terms for distant blood relatives: "shirt-tail relations," "wakes-and-weddings relatives," and "kissin' cousins," each of which is acknowledged as a diluted form of kinship that carries only a vestigial sense of obligation or connection.[31] By contrast, in San Francisco as described by Kath Weston, and Berlin as described by John Borneman, people whose ties biologists and lawyers would mark as contingent or even transgressive themselves experience those same relationships as familial, and they are willing to defy normative thinking in order to formalize them.[32] Borneman, for example, describes a case where, to establish shared property rights, one man legally adopts his male lover, and another where one member of a lesbian couple legally marries her partner's son to gain residence rights. If individuals are so creative in negotiating the bonds of kinship, can we not imagine that states and their leaders might exercise similar ingenuity? Culturalist political scientists, it could be argued, could take from Weston's account of parenting, and Borneman's distinctions between hetero- and homosex, new metaphors for thinking about the new world order and the relations among its members.

MUDDLES IN THE MODEL, FROM BOSNIA TO MACEDONIA (VIA KOSOVO)

Perhaps, though, in suggesting that Samuel Huntington might be the standard-bearer in a war against heteronormativity in American political science, I am getting ahead of my argument. It seems less outlandish, though, to suggest that his analysis of the Yugoslav breakup of the 1990s merits some revision in light of events in the region. As noted above, Huntington represents the conflict in Bosnia as a "fault-line war" in which three sides distinguished on religious grounds enlisted the assistance of their "cultural kin." In 1993, he argued, the alignment of the parties made this evident. The Bosnian Croats were backed by Croatia—both Catholic—and, beyond them, by "Western" Germany. Orthodox Christian Russia backed Orthodox Christian Serbia, which in turn backed the Orthodox Bosnian Serbs. Bosnia's Muslims, a plurality in the republic but lacking a neighboring supporter, drew support from elsewhere in the Islamic world, especially Iran and Turkey. By 1996, however, the world looked different: the war in Bosnia had been ended by the Dayton Peace conference, presided over by the United States, which had taken direct action on behalf of the Bosnian Muslims. Serbia, under President Slobodan Milosevic, had proved ready and willing to negotiate on behalf of the Bosnian Serbs, who were excluded from the peace talks, and to yield—on their behalf—some of their original demands.

The simple kin-state model could not accommodate these anomalies. Accordingly, in his 1996 book, Huntington offered analytical refinements to his model. He distinguished between primary, secondary, and tertiary parties in conflicts, the implication being that these represented successively more influential political powers. If the Bosnian Croats were the primary party, their secondary supporter, or "rallier," was Croatia, and their tertiary kin, Germany. The peace settlement in Bosnia, he argued, represented a case where tertiary and secondary powers successfully used their intracivilizational influence to dissuade their "kin" from continuing to fight. That left the anomaly of U.S. involvement on the side of the Bosnian Muslims; this Huntington explained either as "civilizational realpolitik"—with the aim of offsetting Iranian influence in Bosnia—or as determined by moralistic attitudes, which saw the Bosnian Muslims as victims struggling to preserve multiculturalism.[33]

By such ad hoc means, effectively sneaking self-interest and balance-of-power thinking back in, Huntington preserved his cultural theory without substantially rethinking its basic principles. Subsequent events in the Balkans posed further challenges to his model. Even as he was cohosting an April 1999 conference at Harvard on the theme that "culture matters," the United States was engaged in a war in the Balkans with the stated humanitarian goal of preventing Christian Orthodox Serbs from killing Kosovar Albanian Muslims. In the course of that war, the United States provided arms and training to the Kosovo Liberation Army (KLA), which some analysts, as well as the Serbian military, referred to as a "Muslim guerilla army." Contrary to Huntington's model, other Islamic states did not assist this side: instead, Baghdad and Tripoli expressed support for (Orthodox) Serbia. Russia, in accordance with Huntington's model, protested at the NATO aggression against Serbia and even sent troops to seize the airport in Kosovo's capital, apparently in collusion with Serbia. But Russian plans to fly in reinforcements were thwarted, apparently by the refusal of Orthodox Bulgaria and Romania, under pressure from NATO, to allow Russian aircraft passage through their airspace.[34]

The war in Kosovo was clear evidence that a simple version of the "clash of civilizations" cannot account for the complex web of geopolitics. It was simply not true that kin-states were drawn into conflicts along predictable lines dictated by cultural affinity. Huntington's formal logic of patterned escalation does not fit the Balkans, where, in the words of one ethnographer, "cultural praxis . . . can best be described as mixed, heterogeneous, contradictory, fragmented, and incoherent."[35] Further evidence of this was provided two years later, when a paramilitary Albanian organization called the National Liberation Army launched an armed insurgency against the Macedonian state in early 2001. Some local and international analysts, admittedly, found evidence that civilizations were clashing again and that "kin" rallied in the six months of fighting, as Orthodox Ukraine supplied Macedonian security forces with advanced weaponry and Muslim fighters, or mujahideen, were reported as fighting alongside the Albanian insurgents, who also had ties to the Kosovo Liberation Army. But there was rather more kin-indifference. Within Macedonia, the vast majority of the country's 1.4 million Orthodox Macedonians and five hundred thousand Muslim Albanians maintained a commitment to peaceful resolution of the fighting. (Muslim) Turkey, Bosnia, and Albania, and (Orthodox) Serbia, Greece, and Bulgaria limited their engagement to expressions of concern. The fighting dragged on for six months, until the European Union and the United States brokered a cease-fire settlement.

THE TROUBLE WITH KIN

What, then, do the conflicts in Kosovo and Macedonia in 1999 and 2001, in which Albanians were protagonists, mean for theories of civilizational kinship? Clearly the failure of Islamic countries to rally to the side of Kosovar Albanians, the support of the United States for the Kosovar Albanians, and the disregard of supposed kin loyalties by states on both "sides" in the Macedonia conflict all raise doubts over such theories' applicability. One response is to look more closely at the credentials that groups or countries have for membership in one civilization or another. In this regard, it turns out, Albanians are particularly difficult to pin down. In Huntington's scheme, they are categorized as Muslim. In fact, some Albanians in Kosovo, Macedonia, and Albania are Catholics; in Albania around 20 percent of the population are Eastern Orthodox; and as a modern state, Albania has a defiantly secular history. Still more significantly, as Ger Duijzings points out, Albanians in Kosovo and Macedonia have a strong tradition of Sufism rather than the more mainstream Sunni Islam. Like Shia Muslims, members of Sufi orders have a special devotion to Mohammed's cousin and son-in-law, Ali, and his son

Husayn, whom they believe were unjustly denied their true inheritance. They attach special significance to Kerbela, the site of Husayn's murder by the Caliph Yazid (whose reign they see as illegitimate) in 680. Thus to the Albanians of Kosovo and Macedonia, the Sunni Islam faith declared by the Islamic Community of Yugoslavia and by Bosnian Muslims represents the legacy of traitors and murderers.[36] Tensions between these two branches of Islam are not easily overcome, even where an external foe is in question, so it is hard to dub Albanians simply as members of "Islamic" civilization.

Other Balkan states, especially members of the alleged Eastern Orthodox bloc, also fit uneasily into Huntington's system. Speaking of the frictions between Macedonia and Bulgaria, a Macedonian told me in the spring of 2000, "We hate each other so much, we must be brothers!" This captures a long history of intimate contact and quarrelling over status. Bulgaria's autonomous Orthodox church was born out of an Ottoman decree in 1870 and was bitterly resisted by the Greek-dominated patriarchate. During the Second Balkan War of 1913, World War I, and World War II, disputes over territory and population pitted Bulgaria against Serbia and Greece as Bulgaria sought to win what its people thought of, and in some cases still think of, as their rightful property—most of the modern republic of Macedonia. After World War II, to be sure, Bulgaria was a compliant satellite of Soviet Russia, but in recent years the country has swung dramatically toward the West, and in November 2001 it was admitted into NATO. As with Albania, the country has enough quarrels with its Orthodox neighbors, especially with regard to interpretations of a past its people hold sacred, to make its membership of and cooperation in an Eastern Orthodox bloc fraught with complications.

MAKING (ANTHROPOLOGICAL) SENSE OF THE BALKANS

One way to deal with the civilizational conundrums posed by Albania, Bulgaria, and other countries or groups in the Balkans is to dismiss them as irrelevant details. That is of course the approach of Samuel

Huntington, whose apocalyptic scenario for the next world war, sched-uled for 2010 and precipitated by rivalries between the American and Chinese civilizations, links Bulgaria and Greece to the Orthodox bloc and envisions them launching invasions of Turkey and fighting against Albania in support of a Serbian attack on Muslim Bosnia.[37] Another response to the history of bitter local disputes—a history which indicates that neither Albania nor Bulgaria seems constrained by ties to Islam or Orthodoxy—is to dismiss the utility of Huntington's kin-based civiliza-tions altogether. As I hope this chapter makes clear, a third, more pro-ductive response is to find and utilize metaphors of kinship that are cul-turally appropriate to the processes they are intended to illuminate.

As noted above, descent and marriage are not the only ways in which kinship bonds are created. In Catholic Latin America and in the Orthodox Balkans, ethnographers have charted the significance of fictive kinship, a term they use to describe relations of sponsorship between families. The most important of these is godparenthood, which links a marrying cou-ple or a new child to a sponsor who is unrelated by blood, and who is subsequently prohibited from marrying into the family. In Spanish, the relationship is referred to as *compadrazgo*. In Serbian and Macedonian, the sponsor, if male, is known as the *kum*; in Greek, the term is *koumbaros;* and in Albanian, *kumbar.* The bonds of solidarity thus created are permanent and powerful and may even be considered more sacred than those of blood or marriage.[38]

The concept of *kumstvo,* or godparenthood, gives us an extra resource for thinking about the creation of loyalty in the Balkans. It is especially useful if we are prepared to take one more liberty in thinking of states (or, in one case, future states) as if they were individuals enmeshed in rela-tionships and to reflect that those under discussion here—Bulgaria, Albania, the republic of Macedonia, and Kosovo—are all relatively young or, in the last instance, yet to be born. Huntington himself set a precedent here for classifying countries by age: in his vision, though, the younger (and smaller) members of civilizations find themselves captive and even bullied members of extended families run by senior, stronger members. Bulgaria, in such a scenario, can either stand shoulder to shoul-der with Russia and its other Orthodox brethren (who in fact spent most of the twentieth century rubbing its face in the dirt) or risk being left to fend for itself. Albanian-dominated Kosovo lacks the resources to argue its case in family councils and must put up or shut up, even though its Sufi residents reject core doctrinal beliefs of older Islamic states.

If, however, one takes an expanded view of kin-state to include the "godparent" mode as commonly understood in the Orthodox Balkans, then Bulgaria and Kosovo, like other small states, in fact have other options. Ritual sponsors, traditionally, are not recruited from either blood kin or from families already related by marriage; but the bonds between a *kum* and a child are powerful and benefit both parties. Historically, small, young Balkan states looking for such external assistance have found plenty of offers. When the modern Greek state was created in the mid–nineteenth century—at a time when many members of the rural population around Athens spoke Albanian—Russia vied with Britain and France to control the politics of the new country. Britain, Soviet Russia, and the United States also wrangled over the Balkan countries in the closing days of World War II, when Winston Churchill handed Joseph Stalin the famous scrap of paper that put Greece under Western control, put Bulgaria under Soviet control, and left Yugoslavia as an area of equal influence.[39] Since the end of the cold war and the breakup of Yugoslavia, powerful sponsors are again anxious to recruit client states and exert regional influence. At the birth of brand new states, and the dramatic ide ological reform of others, godparents stand ready in the wings to play a part in leading the new entities through a bewildering world, in which other claimants to their loyalty might lead them astray.

Some might view such interference with suspicion and use metaphors laden with negative connotations (cradle-snatching? pedophilia? brain-washing?) to question the motives of the sponsor state and delegitimate the relationships thus formed. Samuel Huntington himself is certainly convinced that this kind of intrusive meddling on the part of the United States is a recipe for national disaster. Cross-civilizational alliances, he argues, can only be interest driven: their strength can never rival that of cultural kin-ties. But by drawing such an absolute distinction between two kinds of bonds—sentiments based on enduring cultural affinity, and alliances constructed to yield short-term, calculated benefits—he discounts a phenomenon known throughout the Balkans and, in a different form, to ethnographers of kinship everywhere. When people invest belief and trust in relationships, the ties they forge may over time develop a strength that rivals or overmasters those rooted in blood or enshrined in law.

I have already suggested that Samuel Huntington, and others interested in new ways of thinking about kinship in world politics, might enjoy recent works of anthropological theory. They could also learn from Macedonian and Albanian interpretations of U.S. intervention in Kosovo in 1999. Macedonians are certainly critical of that intervention, and do consider Albanians to be members of a non-Western civilization, but they are not bewildered by U.S. assistance to the Kosovo Liberation Army. They describe the United States as playing the role of godfather, or *kum*, to a proposed "Greater Albania." They thus describe the relations of one portion of a people (expansionist Albanians) and a superpower in the way they might describe the relationship between two families who create an enduring connection that dominates other loyalties. Kosovar Albanian familiarity with the concept also surfaced in a human interest story reported by the *Independent* journalist Robert Fisk. A Kosovar Albanian named his daughter "Kfor" after the NATO-led protection force KFOR, and expressed the hope that the British commander, General Jackson, would act as godfather.[40] Perhaps the journalist intended this as a quaint story about local customs and a pathetic gratitude. But it can also be read as an example of how ordinary people, as well as theorists, make links between local cultural forms and international politics.[41] Families have strategies to extend their webs of obligation and common interest and thus create culturally specific kinship ties that have not, so far, informed the theorizing of political scientists. Such anecdotes of culture as practice give an indication of what anthropology—an openness to the categories of others, and an engagement with the messy realities of everyday life—might contribute to the rethinking of world order.

CONCLUSION

What, then, of cultural kinship? The metaphor remains a powerful tool of understanding and illuminating global politics. Other political scientists, though wary of accepting the whole "clash of civilizations" package, nonetheless find inspiration in this particular component.[42] Other recent works in the field, dealing with both international and domestic politics, suggest wider interest in addressing issues of culture and identity.[43] Although Huntington and his discipline are often perceived by anthropologists as doctrinaire and overly scientistic, such culturalist initiatives, and the cross-disciplinary thinking they demand, should be welcomed for what they might well be: signs of intellectual curiosity and vigor. As I have tried to indicate in this chapter, though, Huntington's writing conveys an understanding of culture in general, and kinship in particular, as a somewhat static and limiting force in the world. What it lacks is any reflexive sense of the cultural specificity of that view of culture and kinship. As David Schneider put it almost twenty years ago, "European social scientists use their own folk culture as the source of many, if not all, of their ways of formulating and understanding the world around them."[44] Huntington's adherence to an old-fashioned model of primordially rooted loyalty seems a classic case.

The professional anthropologists I cite here, and at least some of the residents of Macedonia with whom I have worked over the past ten years, offer perspectives also informed by culture. And they present culture differently, as a work in progress yielding ground to human agency and will. If there is a single point I hope readers take from this chapter and reiterate in the important debates kindled by "The Clash of Civilizations?" it is that Samuel Huntington's view of culture and kinship need not define the conversation. For anthropologists and others who explore new ways of thinking about the new world order, the debate over whether culture shapes politics is over: of course it does. The question that remains, and the question that Huntington's lengthy writing consistently skirts, is how.

FOUR

Haunted by the Imaginations
of the Past

ROBERT KAPLAN'S *BALKAN GHOSTS*

Tone Bringa

Robert Kaplan writes that, as he sets foot on the part of the earth he
thinks of as "Balkan," he wonders, "What does the earth look like in
places where people commit atrocities? Is there a bad smell, a genius loci,
something about the landscape that might incriminate?"[1] A few pages on,
he offers his answer: "The earth here had the harsh, exhausted face of a
prostitute, cursing bitterly between coughs. The landscape of atrocities is
easy to recognize: communism had been the Great Preserver."[2] But he has
to hurry before the place loses its primitive, peasant character: "My time
was thus short. Soon, whether in the late 1990s or in the decades following, the entire canvas would go dull, as it already had in Klagenfurt" (on
the Austrian-Slovenian border), where he "saw a man in a purple suede
blazer and Giorgio Armani optics, and women done up by Jil Sanders or
Guerlain," and where "glass display cases in the middle of the side-

walks" were filled with Samsonite luggage, Lego toy space simulation stations, and jewelry from Tiffany's.[3] This is how Kaplan masterfully prepares his readers for what is to come: the other Europe, "anticivilization, alter ego, the dark side within," as Maria Todorova puts it.[4] With an acute sense of urgency, Kaplan searches the Balkans for the last remnants of Europeans' tribal mentality, which he sees as locked into a past where ethnic loyalties and violence reign, a timeless place that is both a great producer and an exporter of evils to the rest of Europe.[5]

I first saw Robert Kaplan's *Balkan Ghosts* in early 1995, when I was working as a policy analyst for the UN peacekeeping operations in Croatia and Bosnia-Herzegovina. I had seen the book in the hands of foreign aid workers, UN civilians, and military personnel as they waited for flights in and out of the war zone. The title alone conjured up the book's hackneyed explanation for the wars in Croatia and Bosnia-Herzegovina: just another legacy of the "Balkan syndrome"—of centuries-old hatreds and a propensity for savage violence erupting once again into the present. A quick browse through the book revealed a lot about monasteries, old monks, and medieval images of evil in the shape of the Ottoman Turks but, to my surprise, very little about Bosnia. From a U.S. diplomat, I learned about the book's influence on President Bill Clinton. He told me that its depiction of centuries-old ethnic hatreds in the Balkans had influenced Clinton's 1993 decision to refrain from military intervention in the war in Bosnia.

It was hard to believe that a book based on the centuries-old-hatred mantra could be taken seriously by people with access to information and sources other than easy-read travel literature. But it was also sad, for the images of the Balkans and its peoples conjured up by Kaplan were the images adopted by numerous foreigners who came to Bosnia to help alleviate the suffering of the people there. With its stereotyping of a kind of Balkan Man, prone to barbaric outbursts of violence motivated by ancient hatred of rival ethnic groups, Kaplan's *Balkan Ghosts* account reinforced countless others that stereotyped Balkan peoples as primitive and violent. Such accounts appeared in newspapers, academic journals, and descriptions of the Balkans voiced by European diplomats and UN officials. It was also, precisely, the line trumpeted by the Serbian and

Croatian nationalist politicians whose rhetoric and actions fed the war. For instance, Radovan Karadzic, the wartime Bosnian Serb leader and war crimes indictee, repeatedly told the Bosnian public, international mediators, and media that there can be no peace (Serbs, Croats, and Muslims living together) in Bosnia for there is "too much hatred, centuries-old hatreds." His mantra served as a justification for his campaign to engineer an ethnically pure Bosnian Serb state. Such stereotyping prevented foreigners from seeing the common human nature at play in the wars, and from recognizing the face of regimes and ideologies that are nationalist fascist rather than "Balkan" in nature. They had not seen these societies in peaceful coexistence and daily interaction, and now *Balkan Ghosts* taught them that the sickening, indeed unbearable, violence they were witnessing was an inevitable product of "Balkan hatreds"— not the result of certain political, social, economic, and cultural factors in the Socialist Federal Republic of Yugoslavia at the end of the twentieth century.

If President Clinton and his colleagues had not read *Balkan Ghosts*, perhaps few people would have cared about Kaplan's Balkan imaginations. But the fact is that it was read, and it did influence thinking about the region generally and the wars in the former Yugoslavia in particular. By way of example—quite apart from the book's influence on the newly elected president as he was formulating his Balkan policy—Senator Dan Coats (R-IN) acknowledged his debt to the "historian" Robert Kaplan's *Balkan Ghosts* in a May 1993 speech in which, in the midst of the shelling of Sarajevo, he characterized conflict in the former Yugoslavia thus: "Fresh laurels for ancient battles. In this part of the world the normal rules of memory don't apply. Nothing that is lost is ever forgotten. Nothing that is gained is ever abandoned. The peoples of the Balkans are bound in the straitjackets of their pasts. They suffer from hemophilia of historical memory. The bleeding will not end. . . . The album of Balkan history might easily be the snapshots of a tourist in hell." The senator continued with an inventory of assassinations, mass executions, and horrors that had taken place from the turn of the nineteenth century onward. He concluded that "[the Balkan region has] nourished the roots of modern terrorism. It witnessed the rise of clerical fanaticism. Its only periods of modern peace have been when repression prevented violence. This is one of history's open wounds—its ancient hatreds radicalized by modern ideologies. This is the region America is now asked to help pacify. This is the history we are supposed to change with carrots and sticks, with embargoes and air strikes, with safe havens or the sacrifice of American soldiers."[6] Thus when Kaplan's book was published, it confirmed commonly held assumptions in the West and a certain political discourse about the ongoing war.[7] Furthermore, it buttressed the claims of ethnonationalist politicians who justified their war against civilians who belonged to the "wrong" ethnic group because "we cannot live together—for there is too much hatred." Those who tried to voice other opinions in the United States and Europe were often dismissed as pro Muslim because they were contradicting the "centuries-old ethnic hatred" thesis that was the constant refrain of Bosnian Serb nationalist leaders and were thus seen as lending support to a multiethnic Bosnia-Herzegovina and its mainly Bosnian Muslim government.

It may seem paradoxical that Kaplan himself argued for intervention in Bosnia to end the war. How then could his impressionistic travel account be used to support arguments against intervention to stop the suffering of civilians in Bosnia? This chapter attempts to answer that question by a careful analysis of the content and context of *Balkan Ghosts*, foregrounding the caricature of the Balkans that Kaplan presents through a selective use of history and fiction. I offer a critical examination, based on anthropological insights, of his portrayal of the "Balkan other." I argue that *Balkan Ghosts* did little to help its readers understand the wars raging in Croatia and Bosnia-Herzegovina or the peoples who were either actively involved or caught in those wars, but that it did much to reinforce Western stereotypes about the peoples living on Europe's southeastern flank.

Indeed, *Balkan Ghosts* depicts a whole region and its different peoples through a brew of negative myths told about each people by outsiders and by themselves. It is an inventory of the negative images neighboring peoples have about each other, but says little about a long history of communality, cultural exchange, and coexistence. In adopting myths as explanatory models and parroting local and Western stereotypes, Robert

Kaplan fails to ask questions that might help his readers understand the role of stereotypes in the dehumanizing process that precedes war and violence among neighboring peoples. For instance, why and how did negative stereotypes of the Other, together with negative views of multi-ethnic coexistence, come to dominate public, and later, everyday discourse? And why and how did individuals eventually act on these views through systematically humiliating and violently attacking the Other, their close neighbors, colleagues, and even friends?

BALKAN GHOSTS IN BOSNIA-HERZEGOVINA

It may seem a curious exercise to discuss *Balkan Ghosts* in relation to Bosnia-Herzegovina, since Kaplan dedicates less than one page to the country. But it was Bosnia that received all the media attention during the first part of the 1990s. This was not because of its many centuries of co-existence among various religious and ethnic communities (Catholic-Croat, Orthodox-Serb, Bosnian Muslim and Jew, as well as Catholic, Orthodox, and Muslim Rom); not because of the many mundane and heroic ways in which ordinary people tried to resist political and military powers forcing an ideology of ethnic purity on them; not because of its community of indigenous Slav Muslims; not because of its Jewish community, whose ancestors found protection there under Ottoman Muslim rule when they were persecuted and thrown out of Christian Spain; nor because, with its Ottoman architecture and spectacular scenery, Bosnia-Herzegovina was a popular tourist destination. Rather, it was because of the atrocities committed on its soil by its neighbors as well as by locals loyal to those neighbors. Many copies of *Balkan Ghosts* were bought by people in the United States and in Europe concerned with trying to understand why those atrocities were happening.

The publisher of *Balkan Ghosts* clearly had such ambitions for the book when it was published in 1993. Despite the fact that the book dealt only marginally with the countries in which the wars that absorbed Western media, diplomats, policy makers, and pundits were raging, the publishers described the book as follows: "From the assassination that set off World

War I to the ethnic warfare sweeping Bosnia and Croatia, the Balkans have been the crucible of the twentieth century—the place where terrorism and genocide were first practiced as tools of policy. This enthralling political travelogue helps us understand that region's anguish."[8] The publisher obviously sought to establish an association between the book's content and Bosnia. Witness, for example, the publisher's choice of front cover illustration for the book, namely an early-twentieth-century photograph of Sarajevo, the capital of Bosnia-Herzegovina, which shows the old, Ottoman part of the city. Kaplan's book, however, did not help its readers *understand* the anguish of that region, since no real understanding can come from an author who fails to anchor observations about people and their statements in the present, and who uncritically reproduces historical myths and negative stereotypes about "the Romanians," "the Bulgarians," "the Bosnian villagers," the Croats, the Macedonians, the Serbs, and so on. One cannot, perhaps, blame the publisher for wanting to make the most of the media coverage of the war in Bosnia and Croatia to increase sales of the book. But it is unconscionable that Kaplan's book was sold as one that could help readers "understand that region's anguish," explicitly including Bosnia's.

THE MISUNDERSTOOD AUTHOR?

In a new foreword to the second edition of *Balkan Ghosts*, published in 1996, when it had became clear that the book had had a significant impact, Kaplan wrote:

> In 1993, just as President Clinton was contemplating forceful action to halt the war in Bosnia, he and Mrs. Clinton are said to have read *Balkan Ghosts*. The history of ethnic rivalry I detailed reportedly encouraged the President's pessimism about the region, and—so it is said—was a factor in his decision not to launch an overt military response in support of the Bosnian Moslems, who were being besieged by Bosnian Serbs. That was disconcerting for two reasons. First, there is exceedingly little about Bosnia in *Balkan Ghosts*. As the reader will see, it is a subjective, broad-brush travel book about the whole Balkan peninsula, not a policy work.[9]

Indeed, Kaplan does not mention that he set foot there, and there is little in the book even about Bosnia-Herzegovina's immediate neighbors and the former Yugoslav republics. Of seventeen chapters (nineteen if the prologue and epilogue are included), only four are devoted to the former Yugoslavia: there is one on Croatia, one on Serbia and Albania, and a five-page chapter on Belgrade and the late dissident Milovan Djilas. The rest is about Romania, Bulgaria, and Greece. There are only nine references in the entire book to Bosnia-Herzegovina, and eight of them refer to history anywhere from half a century to more than two centuries old. Four references mention the massacres of Orthodox Serbs in Croatia by the Ustasha and the forced conversions in Bosnia-Herzegovina by the Catholic Church during World War II; another four references deal with Austria-Hungary's annexation of Bosnia-Herzegovina in 1878, and its political consequences. It is therefore amazing that this book was sold and read as a source of authoritative insights into the causes of the 1992–1995 separatist wars and "ethnic cleansing" campaigns in Bosnia. What it does mention, however, is as significant as what it leaves out, because it so clearly reveals Kaplan's readiness to resort to worn stereotypes and to explain the Other in terms of hatred and violence, including people in places he apparently did not visit. Because of this, Kaplan misses the chance to observe the rich and diverse texture of social life and to learn about the interface between individual and collective expressions of identity politics in the Balkans. I offer an anthropologist's critical reading of a few of Kaplan's statements about local culture in the Balkans. I have picked the one page from *Balkan Ghosts* that talks about Bosnia-Herzegovina, but any chapter or description of a particular country or people in the book could lend itself to a similar exercise, because the book trades in a distressingly simplistic and homogenizing view of the Balkans.

KAPLAN IMAGINES BOSNIA

"On the map, Bosnia is next door to Croatia, and seen from far away—especially during the decades when Yugoslavia was one country—the two regions might have struck a foreigner as indistinguishable. But

Bosnia was always light-years removed from Zagreb. Zagreb is an urbane, ethnically uniform community on the plain, while Bosnia is a morass of ethnically mixed villages in the mountains. Bosnia is rural, isolated, and full of suspicions and hatreds to a degree that the sophisticated Croats of Zagreb could barely imagine." Here Kaplan compares Zagreb, the capital and urban center of Croatia, with rural Bosnia, which is a bit like comparing Atlanta with rural Alabama. While urbanites in both Sarajevo and Zagreb moved easily between the two cities to work or study, some city dwellers in Zagreb were as unfamiliar with the ways of the people in their surrounding villages (including in the ethnically mixed ones) as some Sarajevans were of life in nearby Bosnian villages. After having identified Bosnia with an associational chain consisting of ethnic diversity ("morass of ethnically mixed") backwardness and wildness ("rural, isolated," and "in the mountains"), "suspicions" and "hatreds," Kaplan goes on to explain that sharing territory breeds intolerance and extreme nationalism in ethnic groups: "Bosnia represents an intensification and complication of the Serb-Croat dispute. Just as Croats felt their western Catholicism more intensely than did the Austrians or the Italians, precisely because of their uneasy proximity to the eastern Orthodox and Muslim worlds, so the Croats of Bosnia—because they shared the same mountains with both Orthodox Serbs and Muslims—felt their Croatianism much more intensely than did the Croats in Croatia proper, who enjoyed the psychological luxury of having only their ethnic compatriots as immediate neighbors. The same, of course, was true for the Serbs in Bosnia."[10]

There is one major problem with Kaplan's reasoning: it is based on generalizations that cannot be validated by ethnographic data or empirical facts. First, it is not correct that the Croats in Croatia had only Croats as their immediate neighbors, since there was a sizeable Serb minority in Croatia. Second, Croats in Croatia do not necessarily feel their Catholicism more strongly than Italians in Italy do. (Of course, it is problematic to talk about all Croats and all Italians, since the degree of religious observance and faith varies among members of a society, in addition to which Kaplan makes no distinction between leaders' embracing religious rhetoric for political reasons and the religiosity of the general public.)

Third, Kaplan pays little attention to the important role that religion and the church played as a site for the expression of rituals, beliefs, and practices that countered those formulated by the Communist state, and rushes instead to the conclusion that religion is an expression of nationalism (which it may also be). In Bosnia, it is hard to distinguish an identification with the Catholic faith from an identification with the Croat nation precisely because ethnic and religious identification for historical reasons have become synonymous. But what this "Croat nation" represents to people who call themselves Croats has changed over time. Kaplan's simplifications and disregard for complexities and changing contexts may produce seductive representations, but they have no explanatory power. Finally, Kaplan claims that a religious or ethnic community's proximity to another community leads to more ethnonationalism; but in fact, Croatian nationalism and Croatian separatism were stronger in the western part of Bosnia-Herzegovina than in central Bosnia, although the rural western region of Herzegovina consisted mainly of majority ethnic Croat areas and is near the border with Croatia proper, while central Bosnia is the more ethnically mixed and lies farther away from the Croatian border. In any case, it would be hard to argue that the Bosnian Croats felt their Croatianism more intensely than did the Croats in Croatia proper, primarily because of the lack of ethnographic evidence but also because Kaplan does not give us any clues as to how this "felt Croatianism" may be observed. Before the nationalist wars of the 1990s, many Bosnian Croats had a Bosnian rather than a Croatian orientation. The strong orientation of the Bosnian Croats toward Croatia and Croatianhood is a recent phenomenon and is partly a product of the war and of nationalist ideology disseminated through Zagreb-produced schoolbooks and media during the reign of Croatia's president Franjo Tudjman, the father of modern Croatian nationalism.

Having "explained" the Bosnian Croats, Kaplan turns to the Bosnian Muslims who do complicate the picture somewhat: "Complicating matters in Bosnia was the existence of a larger community of Muslims. These were Slavs, whether originally Croat or Serb, who had been converted to Islam in the late Middle Ages by the Turkish occupiers and whose religion gradually became synonymous with their ethnic identity." Here

Kaplan, instead of checking accounts of the history of the Bosnian Muslims based on scholarship, relies on Croatian and Serbian nationalist historiographies and their claims about Bosnian Muslims.[11] For instance, it is problematic to talk about Serbs and Croats in Bosnia before the end of the nineteenth or beginning of the twentieth century, and Bosnians converted to Islam from the fifteenth century onward. (Bosnia became part of the Ottoman Empire in 1463 and remained so until 1878, when Bosnia was annexed by Austria-Hungary.) Indeed, even as late as the 1980s, people in rural areas of Bosnia were still referring to Catholics rather than Croats, and Orthodox rather than Serbs. And the process whereby "religion gradually became synonymous with their ethnic identity" took place within all three of Bosnia's religious communities, so Bosnian Catholics gradually started identifying with a larger Croatian nation, Bosnian Orthodox with a larger Serbian nation, and, logically, the Bosnian Muslims came to see themselves as a separate ethnic group or "nation" indigenous to Bosnia and Herzegovina. Partly because of Serbian and Croatian political denials of Muslim claims to a distinct ethnic identity and thus to nationality status (within the Yugoslav system), this process started later among the Bosnian Muslims.

Finally, Kaplan concludes his Bosnia page: "Bosnia did have one sophisticated urban center, however: Sarajevo, where Croats, Serbs, Muslims, and Jews had traditionally lived together in reasonable harmony. But the villages all around were full of savage hatreds, leavened by poverty and alcoholism. The fact that the most horrifying violence—during both World War II and the 1990s—occurred in Bosnia was no accident." After first having admitted that at least one part of Bosnia—Sarajevo—bore some resemblance to a civilized society (sophisticated, urban, with reasonable harmony between the people of different ethnic backgrounds), he again slips into his "Balkan hatreds" frame of mind. And he adds a final element—alcoholism—to his Balkan character complex (savagery, hatred, violence, and poverty), drawing a casual link from "savage hatreds leavened by poverty and alcoholism" to the horrifying violence of World War II and of the 1990s.[12] As a description of society and history, Kaplan's conclusion is misleading; as a literary device that connects violence, poverty, and alcoholism, it is a cliché; as an explanation of the political and social dynamics of conflict, it is not particularly useful.[13]

In his benchmark ethnography *The European Moslems*, the anthropologist William Lockwood describes life in ethnically mixed rural communities in Bosnia in the early 1970s. In the part of Bosnia that he studied, villages were either inhabited entirely by members of one ethnic group or were divided into separate hamlets inhabited by different ethnic groups. There were ritual exchanges between villagers of different ethnic backgrounds, but, he argues, they were mainly integrated through the marketplace. Still, he concludes that ethnic relations were largely peaceful.[14] The pattern of interethnic coexistence that I observed in a village farther south in the late 1980s was one of more frequent and friendly interaction between villagers of different ethnic backgrounds.[15] Here Muslims and Catholics (Croats) lived as next-door neighbors and interacted on a daily basis. Although both Muslims and Catholics held stereotypes about each other, such stereotypes were generally not an obstacle to interaction. Sometimes they were a topic of joking. Typically in ethnically mixed company, people would stress similarities and their shared aspects of life—not their perceived differences.[16]

Like Lockwood, I have spent considerable time studying and writing about "the morass of ethnically mixed villages in the mountains" (although, Kaplan notwithstanding, most ethnically mixed villages in Bosnia are not in the mountains but in urban areas and the lowlands). I followed life in one of these villages that Kaplan describes as "full of savage hatreds, leavened by poverty and alcoholism" over a period of fifteen years, from 1987 to 2001.[17] During those years, I observed Bosnian villagers through peaceful times of ethnic coexistence and friendships; through war, fear, ethnic animosity, and forced separation; and most recently, in a period, still ongoing, of reintegration and slow reestablishment of interethnic communication. Although some of those villagers are poor, this does not make them "savage"; although Muslims and Catholics alike drink plum brandy or beer, I have seen no more alcohol consumption in Bosnian villages than in villages in my own Norway. Although the war and nationalist hate rhetoric encouraged some villagers to commit hideous crimes against their neighbors, most of them focused their energies on their own and their families' protection and survival. But daily doses of the official rhetoric of fear and hatred disseminated through the nationalist-controlled media, combined with the ethnically targeted violence that people actually experienced, changed the way neighbors of different ethnic backgrounds saw one another. The previously friendly neighbor you had shared a cup of coffee with was gradually turned into a threatening Other with a perceived secret plan to destroy you. In order to take control of those fears, people learned to hate. The demeaning and dehumanizing images of the Other conjured up by the nationalist hate mongers were absorbed by ordinary people, and these helped them deal with their fears and sense of powerlessness. Eventually, when they were called on by their political and military leaders to attack their neighbors, some joined in the fighting, some fled, and others became silent bystanders to crimes against their former neighbors and friends, while a small number had the courage to find ways of protecting their neighbors who were being persecuted and attacked.

The point about Bosnian society, as with all other societies in the Balkans and beyond, is that it contains both the potential for peaceful coexistence and the potential for conflict among its ethnic communities; there are plenty of examples of both. There were local variations in the history of interethnic relations within Bosnia-Herzegovina before the war and, then again, local variations in the incidence of violence in the 1990s as larger political forces bore down on people in their localities. There were striking differences not only between regions but also within neighborhoods and even within families.[18]

In Bosnia prior to the war in the 1990s, there were many mechanisms for accommodating differences. These ranged from political mechanisms for ethnic power-sharing to ecumenical cooperation among religious leaders and simple practices in everyday life. Examples of the latter included the tradition whereby members of different communities would visit each other on religious holidays to pay respects, and the more informal custom of drinking coffee together, as well as the way in which people switched codes as they moved between multiethnic and monoethnic spheres. (This is reminiscent of the way in which people in the United States say "Happy Holidays" instead of "Merry Christmas" around the Christmas holidays when they cannot be sure everyone present is celebrating the Christian holidays.) But then, in the early 1990s, these mechanisms started breaking down. Administrative mechanisms were actively removed or boycotted in parallel administrative structures set up by new nationalist and separatist leaders. An officially supported attitude of respecting differences was replaced by a new officially promoted attitude of intolerance and hostility as people were exposed to daily doses of fear and hate propaganda from nationalist controlled media.[19]

Kaplan makes the historical grievances of neighboring peoples in the Balkans a central issue. But expressing historical grievances should not be confounded with expressing hatred. The fact that there have been phases of violence and oppression in a society's history does not necessarily cause violent acts in the present. It is the activation of the images that matters: the connection of those historic images and attitudes with the present, and their translation into contemporary demands for action. People have to be made to act upon these images. So we must ask, How do we get from a situation where a local citizen voices historical myths and their accompanying stereotypes about the Other (his neighbor)— exchanged over a cup of coffee in a café with a foreign travel writer—to a situation where this citizen uses such myths and stereotypes to justify violent acts against his neighbor, acts aimed at the ultimate annihilation of him and his fellow Others? This is the crucial complicating step that Kaplan fails to notice, allowing his readers to comfortably dismiss the ethnic cleansing, massacres, and rapes in Bosnia as a natural expression of "Balkanness." As an anthropologist, I observed this process of ethnic mobilization in an ethnically mixed rural community in Bosnia, and it became clear to me that the central issue is not hatred but fear. The hate people started feeling for and displaying toward their ethnic Other was, in a situation of extreme uncertainty, a means to take control of their fears. In other words, what needs explaining is not hatred but fear.

THE HOMOGENIZING EFFECT OF FEAR

Just a few years after Kaplan undertook his travels in the Balkans, war erupted in Croatia and then in Bosnia-Herzegovina as the Socialist Federative Republic of Yugoslavia disintegrated. Violence, atrocities, and intercommunal killings stunned television viewers in the rest of Europe and in North America. Rhetoric by aggressive nationalists and conflict entrepreneurs was filled with demeaning and threatening remarks about members of other ethnic groups and with references to historical grievances such as medieval battles and massacres perpetrated during World War II. These events seemed to support Kaplan's dismal portrait of "the Balkans." But Kaplan could not ask the crucial question in his book that truly would have helped his readers understand "that anguished region," because the selection of voices in his book was both skewed and limited. He could not ask the question, What happened to all those people, so common to the Balkans, who embodied cultural interchange and fluid boundaries through their own multifaceted identities? (This refers to those who saw themselves not primarily as Serbs, Croats, or Muslims but as Sarajevans, Yugoslavs, Bosnians, and, yes, as Serbs or Croats too.) What happened to the voices of the generations of Yugoslavs (Kaplan's own generation) who grew up in the urban, consumer oriented, cosmopolitan, educated social milieus of Josip Tito's socialist Yugoslavia? (This refers to those men and women of multiple ethnic backgrounds who might say, "I grew up in Sarajevo, went to the university in Belgrade, got married in Zagreb, and went on holiday to the Montenegrin Coast.")

What, indeed, happened to all those people, thousands of them, who on the eve of the war demonstrated against nationalist rhetoric and for peaceful coexistence? One must ask why elites found it opportune to promote ideas of irreconcilable differences and conflict at this particular point in history. What made it possible for some racist and fascist leaders to dominate public discourse and intimidate others into leaving the country, shutting up, or adopting their views? What had happened to the alternative views that did not promote conflict and hatred? What changed and why?

Many authors have attempted to answer these questions in the last ten years. There is the big story: The dissolution of the Socialist Federative Republic of Yugoslavia, which had started slowly and almost invisibly with the death of Tito, the founder of modern Yugoslavia, and gained speed with the rise to power of a hard-line communist, Slobodan Milosevic, in the dominant republic of Serbia, where he gradually centralized power and quashed the burgeoning democracy movements. With the end of communist regimes in the rest of eastern Europe, nationalists (often reinvented communists) rose to leadership positions throughout Yugoslavia, and the former official enemy rhetoric of communist Yugoslavia, a tool to create internal cohesion among all of Yugoslavia's peoples, was refashioned to fit the new reality. The new nationalist (and separatist) leaderships directed their rhetoric of fear and animosity toward the other "Yugoslav" peoples or nations within the one Yugoslav nation they were then leading. Slobodan Milosevic of Serbia wanted a Greater Serbia of Serbs and wanted to get rid of Croats in parts of Croatia, and Croats and Muslims in Bosnia. Franjo Tudjman of Croatia wanted a Greater Croatia of Croats and wanted to get rid of Serbs and Muslims who were in the way. In both cases getting to "greater" meant incorporating territory from Bosnia-Herzegovina with Serb and Croat populations, respectively. Academics, historians, sociologists, philologists, and psychologists took an active role in providing "scientific evidence" of the uniqueness of their people and of their "historical right" to certain territories. Such "scientific evidence" was provided not only to justify the nationalists' demands for separation but also to justify discrimination against and dehumanization of neighbors of a different ethnic and religious background. Journalists helped spread the dehumanizing and threatening images of the Others, which were part of the new ideology of ethnic separation and purity.

Then there are the many, many smaller stories that in some way connect to the big story—stories of individuals and local communities. Some became convinced that their only future was within an ethnically homogenous state, and they either silently or actively supported violent actions to rid their territory of people from other ethnic communities. Others continued to believe in tolerance and multiethnic coexistence and sought small, subversive ways of demonstrating this belief. Others were forced, or chose, to flee their country. They believed that tolerance and multiethnic coexistence were no longer possible. The choices people could make depended on their local circumstances. So, while continued belief in multiethnic coexistence was a choice for someone who lived in Sarajevo, it was not a choice for someone who lived in, say, the city of

Banja Luka in the Serbian-controlled part of Bosnia. The Croatian author Slavenka Drakulic writes eloquently about the homogenizing effect of violent nationalism (see n. 32 below); and Chip Gagnon writes lucidly about the ways in which any public discourse other than the nationalist-separatist one was relegated to the realm of nonreality, so that the only way to participate in society was by identifying oneself exclusively with one ethnic or national community. He sees ethnic conflict as an elite strategy to demobilize the general population in a situation where a popular democratic pull was threatening elite control over state power.[20]

It is easy for us to regard the former Yugoslavia with smug complacency, but there are lessons here for societies everywhere. For they, too, have undercurrents of intolerance, racism, and fear of the Other, which, when encouraged by those in power, may turn violent or may be allowed by authorities to blossom with impunity. Such developments may be more likely when societies (or states) undergo dramatic regime changes and are vulnerable to so-called conflict entrepreneurs who communicate, "Vote for me and I will protect you against the evil others, who if not pacified or eliminated will ultimately annihilate you." But in Kaplan's Balkans there is no such historical and social analysis. Instead, the evil, the violence, the historical hatreds are frozen in the blood of the millions of people who inhabit the Balkan peninsula. Kaplan writes almost as if there were a sort of defective Balkan gene that sometimes erupts and spreads its contagion of violence and disorder to the European heartland. Balkan cultural worlds appear unaffected by political, social, and economic developments in the world beyond. Instead, it seems that they created their very own history sometime in the Middle Ages (i.e., during the early Ottoman period) and preserved it in a time capsule.

THE BALKAN TIME CAPSULE

Because Kaplan wants to make a point about the Balkans as a time-capsuled world where people hate and kill with "an age-old sacred fury," he selectively draws on subjective accounts of the past and uses them to depict the present.[21] Thus Kaplan uses selective descriptions of some events in Balkan history, and he relies heavily on accounts by long-dead travel writers, such as Rebecca West, and on the historical fiction of Ivo Andric, whose novel *The Bridge of Drina* chronicles life in a small town in eastern Bosnia over a period of several centuries.[22] This is how he creates his Balkan time capsule, into which he places gory, violent details, Christian orthodox religious iconography, popular literature like the story of Dracula, medieval cruelties at the long-defunct royal courts of eastern Europe, and wars fought in centuries past. It is interesting to note, in contrast, how a Bosnian journalist writes about the violent atrocities of a contemporary war. In his book *The Tenth Circle of Hell*, Rezak Hukanovic, a death camp survivor, describes the horrors of ethnic cleansing and the terror that the inmates of the death camps were subject to at the hands of their Serb tormentors. But in spite of the author's description of acts of atrocities and cruelty, he never falls into easy explanations of centuries-old ethnic hatreds to account for the horror, perhaps because the hatred and cruelty he experienced are phenomena of war—a war where normal rules of social behavior no longer apply. In fact, he also bears witness to acts of human decency and heroism among fellow Bosnians—Muslims, Serbs, and Croats—who shared his hell. Indeed, the whole experience seems so unreal that he writes about himself in the third person. Hukanovic explains that, at the time, it was as if this were happening not to him but to someone else. An explanation of centuries-old ethnic hatreds would simply not make sense for the Bosnian author who grew up in a peaceful, multiethnic community of neighbors, friends, and family.[23]

Balkan Ghosts repeatedly demonstrates Kaplan's view that the Balkans are the source of the anarchy, violence, and ideologies of hatred that have rolled over civilized central and northern Europe in modern history. Kaplan declares that "twentieth-century history came from the Balkans. . . . Here men have been isolated by poverty and ethnic rivalry, dooming them to hate. Here politics had been reduced to a level of near anarchy that from time to time in history has flowed up the Danube into Central Europe. Nazism, for instance, can claim Balkan origins. Among the flophouses of Vienna, a breeding ground of ethnic resentments close to the southern Slavic world, Hitler learned how to hate infectiously."[24] While it is a stretch to include Vienna in the Balkans, or the Balkans as part of the German world where Nazism developed, Kaplan's point seems to be that Vienna, because of its proximity to the southern Slavic world, had been infected with Balkan hatreds. This sweeping statement about the origins of Nazism, while historically and factually untrue, implicitly absolves central European states and their citizens of their roles in creating the intolerant atmosphere that became the breeding ground for violence against and persecution of minorities: the violence was an infection, caught from the contagiously violent Balkans. To Kaplan, it seems, intolerance and hatred toward ethnic minorities can come only from the Balkans. This manipulative use of European history should cause any reasonably enlightened reader to question not only the validity of Kaplan's other references to Balkan history but even the basic premises of his book. In Kaplan's admittedly "subjective, broad-brush" travel account, the Balkans are portrayed as the dark margins of Europe—indeed of civilization—and the originator of the evils that have haunted the West in modern history: xenophobia, fascism, genocide, terrorism, Nazism, and two world wars. People who live not in Kaplan's world of fiction but in their own very real Western societies know this is not true.

KAPLAN'S GHOSTS

When *Balkan Ghosts* was first published in 1993, the war in Bosnia seemed at its most intractable and Western peace efforts were in disarray.[25] Outsiders found it hard to keep track of who was fighting whom. Commentators with little or no prior knowledge of the country attempted to simplify, resorting to crude and ahistorical categories such as "the Muslims" and "the Serbs." In categorizing the war zones in Croatia and Bosnia-Herzegovina as "Balkan," Western commentators invoked the mental map sketched in the English-speaking West by the writings of travelers, journalists (such as Rebecca West), and novelists mostly from the time of World Wars I and II, not all of which were even about Bosnia.

The preeminent example of such writing is *Black Lamb and Grey Falcon*, published in 1941.[26] Rebecca West, a British journalist and novelist who traveled in the Balkans on the eve of World War II, gives a passionate account of Yugoslavia between the world wars. West's account weaves history and contemporary politics into descriptions of Yugoslavia's peoples at that time, providing glimpses into their culture, religion, rituals, and beliefs. Underlying her rich travel account, however, is a sense of urgency: she seeks to warn Europe about the threat of Nazism. "Yugoslavia helped [West] focus her thoughts about the political situation in Europe at the end of the 1930s," writes Felicity Rosslyn. Rosslyn identifies two of the themes in *Black Lamb and Grey Falcon* that would also engage Kaplan's attention more than fifty years later: "what makes men lust after death" and "the interrelation of small cultures and empires."[27] West thus contributed to "imagining the Balkans," a Western tradition explained brilliantly by Maria Todorova:

> By being geographically inextricable from Europe, yet culturally constructed as "the other" within, the Balkans have been able to absorb conveniently a number of externalized political, ideological, and cultural frustrations stemming from tensions and contradictions inherent to the regions and societies outside of the Balkans. Balkanism became, in time, a convenient substitute for the emotional discharge that orientalism provided, exempting the West from charges of racism, colonialism, eurocentrism, and Christian intolerance against Islam. After all, the Balkans are in Europe; they are white; they are predominantly Christian; and therefore the externalization of frustrations on them can circumvent the usual racial and religious bias allegations. As in the case of the Orient, the Balkans have served as a repository of negative characteristics against which a positive and self-congratulatory image of the "European" and the "West" has been constructed.[28]

Robert Kaplan's *Balkan Ghosts* is within this tradition of "imagining the Balkans." Kaplan sets out to retrace West's travels. He tells his readers that *Black Lamb and Grey Falcon* drew him to Yugoslavia, and that he would rather have lost his passport and his money than his heavily thumbed and annotated copy of West's book.[29]

Kaplan followed in Rebecca West's footsteps in the late 1980s on the eve of a new dissolution of the Yugoslav state. While it could not be said about Kaplan that he has any particular sympathies for any of the Balkan peoples he describes (apart from perhaps the Greeks), he uncritically interweaves West's subjective portrait of Yugoslavia between the world wars with his own descriptions of Yugoslavia almost fifty years later. But the context for the tensions and conflicts in Yugoslavia were different in the 1930s (West's contemporary Yugoslav world), in the 1980s (Kaplan's contemporary world), and in the 1990s (when readers of *Balkan Ghosts* had Yugoslav wars of dissolution as their contemporary frame of reference). What the 1930s and the 1980s have in common are a political situation of dramatic ideological shifts and regime transitions causing instability, unemployment, breakdown of state structures, state terror, insecurity, and fear among the general population. And a society in the grip of fear is a fertile breeding ground for prejudices, intolerance, and, if encouraged, ultimately violence. But alongside such views and emotions in any given society, there will always be those of tolerance, courage, and moderation as well. What views in the end come to dominate the public mood depends very much on factors beyond the control of the individual citizen. And what those factors are cannot be deduced from reading fifty-year-old travel literature; it has to be understood in a contemporary context.

Past voices of religious intolerance and ethnic hatred cannot explain why this society descended into war, nor do they give us insight into the way of life that was destroyed in the wars of the 1990s. For the account to have such explanatory power, it would have had to include more voices of people of Kaplan's own generation and secular worldview, and descriptions of their contemporary life. In fact, there is a good example of such a voice in his book, though it is misused by Kaplan. In his chapter on Croatia, Kaplan recounts a conversation with the Croatian writer Slavenka Drakulic. She says to him, "This is happening in Croatia, but that is happening in Serbia or Macedonia. Each situation is unique. There are no easy themes here. Because of Tito's break with Stalin, the enemy in Yugoslavia was always within, not without. For years we were fooled by what was only an illusion of freedom." As a result of this conversation, Kaplan has one of his rare contemporary insights: "I immediately grasped that the counterrevolution in Eastern Europe included Yugoslavia, too. But because the pressure of discontent was being released horizontally, in the form of one group against another, rather than vertically against the Communist powers in Belgrade, the revolutionary path in Yugoslavia was at first more tortuous and, therefore, more disguised. That was why the outside world did not take notice until 1991, when fighting started."[30]

Yet Kaplan fails to take the obvious next step, to conclude that the wars in Yugoslavia were not unleashed by ancient hatreds, but rather resulted from an anticommunist revolt, a counterrevolt, the rise to power of non-democratic and brutal nationalist leaders, and the destruction of the Socialist Federative Republic of Yugoslavia. He brushes aside Drakulic's attempt to convey the complexities and diversities of the region, and instead imposes his own haunted imaginings. Drakulic continues, "You need a few weeks in Zagreb at least. There are so many people to see. The strands here are so subtle, so interwoven. It's all so complex." But at this point Kaplan is not really listening to her; this upsets his *Black-Lamb-and-Grey-Falcon* frame of reference. The native intellectual's attempt to point Kaplan toward some of the historical, cultural, and sociological diversities and complexities of the region is blunted: "Slavenka's fingers seemed to give up in frustration and fall to the table: Here, she implied [Kaplan says, putting words into her mouth with which, one suspects, she might not even agree], the battle between Communism and Capitalism is merely one dimension of a struggle that puts Catholicism against Orthodoxy, Rome against Constantinople, the legacy of Habsburg Austria-Hungary against that of Ottoman Turkey—in other words, West against East, the ultimate historical and cultural conflict."[31] Kaplan's infatuation with West's antiquated and partisan views of the region blinded him to alternative ways to understand social and political life in the Balkans today, even when these were presented to him. Instead, he put his own words into his interlocutor's mouth, saying that she "implied" that this was, in the words made famous by Samuel P. Huntington soon after, a "clash of civilizations."[32]

CONCLUSION

It suited the Bosnian Serb leader Radovan Karadzic to adopt the mantra "We cannot live together, for there is too much hatred." It justified his plan for an ethnically pure Serb state.

It suited President Clinton and other policy makers in 1993 to read *Balkan Ghosts* as evidence that the war in Bosnia was a centuries-old conflict driven by primordial hatreds that could not be stopped by Western military intervention, but would instead have to run its natural course. Thus, Clinton shied away from any decisive action—although he later changed his mind.[33]

It suited Robert Kaplan to stress the potential for conflict in the Balkans in order to tell a dramatic story. He traveled in the Balkans in search of drama and conflict, partly because he was guided by travel books written on the eve of another war, partly because brewing conflict was in evidence, and partly, perhaps, because of Kaplan's own idiosyncratic obsessions. Although he claims that the book is a subjective travelogue with no policy implications, it is clear that his ambitions go beyond those of a travel writer. In the preface to the 1993 edition he says, "Throughout the 1980s, I tried—usually to no avail—to interest editors and the general public in the Balkans and the brewing troubles there." In his 1996 foreword, he points out that in 1989 he was already warning policy makers about the looming crisis in the Balkans (with articles in the *Atlantic Monthly* and the *Wall Street Journal Europe*), and that, since the first half of 1993, he had "publicly advocated military action in support of the Bosnian Moslems on CNN and C-SPAN, in the *Washington Post Outlook* section, and in other forums."[34]

There is obviously a contradiction between the fact that Robert Kaplan pushed for military intervention to stop the slaughter in Bosnia and the fact that his book *Balkan Ghosts* gave President Clinton and his advisors an excuse not to intervene. This is not, however merely a case of misreading the book.[35] For in fact, Kaplan, as shown in this chapter, nurtured stereotypes and clichés that conjure up an image of the Balkans as a place inhabited by naturally violent peoples, driven by "irrational, superstitious hatred."[36] Thus, in the words of Lord Owen, a European Union peace mediator, the only way to end the slaughter of civilians in Bosnia was to treat the country and its people as a body ravaged by an illness for which there was no remedy other than to let the illness work its way through the system.[37]

Robert Kaplan is a serious journalist who has established himself as a public intellectual with his writings on issues of critical interest to policy makers, published in such well-respected journals and newspapers as the *Atlantic Monthly,* the *New Republic, Foreign Policy,* the *Wall Street Journal,* and the *New York Times.* His promotion of crude, negative stereotyping of remote societies, and his sloppy, impressionistic rendering of historical data, is therefore all the more regrettable.

Both journalists and academics have a responsibility as disseminators of knowledge about other peoples and other cultures, and a particular responsibility when they write about areas of the world that are the object of great-power policy interests. I recognize the different constraints of journalists and academics. Journalists work under much shorter dead-lines and necessarily have to be more superficial than academics. However, both the journalist and the anthropologist are trained in the art of observation and contextualization and often use the good anecdote to illustrate core issues. The difference between good and bad journalism, as with good and bad anthropology, is that good journalism and good anthropology undress prejudices and stereotypes and try to convey the diversity of meaning, the rich patterns of social interaction, and the role of power, whether the subject is one's own country or far-flung, seem-ingly exotic places such as the Balkan peninsula. Only then can one start saying anything helpful about the role that prejudices and stereotypes play in public discourse, and about how in a situation of crisis and a cli-mate of fear those prejudices come to dominate public discourse and, ultimately, are acted out by ordinary people in their everyday interaction with the Other.

FIVE Why I Disagree with Robert Kaplan

Catherine Besteman

In 1994, the *Atlantic Monthly* published a provocative essay called "The Coming Anarchy" by journalist Robert Kaplan. A dire portrait of the post–cold war world, replete with warnings to Western readers about their future survival, the essay received tremendous attention and re-appeared as the title chapter in a book of Kaplan's essays.[1] While "The Coming Anarchy" found a wide readership,[2] many anthropologists reacted to it with horror and hostility because of Kaplan's myopic obsession with violence and criminality in Africa, in particular, and in humanity in general. His glib conclusions are contradicted by serious anthropological research in the very same places about which Kaplan writes. Kaplan's portrait is misleading at best; at worst it promotes dangerous ideas about Africa, American foreign policy, and international relations.

Cultural anthropologists make a profession out of understanding and explaining how groups of people organize their social life and interpret the world in which they live. Such a general charter allows anthropologists to comment on a wide range of topics—politics, religion, economics, war, health, emotions, the human use of the environment, and globalization among them—but to do so requires precision, accuracy, and careful field research. "The Coming Anarchy" may be entertaining writing, but it is terrible anthropology. While mere travel journalism does not have to be good anthropology—one reads travel journalism for seductive exotica or for fantasy and the thrill of the foreign—influential travel journalism posing as foreign affairs reportage and policy analysis, like Kaplan's, owes something to the same kinds of research principles as those to which good anthropology adheres. Looked at through my anthropological lens, Kaplan's portrait of future dystopia is a flimsy structure built on a number of insupportable claims; this chapter highlights a few of them.

"THE COMING ANARCHY"

"The Coming Anarchy" presents a terrifying and unambiguous portrait of the contours of the post–cold war world. The essay's primary themes are Third World anarchy and the threat to (Western) readers' safety, health, comfort, and culture posed by what Kaplan foresees as the ongoing and impending collapse of Third World countries. Borrowing an image from Thomas F. Homer-Dixon, a political scientist at the University of Toronto, Kaplan positions his readers as passengers in a comfortable limousine cruising through streets filled with the violent, the diseased, the hungry, the criminal, the deviant, the poor, the corrupt, and the uneducated. The middle and upper classes of North America, Europe, and the Pacific Rim are inside the limo; everyone else is outside it, threatening its security. The readers are made into fascinated and terrified spectators riding along in comfort, watching through the windows as those less fortunate kill each other, steal from each other, starve to death, and die of disease. Kaplan warns his readers that "outside the stretch limo would be a rundown, crowded planet of skinhead Cossacks and juju warriors, influenced by the worst refuse of Western pop culture and ancient tribal hatreds, and battling over scraps of overused earth in guerrilla conflicts that ripple across continents and intersect in no discernible pattern—meaning there's no easy-to-define threat" (62–63). Although Kaplan's readers are comfortably inside the limo, he warns that they should be concerned about what is going on outside it, because the criminals, the diseased, and the warlords—all those desperate people outside the limousine—are going to take the readers down with them: they are going to engulf the West in their anarchy and destroy Western civilization.

The imagery is powerful. To provide readers with an illustration of the coming anarchy that he predicts, one that smacks of realism, Kaplan offers West Africa as the model of what is happening on the streets outside the comfortable limo—in other words, the model of our global future. Africa, Kaplan says, is reverting to its premodern past when, as Victorian England saw it, the continent was "blank" and "unexplored" (48). "Precisely because much of Africa is set to go over the edge at a time when the Cold War has ended," he explains, "when environmental degradation and demographic stress in other parts of the globe is [sic] becoming critical, and when the post–First World War system of nation-states . . . is about to be toppled, Africa suggests what war, borders, and ethnic politics will be like a few decades hence" (54).

Kaplan offers numerous impressionistic anecdotes of his experiences in West African cities, detailing corruption, slums, crime, disease, and pollution. He claims that animism, "juju spirits," and "loose family structures" resulting from polygamy are contributing to urban violence (46). He describes the "stick-and-gun-wielding [restaurant] guards" (45) and "young men with restless, scanning eyes" (46) who surround his taxi in Abidjan. He recounts the inefficiency and corruption that accompany his border crossings along the West African coast; the "children . . . as numerous as ants" (54); the money he had to spend on vaccinations to avoid disease; and the "nightmarish Dickensian spectacle" of Guinea's capital, complete with garbage floating in puddles, dead rats, and "scabrous" homes "coated with black slime" (54). As Africa's political infrastructure continues to fall apart, the "dangerous, disease-ridden coastal trading posts" (54) through which he has traveled and which his article describes so gruesomely, will become, he warns, Africa's gateway to the rest of the world.

After fixing this nightmarish spectacle of Africa's present condition in the minds of his readers, Kaplan offers his theory of what is pushing Africa over the edge and how Africa's descent into anarchy will affect his Western readers. He argues that population pressure and a changing global climate are causing widespread environmental degradation. A rising population in the midst of environmental constraints is resulting in resource scarcity, which, in turn, is causing people to move across borders and from the countryside into overcrowded cities. Such border crossings are bringing together people from different cultural, religious, ethnic, and racial backgrounds and are creating clashes of cultures or, as Samuel Huntington would say, of civilizations. Cultural differences (which are real and natural, he says, citing Huntington) are creating an increase in ethnic strife. Ethnic strife is fueled by a natural human propensity for violence and warfare that struggling poor people may find liberating "in areas where the Western Enlightenment has not penetrated" (72). The result, he says, is "re-primitivized man: warrior societies operating at a time of unprecedented resource scarcity and planetary overcrowding" (73). The creation of "re-primitivized man" is acute in Africa's urban slums, Kaplan argues, where weak cultural bonds—"unstable social fluid . . . clearly on the verge of igniting"—produce "hordes" of young men (also referred to as "loose molecules") who turn to violent crime (46).

Kaplan concludes by arguing that his readers in the West must pay attention to the chaos occurring elsewhere, because some of the components of his model are also found within the United States. He suggests that, whereas in the past Irish and Jewish immigrants to the United States were forced to conform and assimilate through public education, African Americans refused. Their refusal is contributing to the transformation of the American nation-state, making it less coherent and more fragmented. At the same time, African Americans' sensitivity to media depictions of and political involvement in collapsing African states may hinder a rigorous analysis of Africa's problems. As a result, Kaplan says, "Africa's distress will exert a destabilizing influence on the United States." The United States will become "less of a nation" (73), and this, to

Kaplan, seems to be the most immediate threat. Like Huntington, Kaplan sees in American multiculturalism the threat of increasing weakness and instability.

Kaplan's portrait of African dystopia received a tremendous response, both positive and negative. It influenced the highest policy circles in Washington, and, according to the anthropologist Paul Richards, was faxed to every U.S. embassy in Africa.[3] However, it outraged many academics who objected to Kaplan's sensationalist imagery, his pessimistic generalizations, and his unwarranted environmental determinism. Many anthropologists—particularly those who study Africa, ethnic violence, or environmental issues—saw that the essay committed major anthropological errors that might have enhanced its sensationalist appeal but destroyed its empirical validity. Kaplan's methods fall far short of anthropological standards, which perhaps explains why anthropological research on Africa offers direct challenges to Kaplan's vision of anarchy and despair.

KAPLAN'S BLUNDERS

Although many anthropologists might not appreciate the comparison, travel journalism and anthropology are somewhat similar undertakings: both professions use writing to evoke a place and describe a way of life. Both use descriptive imagery, claims to firsthand experience, and knowledge of the Other to construct portraits of foreign or sometimes familiar places. When anthropological writing is dry, overly esoteric, or drenched in academic jargon, it could probably benefit from a dollop of journalistic style. Travel journalism, in turn, is at its best when it is accurate. Ethnographic inaccuracy results from committing various anthropological blunders, some of which are prominent in Kaplan's article.

Overgeneralizing

Travel journalism, like anthropology, depends on the writer being there and witnessing. Practitioners of either must convince their readers that they have the knowledge to describe another part of the world accurately. Kaplan's descriptions of his visits to "cities in six West African countries" (46), his border crossings by "bush taxi," his arrivals at airports and bus terminals, and his conversations with an African ministry official and a "foreign resident" in Sierra Leone are meant to establish his authority as an informed eyewitness who has logged time in these places, and his shocked tone in describing what he saw is compelling. However, readers are given no information about how long Kaplan stayed in these cities, where he stayed, or with whom he spoke and in what language (other than the African official and the foreign resident noted above). Anthropological writing, in contrast, depends on long-term, systematic research, not short visits and limited interviews.

Like travel journalists, anthropologists often pen colorful and compelling descriptions of their field sites to convince their readers that they are intimately familiar with the place about which they write. Kaplan's essay, however, moves from descriptions of specific West African urban slum environments to broad statements about "West Africa," which he expands to generalizations about "Africa." Arguing that Africa's state borders are increasingly irrelevant, he slips into writing about a generic "Africa" despite his extremely limited experience with that vast continent's enormous diversity. Imagine visiting Beverly Hills; Greenwich, Connecticut; and New York's upper-east-side stretch of Park Avenue and believing that these places represent the lifestyle of all Americans! Does the crime he describes in urban Abidjan characterize life in rural Botswana? Does the crime rate in Los Angeles reflect crime rates in rural Oregon? I read in a South African newspaper in 2001 that an average of twelve schoolchildren a day are killed by guns in the United States: should readers assume that dodging bullets is part of the normal American school curriculum?

Misuse of the Term Culture

Culture seems to be a favorite term these days. We hear about "the culture wars," that "multiculturalism" is wonderful or that it threatens American culture, that people's culture determines their behavior, that culture is tied to race or ethnicity. Kaplan embraces the concept of "culture" as a force that can motivate people to action and cause them to kill each other in a context of resource scarcity. His use of phrases such as "cultural and racial war" (62), the present "age of cultural and racial clash" (76), and even "intractable culture zones like Haiti and Somalia" (whatever those are) (72) affirm that cultural and racial differences are innate, antagonistic, and capable of generating violence.

We anthropologists claim some responsibility for the concept of culture, which has been our stock in trade for a century. But our definition of the term has undergone major revision from the old days, when we listed the primary traits of culture X or stated that "culture Y believes such and such." The antiquated assumption that cultures were unique, internally integrated, bounded entities that shared borders but not content has been thoroughly dismantled over the past several decades as anthropologists have come to understand how five hundred years of growing global interconnections continuously reshaped peoples' ideas about their identities. The rapid mobility of people, ideas, goods, practices, and styles, and the overarching political and economic power structures that integrate our contemporary world, make any notion of discrete, unchanging cultures problematic. To which culture does a Haitian-born woman who lives with her American-born children in a Brooklyn neighborhood of Puerto Rican immigrants belong? To which culture does a young immigrant from rural Côte d'Ivoire living with his sister's husband's relatives in Ghana belong? Does a wealthy member of the jet-setting elite in Rio share "a culture" with rural cane-cutters of the north of Brazil simply because they are all Portuguese-speaking Brazilians?

Anthropologists continue to grapple with an acceptable definition of culture that captures a sense of "groupness" while recognizing people's profound worldliness, participation in multiple cultural milieus, and propensity to change perspectives and behaviors over time. Unfortunately, travel journalism has generally not caught up; it often continues to depend on a bounded and timeless view by which culture X is described with exotic images that promote perceptions of overwhelming difference and inspire desire, fear, or both.

This has consequences: once a culture is imagined to be bounded, distinct, and unchanging, then one can attribute all kinds of actions, behaviors, and beliefs to it. For example, "cultural differences" can stand in as a facile explanation of why people are at war with each other. I cannot count the number of news articles I have read in the United States that claim "the war in [name of African country] results from ancient cultural [or ethnic, tribal, clan] differences." But such explanations make most anthropologists recoil. We cannot assume that culture "naturally" defines allies and enemies. We cannot assume that cultural differences will produce hostility rather than mutual interest. We cannot assume that cultural differences must be reconciled through conflict rather than syncretism or mediation. We cannot assume that the natural human tendency is to kill those whom we perceive as different rather than accommodate them or cooperate with them. The history of humanity suggests a far different tendency. As the anthropologist Mary Catherine Bateson wrote, "If, in the course of evolution, human beings really had practiced Hobbes's 'war of all against all,' our species would not have survived. Nor would we have survived if our families, tribes and communities had been based solely on calculated advantage."[4] An assumption that people are naturally violent, or that they are naturally inclined to use violence in the struggle for resources against those they perceive as culturally different, would be contrary to what anthropologists know about humanity past and present. Rather, most of the time, in most of the world, people of different cultural backgrounds peacefully coexist, intermarry, do business, and build relationships. Even field research in war zones like Somalia in the 1990s and Mozambique in the 1980s shows that most people are not combatants but work together to protect their communities from the well-armed, violent few.[5] In short, discrete cultures do not exist and cultural differences do not naturally produce competition or violent conflict. Kaplan is simply wrong to assert this.

Describing Cultures in Biological Terms

Along with the tendency to envision culture as a closed, bounded, competitive entity comes the inclination to conflate culture and biology. When journalists and pundits talk about culture in biological terms, or as if it resulted from genetic inheritance, this makes many anthropologists want to tear their hair out. The idea that cultural behaviors or qualities are biologically inherited ("the people of culture X are innately bellicose; the people of culture Y are naturally more studious") has been thoroughly repudiated by anthropological research. Similarly, treating a culture like an organism (culture X is sick; culture Y is pathological) tells us nothing about the historical circumstances that have produced a set of destructive cultural practices or behaviors.

Kaplan suggests that African urban cultures are weak, and he blames the criminal violence in areas of urban poverty on cultural deterioration. According to Kaplan, some cultures are strong enough to stave off dissolution in crowded, economically unstable urban areas. In contrast to African urban slums that have created zones of violent crime and cultural deterioration, Kaplan presents the "Golden Mountain" urban slum of Ankara, Turkey, as a "wholesome," crime-free, dignified, clean, orderly, "real neighborhood" (63). Unlike African culture, Turkish Muslim culture is "formidable" (63), Kaplan argues, with "natural muscle tone" (66) "Slums are litmus tests for innate cultural strengths and weaknesses. Those peoples whose cultures can harbor extensive slum life without decomposing will be, relatively speaking, the future's winners. Those whose cultures cannot will be the future's victims" (63–66). Viewed through this lens, Africa's urban distress and criminal violence is a product of its innate cultural weaknesses. What annoys many anthropologists about this kind of biological reductionism (with its fascist overtones) is its total disregard for historical and political circumstances. Cultural behaviors are shaped out of particular historical conditions; they do not emerge from genetic codes. This point leads us to blunder number 4, Kaplan's tendency to ignore historical context.

Ignoring Context

"Physical aggression," Kaplan asserts, "is a part of being human. Only when people attain a certain economic, educational, and cultural standard is this trait tranquilized" (73). For Kaplan, poor urban slum dwellers with dissolving cultures have become "re-primitivized"; as their cultures deteriorate in the dense, competitive urban environment of scarcity, their inclination to violence naturally emerges.

This argument is shocking on two accounts. One, it ignores the fact that some of the most violent countries on earth, including the United States and Great Britain, are those Kaplan would characterize as having achieved the tranquilizing "economic, educational, and cultural standard." Second, it blames violence on cultural weakness rather than political or economic circumstances. In contrast, anthropologists reject the idea that cultures deteriorate like sick organisms and that humans are naturally inclined toward violence; instead, they seek explanations for violence by analyzing the changing political, economic, and historical contexts of violent places.

One passage from Kaplan's essay is particularly egregious. Kaplan writes, "Because the demographic reality of West Africa is a countryside draining into dense slums by the coast, ultimately the region's rulers will come to reflect the values of these shanty-towns. There are signs of this already in Sierra Leone—and in Togo, where the dictator Etienne Eyadema, in power since 1967, was nearly toppled in 1991, not by democrats but by thousands of youths whom the London-based magazine *West Africa* described as 'Soweto-like stone throwing adolescents.' Their behavior may herald a regime more brutal than Eyadema's repressive one" (52).

In borrowing the image that "Soweto-like stone throwing adolescents" might bring to power a brutal regime, Kaplan ignores the South Africa context of apartheid brutality and the oppositional pro-democracy movement. Those stone-throwing youths in Soweto were part of a much larger context of violence and antiapartheid struggle shaped by the appalling policies of the apartheid government. Invoking a frightening image of violent youth and suggesting their behavior is contrary to democracy does nothing to clarify why they are throwing stones or their attitudes about democracy.

ANTHROPOLOGICAL EVIDENCE

No one can deny that many African communities have suffered terrible violence in the past decade. But few anthropologists would explain these

violent situations as the result of "weak cultures" deteriorating into criminal violence because of resource scarcity. How do anthropologists
explain violent criminality and conflict in places like Sierra Leone,
Rwanda, or Somalia? Is Kaplan at least right about the role of environmental scarcity and degradation in triggering wars over scarce resources
where the combatants are defined by their cultural groupings? Anthropologists who have studied these places in depth provide evidence for us
to examine.

Sierra Leone

The anthropologist Paul Richards, who has worked in Sierra Leone
for decades, tests Kaplan's "New Barbarism Thesis" against evidence
presented in his 1996 book *Fighting for the Rain Forest: War, Youth, and
Resources in Sierra Leone*. Richards finds that in Sierra Leone it is not environmental degradation but rather political and economic transformations that are producing intense conflict in the resource-rich parts of the
country. A reduction in international aid, and the new economic policies
of structural adjustment required by the International Monetary Fund
following the end of the cold war, created a crisis in the aid-supported
government. Sierra Leone's government provided inept and corrupt
political leadership during this crisis.

Facing an uncertain economic future, young men were drawn to the
diamond mining areas near the Liberian border, where they came under
the influence of the rebel army, the Revolutionary United Front. Far from
being a localized group with narrow ethnic interests, this army was led
by a well-educated, intellectual elite tightly connected to the international trade in diamonds. Violence in Sierra Leone is in fact more about
the control of the diamond trade than anything else. None of the factors
blamed by Kaplan—population pressure, environmental degradation,
scarce natural resources, ethnic and cultural cleavages—created the brutal warfare in Sierra Leone. Rather, Sierra Leone's problem results from
an abundance of internationally desired resources that people are fighting to control, a willingness by the international diamond industry to buy
diamonds from violent guerilla militias, and poor governance.

Rwanda

Rwanda might seem to present a better fit for Kaplan's theory of population pressure, resource scarcity, and cultural clash. Tiny Rwanda was one of Africa's most populous countries, and the 1994 genocide targeted one group, the Tutsi (as well as politically moderate Hutu). But Peter Uvin, Christopher Taylor, Alison DesForges, and the journalist Philip Gourevitch, all of whom have worked in Rwanda, reject the argument that environmental degradation resulting from population pressure generated conflict along ethnic lines over increasingly scarce resources, as Kaplan would have it. Rather, these researchers emphasize how international involvement in Rwanda contributed to its recent period of intense violence.[6]

Rwanda is characterized by linguistic, religious, and cultural unity; however, during the colonial era, colonial religious, political, and academic elites fostered intensely racist ideas that distinguished among Hutu, Tutsi, and Twa racial identities. Part of the colonial project in Rwanda was the construction of a rigid social order of mutually exclusive, hierarchical racial groups, to one of which every Rwandan was assigned. In imposing a new racial order, colonial authorities issued mandatory identity cards designating the carrier's race, engaged in a "scientific" process of measuring noses and skull sizes to assign racial identity, created a descriptive terminology for each racial group, and practiced a race-based allocation of favors and opportunities. "Hence," as Peter Uvin explains, "social relationships in Rwanda became more uniform, rigid, unequal, and exploitative than ever, with a clear hierarchy from Bazungu [colonist] to Tutsi to Hutu to Twa, with each higher level having privileges denied to the lower level and with an ideology of racial superiority underlying this system of inequality."[7] Rwandan independence in 1962 was marked by intense ethnic violence, as the departing Belgian colonists shifted their support from the Tutsi, favored during the colonial period, to the Hutu majority, who would take control of Rwanda's postcolonial government.

The racist distinctions fostered during the colonial era pervaded postcolonial Rwandan society, and regimes supported by massive international aid fostered state-sanctioned racism and status inequalities. In the 1980s, a drop in world prices of coffee (Rwanda's most important export), and the structural adjustment demands mandated by the International Monetary Fund, contributed to a climate of economic insecurity. Political insecurity arose over internationally mandated multiparty elections and the threat posed by a rebel Tutsi-dominated army of Rwandan refugees on the Ugandan border. Rwanda's Hutu-dominated authoritarian government responded to these insecurities with an anti-Tutsi racist campaign designed to enhance support for the government among the Hutu majority and to marginalize moderate Hutu who favored power-sharing political reforms. Due to the doctrine of Hutu-Tutsi racial difference and inequality promoted by European elites during the colonial period, many Hutus among the impoverished, intimidated, and politically marginalized peasantry were receptive to the government's message. This government was almost entirely funded by international aid, despite its record of human rights abuses, virulent racism, and contemptuous, authoritarian treatment of its population. Contrary to Kaplan's notions, the ecological environment was not degraded, cultural differences were absent, and the government was not weak. Rather, a strong, internationally supported government embarked on a racist campaign of massive proportions in order to convince a politically and economically disenfranchised population to murder anyone suspected of not supporting the government. The result was that, within one hundred days, 1 million Tutsis and moderate Hutus were killed.[8]

The slaughter in Rwanda was not a "natural" result of cultural or racial differences in a context of overpopulation and cultural deterioration, as Kaplan suggests. In part, Rwanda's trajectory of racist hatred was shaped by local and international politics and abetted by local and international financing.

Somalia

My own research in Somalia offers another challenge to Kaplan's thesis. In the American mass media, Somalia's collapse was explained as the inevitable result of ancient clan hatreds that simmered just under the surface throughout the period of colonial control and "pacification." Journalists argued that the modern state structure left in place in Somalia following colonialism could—for reasons usually left unexplored—no longer contain these ancient antagonisms among clans, which exploded in the 1980s and 1990s, when there was easy access to advanced military technology. Western news reports described the Somali environment as arid, harsh, and resource poor; Somali politics as based in rigid, autonomous, kinship-based clans; and Somali culture as inherently war-like and antagonistic. This portrait of Somalia's collapse was depicted as the inevitable result of a warrior culture historically divided into antago-nistic, mutually exclusive primordial kinship units battling over scarce resources. Such a picture was simple, accessible, and easy to understand, and it seemed both to support and be explained by Kaplan's general explanation of Africa's current distress.

In fact, these assumptions about Somalia ignore the most critical fac-tors contributing to Somalia's violence. First, Somalia is simply not over-populated; this fact immediately negates Kaplan's emphasis on this issue. Somali society does consist of a network of mutually exclusive clans. However, the clan basis of Somali society is quite complex, because not all Somalis are members of clans, and in southern Somalia—the scene of the worst violence in the 1990s—people could, and did, switch clan affiliations with ease. Throughout the south, people of different clan memberships intermarried and formed villages together. Furthermore, although violence between clans has certainly occurred in local contexts in the past, clan interrelations carry a long history of mediation and con-flict-resolution customs.

Most important, journalists' misplaced emphasis on Somalia's clan structure as the source of the violence ignores the political and economic context of life in Somalia in the 1980s. Somalia's dictator since 1969, Siyad Barre, had adeptly utilized the cold war system of international relations to his benefit, becoming the second largest African recipient of U.S. aid during the 1980s. United States–led "development" and military assistance in the 1980s strengthened the repressive dictatorship and paid for a tremendous arms buildup. The government used its power to take land away from rural farmers and give it to state employees, to incarcerate its critics, and to bomb its citizens when they protested against government abuses.

By the 1980s, Somalis began rebelling against Siyad Barre's dictatorship. The oppositional movements contained people from diverse backgrounds, but as the struggle intensified, politicized clan identities emerged as the most salient groupings on the national level. During chaotic times of intense state violence or collapse, clan affiliations can help people identify networks of support and alliance. The clan structure also provided a way to channel and define the lines of conflict, but it did not produce the conflict. Civil war in Somalia was simply not caused by ancient clan hatreds (or what Kaplan termed *intractable culture*) made unbearable by resource scarcity resulting from population pressure. Rather, Somalia's civil war resulted from a rebellion against a brutal United States–backed dictator whose policies militarized the country, dispossessed rural people of their land, and diminished local forms of authority and mediation.

THE LARGER PICTURE

Kaplan's Africa-in-a-vacuum portrait completely ignores several dimensions of state collapse as it happened in Sierra Leone, Rwanda, Somalia, and elsewhere. First of all, his model ignores the effect of international politics in transforming the countryside and cities of Africa's states. Viewing African states in isolation from their involvement with the rest of the world, Kaplan makes Africans appear to be absolutely inept and corrupt state-makers. Certainly some African regimes have exhibited deplorable political leadership, but they have been able to operate ruthlessly and selfishly because of the international backing they received during the cold war years. Media coverage of Africa is skewed not because African Americans are overly sensitive to Africa's image in the U.S. media, as Kaplan suggests, but more significantly because the U.S. government is deeply implicated in support for dictators, the militarization of African countries, and the ensuing collapse of several African states.

A second dimension of state collapse ignored by Kaplan is how the local political and economic systems—which are supported in part by international political patronage—structure who gets access to resources and who does not. For example, in Somalia, pressure on agricultural land resulted from government policies that took land away from farmers and distributed it to political and business elites. This point must be stressed: contrary to Kaplan's assertion that rising population pressure in Africa produced resource scarcity, in Somalia scarcity was artificially created by politically motivated land expropriation and by development projects that distributed land unequally. Peter Uvin argues that internationally funded development projects in Rwanda similarly contributed to an unequal distribution of resources that exacerbated resource scarcity in some areas.[9] Kaplan's generalized notion of "environmental pressure" completely ignores political and economic dynamics that determine how resources become valued, competed for, and allocated. Political policies, the world market for Africa's commodities, and international economic interactions have played critical roles in creating inequality in accessing resources in Africa. Kaplan's simplistic neo-Malthusian explanation of scarcity is simply wrong.

The third dimension ignored by Kaplan is how ethnicity emerges from political contexts. Ethnicity is not "primordial," but rather becomes relevant in particular ways in particular situations. In focusing solely on population pressure and resource scarcity, Kaplan simplifies and minimizes what are in reality highly complex social, political, and economic contexts. Furthermore, he profoundly ignores history. To understand the wave of destructive changes sweeping across some African states, both the historic local context and global geopolitics must be taken into account. While there are no simple models that can account for what has been happening in some parts of Africa, the evidence is clear that ethnic and tribal differences do not "naturally" produce conflict.

KAPLAN'S "REALISM": HOW REAL IS IT?

One more thing is wrong with Kaplan's portrait. He claims to be writing from a "realist" stance that describes how the world "really" is, rather than how politicians or international relations experts think it should be. He emphasizes what he imagines to be the real conditions of being human: aggression, conflict, struggle over resources, and the potential threats to state security and international stability. But in fact, his portrait of Africa is a result of his own selectivities and biases rather than an accurate assessment of the continent's realities or its potential threats to the United States. Kaplan is apparently attracted to violence and criminality and prefers a Hobbesian dog-eat-dog vision of human nature. Because his portrait of Africa is designed to support his particular version of reality, we get no glimpse of the millions of Africans leading peaceful, fulfilling lives: raising their crops, herding their livestock, building their businesses, and working together to support their families and communities. The anthropological literature on Africa is filled with just such descriptions. These realities—of peace, community, family, work—are ignored in Kaplan's account because he is focused on peddling a particular image of the post–cold war world: an image of destructive possibilities lurking throughout the globe at this historical moment. In selecting particularly disturbing images from Africa to support his larger thesis, he emphasizes population pressure, environmental degradation, and resource scarcity. It is a shame that, while Kaplan identifies these areas of importance to Africa's future—the environment, control of resources, and the youth demographic—his ability to offer serious insights is derailed by his adherence to such a flawed understanding of human nature and social interaction. Anthropologists identify the environment, control of resources, and the youth demographic as important areas to understand for contemporary Africa, but recognize that the significant questions have much to do with how social relations of inequality are created by the political and economic context within which particular groups struggle to control Africa's resources.

U.S. DISINTEGRATION?

Kaplan's real focus in presenting his analysis of Africa is the West. While his article predicts an anarchic future in many areas of the world, he is most concerned with how this predicted anarchy will affect the United

States. In the final paragraphs of his article, Kaplan suggests that the threat to the United States presented by Africa's collapse will take the form of increased cultural and racial clashes within U.S. borders. He does not explain clearly why this will be so, but he seems to be suggesting that Africa's collapse will incite racial tensions within the United States. Kaplan sees the United States as newly divided and fragmented by "racial polarity, educational dysfunction, [and] social fragmentation of many and various kinds" (76). As evidence, he notes the "violent affirmation of negritude" that characterized black students' responses to assimilation attempts in the public schools. He mentions that the Washington, D.C., public school system is "already experimenting with an Afrocentric curriculum." Moreover, he claims that, "because America is a multi-ethnic society, the nation-state has always been more fragile here than it is in more homogeneous societies like Germany and Japan" (76). (Kaplan fails to mention the twentieth century's most significant contribution to German "homogeneity.")

What is so disturbing about this argument is his implication that multiethnicity—and the self-affirmation of minorities in particular—is making the United States less of a nation, and that the collapse of African states will contribute to cultural fragmentation in the United States by further polarizing racial groups. Because of these tensions, he implies, American culture is becoming weaker and thus less able to withstand the kind of cultural deterioration he describes in urban Africa. Here, he seems to be assuming that a discrete, definable "American culture" is, like a biological organism, under attack from invading foreign cultures. However, a very different cause of racial polarities in the United States is easily identifiable; they are intimately bound up with the system of stratification by class, race, and gender that has long characterized American society. Where Kaplan argues that multiethnicity is making us less of a nation, I argue that the blame lies with extreme and growing inequities in wealth and opportunity. The destructive effects of inequality and class polarization is, of course, the great American public secret.

Averting our eyes from the effects of inequality in the United States makes it easier to ignore the economic dimensions of violence in African states. Certainly, it is easier to lay the blame for violence at the feet of culture, imagining violence to be a result of internal issues and cultural deterioration. But peddling this kind of an explanation of violence in Africa, with the assistance of exotic descriptions that titillate readers' fearful fantasies, is not only wrong; it is inhumane.

SIX Globalization and Thomas Friedman

Angelique Haugerud

Who could possibly be against globalization? Only "a Noah's ark of flat-earth advocates, protectionist trade unions and yuppies looking for their 1960s fix," according to Thomas Friedman, foreign affairs columnist for the *New York Times*.[1] "Senseless in Seattle" was his epithet for the thousands of protesters—many dressed as monarch butterflies and sea turtles—who disrupted the December 1999 World Trade Organization (WTO) meetings in Seattle.[2] Unfortunately, Friedman utterly mistakes the protesters' agendas, starting with the antiglobalization label itself, which they reject as a media invention. The activists' real aims are global social justice and new forms of global democracy. But these goals are not Friedman's concern. Instead, in his best-selling book *The Lexus and the Olive Tree: Understanding Globalization*, Friedman praises globalization as an inexorable force that can solve many of the world's problems. Friedman's hype, however, is at variance with decades of anthropological research about the processes he describes. His globalization tale is, at best, wishful thinking, and potentially harmful if it shapes public policy.

Cultural and social anthropologists have long studied startling changes like those that excite Friedman and some of his readers. The anthropologist's quarry includes economic, political, cultural, legal, spiritual, and environmental transformations in locales that North Americans and Europeans consider remote, as well as those they find familiar. Careful ethnographic and historical research long ago led anthropologists to discard overwrought images of primordial "tribes" whose cultural differences supposedly cause them to kill one another. Also rejected are notions that any contemporary peoples are Stone Age homologues or tradition bound exotics who stubbornly or irrationally resist change. Gone are yesterday's notions of boundaries as fixed, natural, or inevitable. Contemporary anthropology, however, appears to be unknown to Friedman, whose writings on globalization offer a caricature of a world torn between olive trees and Lexus luxury cars, between stasis and change.

Although Friedman's writing style is powerful and persuasive, its empirical underpinnings are deeply flawed. Influential policy makers and opinion shapers—even when they are journalists and not scholars—should be held to high evidential standards. This chapter shows why Friedman's approach, assumptions, and claims fare poorly under anthropological scrutiny. It begins by briefly outlining his tale of globalization as the key to understanding the post–cold war era, notes some limitations of his methods, and then identifies four fundamental flaws: an overly narrow observational frame, misunderstanding of tradition, misconception of ethnicity and culture, and failure to address the morality of economic neoliberalism. Next it sketches anthropological alternatives to Friedman's misconceived olive groves and his narrow view of the 1999 WTO protests in Seattle. Contrary to what Friedman believes, globalizers include precisely those village societies he deprecates as rooted in olive groves, together with migrants to the industrialized North who sustain ties with their countries of origin and forge complex transnational networks. What villagers, migrants, shantytown dwellers, and protesters seek is global and local social justice, not isolated olive groves of tradition.

FRIEDMAN'S GLOBALIZATION WRITINGS

In this chapter, I use the term *globalization* to refer to accelerated flows or intensified connections—across national and other boundaries—of commodities, people, symbols, technology, images, information, and capital.

Friedman celebrates the recent emergence of a global market economy, driven largely by an "electronic herd" of global investors wielding such technology as the Internet, satellites, cell phones, and personal computers. He displays little patience with individuals or groups concerned about the increasing power of corporations that are not accountable to the public, or about declining living standards, curtailment of social expenditures in poor nations, harm to the natural environment, or growing global economic instability and inequality. The primary task of world leaders now, as he presents it, is to keep investors happy so that their corporations will not leave for other countries. For Friedman, a particular type of globalization known in much of the world as economic neoliberalism is an inevitable new world order worth applauding.[3] Neoliberalism refers to supposedly free markets and minimal government direction of flows of goods, services, and finance—a set of policies Friedman terms the "golden straitjacket":

> The Golden Straitjacket is the defining political-economic garment of this globalization era. . . . If your country has not been fitted for one, it will be soon. The Golden Straitjacket first began to be stitched together and popularized in 1979 by British Prime Minister Margaret Thatcher. . . . That Thatcherite coat was soon reinforced by Ronald Reagan. . . . It became a global fashion with the end of the Cold War. . . . Thatcher and Reagan combined to strip huge chunks of economic decision-making power from the state, from the advocates of the Great Society and from traditional Keynesian economics, and hand them over to the free market.[4]

In poorer nations, the neoliberal golden straitjacket often means imperatives by the World Bank and International Monetary Fund (IMF) to reduce government subsidies for education and health care, privatize state-owned firms, liberalize trade, devalue currencies, emphasize production of primary goods for export, and deregulate financial and labor markets. The underlying logic is that market competition ensures efficient production of goods and services, and that market deregulation stimulates productive economic activity that benefits all in the long term. Friedman portrays those who do not celebrate this new economic order's competitive realities as "irrational backlashers" destined for Darwinian failure.

While urging everyone to jump on the globalization train, however, Friedman acknowledges that "both the booms and the busts will be coming faster," and he hopes that the entire system does not collapse (p. 462). Although he wishes he could slow this train down, "there's no one at the controls," and the system is "so new and so fast" that no one really "understands how it works and what happens when you pull a lever here or turn a dial there" (pp. 343, 459).

In addition to praising a system that, he concedes, risks catastrophic breakdown, Friedman argues that it is pointless to try to fight the powerful lobbies of American banks or to imagine a global central bank to regulate the global economy the way the U.S. Federal Reserve manages the American economy. Instead he finds hope in the market's capacity to discipline itself, noting that the 1998–1999 financial crises led to the ouster of chief executives of some of the world's largest banks and prompted many major banks to demand more transparency from those to whom they lend and to implement more serious risk management techniques.[5] Such ad hoc approaches, he says, will have to suffice "until the day when some new global financial regulatory system can be erected" (460–61). In short, his advice is to let the market work as it will and not to be unrealistic about change.

Just as Friedman considers globalization to be an inevitable and positive force, he views resistance to it as an act of irrationality or ignorance. People either "get it," embrace globalization in its current guise, and join the "fast world," or they are ignorant "turtles" (his terms) left out of the race. There are two extremes in Friedman's world: that of the Lexus and that of the olive tree. Inspired by his visit to a Tokyo car factory where sixty-six human beings and 310 robots each day produce three hundred Lexus sedans, Friedman sees half the post–cold war world as "intent on building a better Lexus, dedicated to modernizing, streamlining and privatizing their economies in order to thrive in the system of globalization" (p. 31). The other half of the world is "still caught up in the fight over who owns which olive tree." Olive trees, he suggests, represent "everything that roots us, anchors us, identifies us, and locates us in this world—whether it be belonging to a family, a community, a tribe, a nation, a religion, or most of all, a place called home" (p. 31).

In Friedman's shorthand, then, the tale of globalization is a struggle between Lexus and olive tree, and the two must be kept in a "healthy balance." Yet in many respects, Friedman suggests, the outcome of the story is already known. Although olive trees should survive, and although the Lexus threatens the olive tree and so may provoke a "backlash" from the protectors of the tree, "sooner or later the Lexus always catches up with you" (p. 39).

His analytic vision thus circumscribed by the modern Lexus, on the one hand, and the ancient olive tree, on the other, Friedman ridicules those who dare to imagine more humane, environmentally safe, and democratic forms of globalization. In his view, those who protest the economic status quo are, at best, myopic denizens of olive groves. His descriptions of them are often much harsher.[6]

Such language sells newspapers and books and has helped to make Friedman a visible television commentator on the Public Broadcasting System's *NewsHour, Washington Week in Review,* and elsewhere. Corporate leaders, financial analysts, and mainstream policy makers are likely to appreciate his arguments about the inevitability of the golden straitjacket, or neoliberal form of economic globalization, and his idea that globalization is the "one big thing" on which people should focus in order to understand the post–cold war world.[7] Indeed most mainstream media representations of globalization are deferential toward big business and downplay the negative effects of neoliberal economic policies on education, health, and the environment; the reduction of labor's share in income; the astonishing rise in economic inequality; and the increasing power of corporations with little accountability to the public. Friedman has easy access to the powerful: in the acknowledgments to *The Lexus and the Olive Tree*, among those he particularly thanks are former treasury secretaries Lawrence Summers and Robert Rubin, the World Bank president James Wolfensohn, the vice chairman of Goldman Sachs, the chairs of Monsanto and Cisco Systems, members of the Davos World Economic Forum, and the Federal Reserve chairman, Alan Greenspan.

His stock is not so high with most academics. For example, political scientist Mark Rupert of Syracuse University; Rupert writes on his Website that "Friedman is frequently mistaken for an authority on globalization."[8] Rupert notes Friedman's failure to engage the "vibrant scholarly literature on globalization" or to take seriously the alternatives to standard economic neoliberalism that are more democratic, sustainable, and egalitarian, put forward by an emerging global civil society of nongovernmental organizations, activist groups, and others.[9]

Friedman sides with so-called realists who understand the status quo and the weighty forces that define the distribution of power and wealth, and who urge individuals to figure out how to profit from the system as it is. In belittling people who struggle to improve globalization by striving for better wages, labor rights, food-safety standards, and environmental safeguards, Friedman—whether intentionally or not—affirms the power and ostensible rationality of the elite architects of the status quo. Such a stance ignores a rich history of successful struggles against seemingly inexorable forces such as racism, sexism, environmental destruction, economic exploitation, and abuse of power.

Friedman describes himself as "a tourist with attitude," and he says he has the "best job in the world" as foreign affairs columnist for the *New York Times.* Is being a "tourist with attitude" enough to provide useful insight into issues of such profound importance? Admittedly anthropology, like journalism, has its touristic moments, but both anthropologists and journalists must do more than tell travel stories. They must work to understand and interpret other places and lives, try to balance objectivity and subjectivity, and acknowledge observer biases and effects as they record, describe, and analyze. Both anthropologists and journalists must make judgments about what is worth reporting, but anthropologists know that they should do so only after immersion in the social communities and networks they analyze. Moreover, anthropological research carries the professional imperative of systematic collection of information from individuals in a variety of situations, and careful attention to the kinds of biases that can accompany the selection of interviewees. An anthropologist's observations during extended field research offer opportunities to test inferences and conclusions and to complicate, enrich, and refine them. Without expecting journalists to become anthropologists, the former can learn from the work of the latter. So how might an anthropologist approach the task Friedman took on, that of making sense of globalization?

FRIEDMAN'S FLAWS

At first glance, Friedman's globetrotting approach might seem similar to that of modern anthropologists who have shed their discipline's earlier attachment to long-term field research, as both participant and observer, in a single, out-of-the-way locale. Today many anthropologists prefer multisite field research, which means that those studying economic development and social change in a Kenyan or Zambian village may now find it useful to interview not only African villagers but also migrants to New York and Lusaka, as well as project managers for the UN's Food and Agriculture Organization and the World Bank in Rome and Washington.[10] Contemporary anthropology also values ethnographic writing that includes revelations about the author, as well as unstaged dialogues between the anthropologist and those being studied. Many anthropologists today are skeptical empiricists who find those authors who frankly express their own opinions or biases, and reveal their own effects on the data they collect, more credible than those scholars of human behavior who claim to be neutral, objective, or value-free observers. Friedman, too, pugnaciously declares what he thinks in a way many readers find engaging, and his prose is similarly enlivened by his reporting of such dialogue and self-revelations. Indeed, anthropologists may find Friedman annoying precisely because his work has some of the trappings of "a seductive, and thus extremely effective, form of the ethnography of globalization to which many of us vaguely aspire."[11] Yet no serious anthropologist would recommend to students Friedman's approach. Seen through an anthropological lens, Friedman's work on globalization contains a number of fatal flaws.

Overly Narrow Observational Frame

Friedman's disposition to view the 1999 Seattle protesters as "crazy" and "ridiculous" prevents him from exploring their perspectives and aims; he simply overwhelms the reader with his own. Anthropologists, on the other hand, are judged by how deeply they penetrate or make sense of the motivations and behavior of others. Thus they are trained not to rely too heavily on a narrow segment of the population under study; rather they must observe and interview widely and record, describe, and analyze an event from multiple perspectives. The write up should be a respectful portrait rather than a caricature.

Friedman fails anthropologists' test, then, by substituting ridicule for careful observation and analysis of others' understandings and aims. That error is compounded by his apparently heavy reliance on elite, mainstream sources in business and government and his failure to explore any but the most distant connections to other types of people. His book *The Lexus and the Olive Tree* depicts how the world's less fortunate peoples experience globalization through anecdotes and vignettes gleaned from Friedman's brief stays abroad, usually in luxury hotels in capital cities. (This globetrotting approach differs sharply from that of his earlier book, *From Beirut to Jerusalem*, which was based on many years in the Middle East.) Friedman's easy access to elites contrasts the way that the less privileged enter his global framework: through his casual conversations with street vendors, hotel clerks, room service waiters, shoe shiners, cooks, and other tourist service workers whose lives are profoundly affected by (and who also help to shape) the globalization processes he describes. Anthropologists too must deal with uneven access to different categories of people, but Friedman does not appear to have made much effort to overcome this bias in his sources. Moreover, what he does convey would be more persuasive if his own opinions did not obliterate those of so many other people who do cross his path.

Tradition Misunderstood

Friedman views tradition as an obstacle to progress, a romanticized domain to be protected, or a source of destructive backlash. Anthropologists, on the other hand, view tradition as a dynamic, adaptable, complex set of meanings and symbols manipulated to serve present interests and needs. Friedman appears captivated by misleading notions of an inevitable clash between a frozen "tradition," on the one hand (symbolized by the "olive tree"), and "modernity" (the Lexus), on the other. Missing the subtleties and complex capabilities of tradition (and culture), Friedman misrepresents resistance to some forms of economic globalization as simply a stark refusal of "modernity." Anthropologists, by contrast, recognize that resistance may very well signal rejection not of modernity per se but of the social injustices, environmental destruction, and brutal economic inequality that can accompany industrialization and economic neoliberalism. Viewing resistance simplistically as mere rejection of change or modernity leaves Friedman blind to profound historical processes and social movements that are redefining our era. He thus misses the main story.

Friedman simply fails to see the dynamism of societies that appear to him as static relics of an ancient past, such as when he gazes out his train window in Egypt and imagines that the "barefoot villagers" are contemporary survivors of the Egypt of 2000 B.C. (p. 339). In his perception, a dichotomy exists between two rigidly separate worlds: that of the constantly ringing cell phones in his train car full of forward-looking middle- and upper-class Egyptians, and that of the "barefoot Egyptian villagers . . . tilling their fields with the same tools and water buffalo that their ancestors used in Pharaoh's day." The latter image of what he takes to be a static "traditional" Egypt of course is utterly false: it is contradicted by Egypt's long history of agricultural innovation, production increases, economic growth, labor migration, and participation in far-flung trading networks.[12] The sharp dichotomy he imagines between two worlds—one traditional and the other on the globalization train— obscures the dense networks of social and economic relationships and reciprocities that actually bind these worlds together.

The force of such ties is illustrated, for example, in anguished questions put to him by educated Egyptians, such as a woman who asks, "Does globalization mean we just leave the poor to fend for themselves?" Or an Egyptian professor who wonders, "How do we privatize when we have no safety nets?" (p. 341). Friedman does not directly answer these questions, but instead tells us that such conversations led him to realize that "most Egyptians—understandably—were approaching globalization out of a combination of despair and necessity, not out of any sense of opportunity. . . . When you tell a traditional society it has to streamline, downsize, and get with the Internet, it is a challenge that is devoid of any redemptive or inspirational force." Again, in Friedman's world, people either embrace contemporary (neoliberal) globalization and join the "fast world," or they are ignorant "turtles" left out of the race. If the government's social safety nets are shredded in the process,[13] or if the capacity to create such safety nets is eliminated, or if ties to one's rural cousins must be broken, so be it.

Ethnicity and Culture Misconceived

Friedman sees ethnicity as cultural attachment to ancient identities (the olive trees again). Ethnicity, to him, is a potent natural and primordial source of conflict that must be contained. Contemporary anthropology, on the other hand, emphasizes the modern political and economic origins of conflicts often labeled as ethnic.[14] Ethnic identities are not primordial, essential differences but—like any supposed traditions—manipulable symbols and dynamic understandings, myths, and narratives. Individuals may accentuate, efface, or disguise ethnicity: like any identity, it is situationally contingent. Friedman, however, clings to outdated stereotypes of ethnic conflict. Indeed, in his schema entire countries can be "olive trees," a characterization he attributes to Rwanda.

In briefly discussing genocide in Rwanda, Friedman invokes stereotypes of a country emerging from "an orgy of tribal warfare." He calls it a place where "Tutsi and Hutu tribesmen [have] tak[en] turns downsizing each other to grab more resources for themselves."[15] He does not mention the ways modern political party competition, regional (not just ethnic) oppositions within Rwanda, patronage politics, hate radio, and governmental structures all helped to fuel the 1994 genocide, which was carried out by well-organized extremist militias using lists of targeted individuals drawn up years before. The genocide was made possible by the capacities of a strong state that had received substantial external support when it adopted precisely the kinds of neoliberal economic policies Friedman praises.[16] In short, far from being an atavistic resurgence of "ancient tribal hatreds," the genocide emerged from very modern political and economic forces. Those contemporary political and economic complexities, however, seem to have escaped Friedman, who instead lazily invokes familiar stereotypes of perennial conflict in a "tribal" Africa. He ignores the many careful, scholarly accounts of the Rwanda genocide produced by anthropologists, historians, and political scientists as well as Friedman's fellow journalist, Philip Gourevitch.[17] To reduce the modern political complexities of Africa—or any region—to "ancient animosities" or simplistic tribal or ethnic conflicts is not only misleading but also dangerous when they inform U.S. foreign policy or become an official pretext for inaction.

The Ethical Bankruptcy of Blind Faith in Markets

Friedman asserts that "countries basically get the economic outcomes they deserve" (pp. 455–56). This position makes no allowance for the unequal starting positions of countries, classes, or individuals in today's race to globalize. Does he believe that a child born into poverty in Ethiopia or Haiti or Peru gets the outcome she or he "deserves?" The ethical bankruptcy of that argument is obscured by Friedman's portrayal of the economic system as "rational" (notwithstanding his concession that it risks spinning out of control and leaving casualties in its wake).

Friedman does acknowledge that globalization impoverishes as well as enriches, and it disempowers as well as empowers. He insists nonetheless that free trade and globalization offer the poor the "best ladder out of misery," and does so with a fine disregard for what scholars term *structural violence*—widespread hunger, disease, and unemployment—caused or exacerbated by economic neoliberalism.

Moreover, it is simplistic to talk as if markets are entirely "free," unfettered, or unshaped by government laws. An anthropologist might inquire instead, Who benefits from the rules that define market competition? Who has the power to define the rules? Government intervention in the market is an everyday practice; without it we would lack many of the services, goods, and protections many of us take for granted, such as relatively safe food, water, and workplaces. But, the anthropologist might ask, What political dynamics encourage vilification of poor recipients of welfare benefits while winking at government assistance for wealthy corporations? Why do most free market cheerleaders not condemn tax breaks or subsidies for developers of a sports stadium or government bailouts of failing airlines? Economic neoliberalism as both theoretical edifice and societal vision deserves careful scrutiny rather than enshrinement.[18] Even that iconic champion of the market, Adam Smith, cautioned against low wages, too sudden removal of protectionist tariffs, and the runaway greed of the powerful.[19]

By treating a particular form of economic globalization as if it were natural and inevitable, and then hyping it, Friedman also rationalizes the growing poverty of much of the world's population, as well as environmental destruction, human rights and labor abuses, and denial of basic freedoms to people who inconvenience the large corporations, the focus of nearly all his deferential attention. His view seems to be that nothing should stand in the way of corporatism—a powerful partnership of transnational corporations, global regulatory and financial institutions, and the state (which offers corporations contracts for weapons, antibiotics, prison management, and security services).[20] Friedman's world citizens in turn are reduced to consumers or brand boycotters who can protest only with their wallets—assuming they have anything in them.

Friedman weaves symbols such as the Lexus and the olive tree into seductive tales based on false pictures of "free" markets and about the Other: the region, country, or individual that differs from "us." His picture of the olive tree is particularly distorted: into the olive grove, he dumps an improbable array of phenomena, including the politics of conservation, consumer protection, welfarism, labor, human rights, culture, nationalism, and ethnicity. Although, astonishingly, he makes them all expressions of something he labels "tradition," they are—to the contrary—profoundly important forces of change.

Anthropologists have, in fact, for several decades analyzed how those who resist or challenge status quo inequalities of race, class, and gender may contribute to change that is ultimately progressive.[21] There is no reason, and Friedman does not offer one, to assume along with Friedman that resistance to the golden straitjacket is necessarily ignorant, regressive, irrational, or foolish.

Friedman romanticizes and demonizes the olive grove and treats it as a repository of all that is irrational, but he never analyzes it with attentiveness or insight. His narrow observational framework, his misconceptions of culture and tradition, and his refusal to take a morally grounded point of view all produce a globalization narrative that is more panegyric than analysis, more fiction than truth, more arrogance than understanding. For Friedman, there is nothing to be done about globalization except to proclaim it to be inevitable and desirable and then celebrate.

But the term *globalization* need not be limited to international financial markets, capital flows, and Disney-fication; instead, it could also signify an increasing capacity for political alliances and declarations that transcend the nation-state. Imagine that we identify as "globalizers" precisely those village societies that Friedman deprecates for being rooted like olive groves, together with the new transnations they constitute with migrants in the industrialized North and the complex traffic in culture, social ties, and cash remittances that connects them. How then might we reread Friedman, drawing on anthropological evidence and approaches?

THE LEXUS AND THE . . . MIGRANT?
SHANTYTOWN? SWEATSHOP?

First, let us replace Friedman's imaginary notion of who inhabits olive groves with some real people: for example, rural and urban East Africans

(Kenyans), among whom I have carried out field research at various times during the past two decades.[22] Even rural Kenyans do not fit Friedman's binary between modernity and isolated olive groves of tradition. Many Kenyans are on the move between town and countryside, office job and farm, small business and outdoor market, constantly adjusting to rapid economic and political shifts and careful to diversify their economic activities. Small-scale farmers in central Kenya keep an eye on world coffee prices and frosts in Brazil that might signal higher prices for their exports. Many sustain relationships with relatives and friends abroad, some of whom have used the Internet to create international networks and discussion groups. Rural-urban migration patterns once thought to be one-way, from countryside to city, no longer are seen to be so, as urban economic decline sends migrants back to rural areas, and as growing numbers of urban civil servants who have retired or lost their jobs (often as a result of retrenchment mandated by the IMF and World Bank) decide to move back to the countryside.

Familial, social, and economic relations underwrite networks of reciprocity linking rich and poor, educated and uneducated, city dweller and farmer. Such relations of sociality, reciprocity, and clientage often are strengthened rather than attenuated by agrarian commercialization, industrialization, and globalization (the opposite of what earlier evolutionary models of social and economic change predicted). Rural land rights, even if one possesses an official title deed, often are not more secure or predictable than urban employment or business or other income. Thus, urban workers attempt to maintain rights in rural land, which entails material and social exchanges with rural kin and acquaintances. Uncertain economies, institutions, and politics place a premium on flexibility and encourage people to multiply social relationships and networks in order to acquire and safeguard access to markets, credit, and laborers. It is advantageous to spread one's risks by cultivating access to a range of people, resources, and income-earning opportunities.

Many educated urban Kenyans whom Friedman might characterize as having joined the "fast world" do not embrace globalization in its current neoliberal guise. Rather, they worry about deteriorating infrastructure (such as roads in disrepair or unreliable phone and electrical services), growing poverty and economic inequality, and declining access to health care and education following reductions in government spending and imposition of user fees for social services. These Kenyans who oppose standard neoliberal policies do not fit easily into Friedman's categories: neither ignorant "turtles" nor sentimental denizens of isolated olive groves, they are informed citizens who resent their government's diminished control over its own economic policies due to IMF and World Bank intervention.

Looking beyond Kenya, we can find others who are not part of the Lexus class but who do not sit under the olive tree either. A recent survey of popular attitudes to markets in four African countries—Ghana, Malawi, Nigeria, and Zimbabwe—found that substantial majorities were dissatisfied with their government's structural adjustment programs mandated by the IMF and World Bank, and that they disagreed with the statement that government policies in the era of structural adjustment have helped most people.[23] Some distinguished economists share that opinion, including former supporters of neoliberal economic policies. Joseph Stiglitz, a Nobel Prize–winning economist and former chief economist at the World Bank, has criticized the economic consequences of standard IMF policies in Asia and elsewhere.[24] Jeffrey Sachs, a former supporter of structural adjustment programs, has become a prominent advocate of the Jubilee 2000 debt cancellation movement.[25]

Today nearly half the world's population lives on less than two dollars per capita per day.[26] By the mid-1990s, the wealth of the world's 447 billionaires was valued at $1.1 trillion, which was equivalent to the total income of the poorest half of the world's population. By 1998 the combined assets of the world's wealthiest three billionaires exceeded the total gross national product of all the least developed countries and their 600 million citizens. The wealthiest fifth of the world's people receives over four-fifths of the world's income. The poorest 60 percent receives only 6 percent of the world's income. The golden straitjacket Friedman touts not only has failed to offer a solution to growing poverty and rising economic inequality but also does not even recognize them as problems. Instead it grants extraordinary freedom to corporations accountable only to their most powerful shareholders.

This sketch only hints at the complexities of globalization, such as the capacities for reform as well as violence of a postcolonial state controlled by historically advantaged elite classes, and the viability of nationalisms that envision strong states capable of resisting or reshaping IMF and World Bank conditions. Those who protest the status quo sometimes have contradictory agendas, and these too require careful study rather than Friedman-style ridicule or dismissal.

Friedman's misleading caricature of opposition between the Lexus and the olive tree, or between one kind of "modernity" and a supposedly static tradition, should be replaced with more accurate symbols. Friedman's binary vision obscures vital struggles under way—not over the protection of isolated olive groves of tradition but over social justice and economic opportunity on global as well as local scales. Perhaps he— or we—should be looking at the Lexus and the migrant, the shantytown, or the sweatshop.

REFORMING THE GLOBAL MARKET?

Now let us imagine anthropological alternatives to Friedman's narrow observational frame in looking at the 1999 WTO protests in Seattle. Instead of simply dismissing the protesters as lunatics, an anthropologist would ask questions: How does the WTO work and why do some favor reforming it or abolishing it? How and with what consequences does the WTO exercise its power to overturn a country's laws protecting environmental or health standards in the name of international free trade? What political inequalities are embedded in the sorts of trade negotiations that provoke growing criticism from poorer nations that would, for example, like to see an end to some European and North American farm subsidies?[27]

An anthropologist also would want to know what modes of organization characterized the 1999 Seattle protesters. In Seattle in 1999, broad coalitions of labor, environmental, farm, and human rights groups called for a less secretive and more democratic WTO; some demonstrators wanted to abolish the WTO, others to reform it. What alternative visions of globalization inspired thousands of protesters from around the world

to march through the streets of Seattle? Why did the anti-WTO demon-
strations draw together such unlikely allies as the United Steelworkers of
America and the Rainforest Action Network? Here was a chance to examine both the obstacles and the possibilities facing such movements.[28] An
anthropologist would explore the political networks and organizational
modes that produced the street theater in Seattle as well-organized and
peaceful "turtle" marchers formed an improbable alliance with teamsters,
with shouts of "turtles love Teamsters!" and "Teamsters love turtles!"

Friedman, however, shunned such knowledge or inquiry. His first critical column on the Seattle protests, for example, does not address at all
the issues raised by the protestors concerning WTO secrecy and lack of
democratic accountability.[29] Friedman dismisses the Seattle protesters'
concerns about the broad impact of WTO rulings.[30] He mentions just one
example of the type of ruling protesters find problematic, and terms it a
"narrow case": namely, the WTO ruling that the U.S. prohibition on
catching tuna in nets that also trap dolphins was an illegal barrier to
trade. He suggests that it is "nonsense" to conclude from such rulings
that the WTO "is going to become a Big Brother and tell us how to live
generally."[31]

Friedman suggests that, rather than targeting the WTO and urging it
to set different rules, the protesters should recognize that the global market itself encourages reform. Here he cites Microsoft's application of
pressure on Sri Lanka by refusing to sell its products there until the latter
passed stronger intellectual property laws. He also points to reforms
achieved through the "hard work of coalition-building with companies
and consumers," by, for example, showing corporations how they can be
"both green and profitable." Thus he notes that DuPont and Victoria's
Secret modified their practices in response to pressures from activist
groups who mobilize consumers and who publicize environmental damage or harsh child labor or sweatshop conditions on the World Wide Web.
Friedman contrasts such Web-based tactics with the Seattle protesters'
"1960s tactics," accusing them of the "fool's errand" of "blocking trade,
choking globalization or getting the WTO to put up more walls." In reality, however, many of the activist groups represented in the Seattle
protests exercise precisely the kinds of consumer mobilization and Web-

based tactics Friedman praises, and many of their battles have yielded the kinds of reforms and democratically enacted laws that the WTO has the power to overturn. Friedman presents contradictory arguments about when activism is appropriate and what it should look like.

A week after his "Senseless in Seattle" column on the WTO protests, Friedman returned with "Senseless in Seattle II," in which he reported that he had checked every can of tuna in his local supermarket and found that they were all labeled "dolphin safe" notwithstanding the WTO ruling that the law requiring this was an illegal barrier to free trade.[32] The dolphin-safe tuna he credits to "smart activists" who ignored the international trade body's ruling and mobilized consumers to put economic pressure on the tuna companies. Mexican fishermen, not wishing to lose customers, responded to these pressures by using dolphin-safe nets.

When the save-the-dolphins-from-tuna-nets activists first mobilized a couple of decades ago, however, one could expect from his other writing that Friedman would have dismissed them as hopeless idealists. The activists' success in this instance (assuming—possibly a stretch—that the tuna labels are true) may have depended in part on the affection American consumers already had for dolphins. If securing more humane, healthy, and environmentally friendly forms of globalization depends on intangibles such as which mammals Americans find charismatic, then the reform tactics favored by Friedman will often fail. Reforming globalization demands diverse tactics and forms of struggle; these deserve to be documented and analyzed.[33]

By mid-2001, Friedman began to suggest that the "serious protesters" (those concerned with how we globalize) had made their point, and he urged them to "design solutions in partnership with big businesses and governments."[34] Such a formulation has unfortunate affinities with the "constructive engagement" posture of apartheid apologists some years ago, and today it might simply be called "corporatism": the assumption that huge corporations, states, trade unions, and consumer groups can reconcile their competing (never contradictory) interests in a manner that will improve the welfare and prosperity of everyone.[35] Corporate scandals in the United States, such as Enron's meltdown and public revelations about top executives of other firms who prospered during their company's decline or collapse, as thousands of employees lost their livelihoods or retirement funds, suggest a much darker view of the potential Friedman sees in ordinary citizens' partnerships with big business.

In 2003, global trade dilemmas that derailed the 1999 WTO meeting in Seattle again surfaced spectacularly as world trade talks collapsed in Cancun. Representatives of many poor countries were elated at their success in banding together this time and standing up to the rich countries that refused to eliminate their farm export subsidies. Others warned that poor countries would suffer most from the failed negotiating round in Cancun. Yet even *The Economist* termed rich countries' farm subsidies "grotesque" and noted that "America's unwillingness to curb its cotton subsidies—which have an especially severe effect on poor-country producers—is unforgivable. So too is Japan's unyielding defence of its own swaddled rice farmers."[36] Nongovernmental organizations such as Oxfam helped to shine a spotlight on the crushing effects of rich-country cotton subsidies on poor cotton farmers in West Africa. In short, global markets are far from free and open, and the challenges of constructing a fair multilateral trade system remain enormous. In addition to the subsidy hypocrisies and corporate scandals, the costs of globalization in its present form are starkly apparent in the colossal and continuing loss of U.S. jobs to countries where labor is much cheaper and where environmental and worker protections are weaker. These challenges demand attention to more humane forms of globalization (not alternatives to globalization). Far from meriting Friedman's ridicule or smug dismissal, activists in the global movement for social justice deserve praise for sounding an alarm about a careening economic globalization train.

SEVEN

On *The Lexus and the Olive Tree,*
by Thomas L. Friedman

Ellen Hertz and Laura Nader

You can fool some of the people all of the time, and all of the
people some of the time, but you can't fool all of the people all
of the time.

It is intriguing to read a book such as Thomas L. Friedman's *Lexus and the Olive Tree: Understanding Globalization,* a book that received accolades from all the major newspapers, only to realize that one disagrees with almost every bit of praise heaped upon it.[1] To put Friedman's argument in a nutshell, globalization—or the New World Order—is driven by free market capitalism of a new kind. Since the technology and information revolutions of the 1980s and 1990s, and because of the growing importance of financial markets in the production and distribution of wealth in the world, this new capitalism is more volatile and more dynamic than ever before. It is also increasingly American led. It places the bulk of its faith in the power of markets to come up with solutions to social problems. Accordingly, it promotes the downsizing of government, both consciously as a matter of policy formation and through the unintended consequences of financial markets that weaken governments' power to determine the course of national and international events. Although this poses the problem of how to preserve traditional values and community (the olive tree in the book's title), this new capitalism is fated to exist and expand because of its superior capacity to improve standards of living through consumerism (the Lexus in the book's title) and its tendency to weaken governments and thus to democratize authoritarian regimes.

In our view—that of two anthropologists and concerned world citizens—Friedman's arguments are based on glib phrase-mongering rather than reasoned analysis. He neither takes the time to understand local situations, nor cites any experts who do not agree with him (and he plays fast and loose with the experts he does cite). In other words, he does the exact opposite of what anthropologists are supposed to do: stay a long time on-site to gain in-depth knowledge of the way our informants see the world, learn the local language, apply rules designed to avoid bias in the gathering of evidence, and, perhaps most important, listen. Critics have dubbed Friedman the most traveled blind man ever, and yet his vision of the changes reshaping the globe at the beginning of the twenty-first century speaks to his readers. Clearly, it is not merely the beliefs expressed in Friedman's message that make this book a best-seller. What is it about the medium in which this message is conveyed that is so attractive?

As anthropologists, we must address these questions of form with as much attention as we pay to the content of Friedman's arguments, for it is, in large part, the packaging that caused Friedman's book to be so widely read. Indeed, we go further and suggest that it behooves anthropologists and other scholars to replicate the effectiveness of that packaging once in a while if we wish to convince people of what we have learned, based on our research, about the real effects of globalization and the reasons why many people worldwide, not just Friedman's sentimental denizens of notional "olive groves," raise objections to it. In this chapter, we take up various strategies for analyzing Friedman's success with the media. We focus primarily on one example of his writing, *The Lexus and the Olive Tree*, having also read many of his columns and examined his 2002 book, *Longitudes and Attitudes*. Many of the characteristics we find in *Lexus* are present in his other writing, oversimplification being the overriding theme. In what follows, we describe and then parody Friedman's rather accomplished style. We then review the main themes and flaws of this type of journalism, highlighting Friedman's techniques of persuasion. We conclude with a discussion of how responsible social science scholarship and reporting approaches the questions central to this book, and discuss the dangers of the kinds of simplifications Friedman uses.

FRIEDMAN'S STYLE

Friedman's New World Propaganda is breezy, sarcastic, anecdotal, accessible, and optimistic—the kind of not-too-serious writing that people might choose to read at the end of an all-too-serious workday. His exaggerated writing style draws on the techniques of advertisers, whom he admits he prefers to academics. Readers may like Friedman because he sounds proud of his country; because he is optimistic about electronic technology, free markets, and "democracy"; and because he doesn't take his own caveats too seriously. He uses ridicule to tarnish governments and peoples who have not opened their doors to the version of globalization he touts, and he lightly prophesizes their demise for not "getting on board." Friedman (hereafter referred to as TLF) is confident he has the key to the future. To make his points he uses colorful images geared to arouse emotions of fear and self-satisfaction. His depiction of "Us" versus "Them"—the civilized world versus the backward and irrational traditionalists—portrays those who are not on board the globalization train as misguided unfortunates. His contempt for alien cultures is blatant, his picture simplicity itself. Furthermore, we have heard all this before—in ads, in *Business Week*, and in Friedman's own columns. So it is familiar—a characteristic frequently mistaken for smart.

SOMEONE LIKE FRIEDMAN ON FRIEDMAN

Globally speaking, TLF's book is about globalization. This is a problem, because TLF couldn't understand globalization if it hit him over the head (and somebody should). If globalization were really as simple as TLF would have us believe, if it were really just "the One Big Thing" he says it is (p. xviii), then *The Lexus and the Olive Tree* would be the twenty-first century's answer to Mao's little red book, and we'd all be wearing Armani suits and waving it as we prostrated ourselves in the parking lot outside that pathetic little Beltway bakery where TLF can be found having his coffee every noninternational morning (p. 243). Indeed, TLF would be President of the World, just like he imagines he is, as illustrated by his truly embarrassing daydreams about telling off world leaders, from Malaysia's Mahathir ("Ah, excuse me, Mahathir, but what planet are you living on?" p. 93) to the former Algerian prime minister. ("I listened politely to his remarks[,] . . . and then I decided to respond in a deliberately provocative manner, in hopes of bursting through his fixed mind-set. I said roughly the following [with my profanities edited out]: . . . We don't give a flying petunia about you!" [p. 316]). Now that's tellin' 'em, Tom!

If we've moved rather rapidly here from the subject of globalization to that of TLF's globally proportioned ego, it is because that's what his book is about. TLF is not writing about globalization; he's writing ad copy— for himself and the people he associates with. He lives in a Lexus and drives in a dream world, surrounded by friends living in Lexuses driving around in dream worlds. TLF has talked to people all around the world who drive Lexuses like himself and live in their own particular dream worlds: American expatriates in Thailand—TLF refers to them democratically as "people"—who talk about the life-imperiling congestion and urban sprawl of Bangkok as "the Mother of all Traffic Jams" (p. 222). Or journalists for large American newspapers who tell "wonderful stories" about rioting in the streets and devalued currency in Mexico (p. 343). Or his very own self, engaged (p. 4, we're not making this up!) in time-consuming negotiations with room service at a four-star hotel in a dreadfully poor country to try to get them to stop peeling his oranges so that he can take them with him and drip orange juice on Lexus upholstery all around the world. In short, TLF has not talked to very many different kinds of people on his jaunts across the four-star-hotel-dotted globe. He's talked to the global representatives of Madison Avenue.

TLF brags about his "attitude" (p. 5); he even named his next book after it.[2] Yes, he has an attitude, and it's a bad one. For TLF has not done his homework. For example, unlike our kinda-elected president George W., TLF thinks that nuclear annihilation is a thing of the past (p. 7). He believes that France is a dying country (or is it a soccer team?) because it has introduced the thirty-five-hour work week (p. 10). He thinks everyone in America has home computers, credit cards, and access to the Internet (p. 66). And he thinks countries are like companies are like sports teams; that cultures are like animal species, doomed to evolve; and that "the world is only ten years old" (p. xiii). But perhaps we are being unfair. TLF doesn't really think the world is only ten years old. He admits that he stole this idea from a Merrill Lynch ad.

TLF thinks that some countries suffer from microchip immune deficiency syndrome, or MIDS, a very funny takeoff on that hilarious condition known as AIDS. He is wrong. What is right is that TLF himself suffers from TIS ("the inevitability syndrome," also known as BAHHUMBUG). He believes that globalization is inevitable, much like the fact that "the sun comes up every morning" (p. xviii). TLF pithily defines globalization as "both clashes of civilization and the homogenization of civilizations, both environmental disasters and amazing environmental rescues, both the triumph of liberal, free-market capitalism and a backlash against it, both the durability of nation-states and the rise of enormously powerful non-state actors" (p. xviii)—in short, everything and its opposite. The trick would have been, for a book of such weighty stature and magnificent price, to define it as something. Were he to do so, he might be able to see what it means to be "for it" or "against it," indeed what it means, full stop. Instead Friedman dins us with platitudes: "The answer is free-market capitalism" (p. 86). But neither Pat Buchanan nor Ralph Nader—to mention just two examples from what is obviously the most important country in the world—is "against" free market capitalism. It all depends on what you mean by "free market capitalism," what kind of "free market capitalism," and how it is carried out. Now "there is the rub," to quote one of the sexiest admen of the seventeenth century.

Sometimes TLF does define things as something rather than everything. For example, TLF defines the "democratization of finance" as "workers [moving] their money around like chips on a roulette table"

(p. 51). Now, aside from the fact that this represents a dangerous misperception of those upstanding mafiosi who so democratically run our roulette tables in a state west of Delaware, this is a just plain odd definition of democracy. Thankfully, TLF also gives us other definitions, in direct contradiction with this one. "Panic has been democratized," explains Egypt's minister of economy helpfully from his Lexus car phone, while the "short-horn cattle" (that's Friedmish for large funds on financial markets) run roughshod over his country (p. 110). If this isn't clear yet, another example should help: Dell Computers, says TLF, has really "democratized" a lot by decentralizing certain functions and assigning them to its individual sales and service centers so that they can "tailor [their] services to [the customers'] particular needs and tastes" (p. 70)— as clear and heartwarming a definition of democracy as his blast-from-the-past namesake Thomas Jefferson ever gave us.

You see, TLF, who has great patience for stories involving TLF, has little patience with "technicalities." He likes "simple stories" (pp. 15, 22— for simple people, Tom? Positive your paternalizing populism!). Markets are good things. Laws are good things. Sure. Any fool and even some economists know this. The problem is, sometimes these good things lead to conflicts of interests and values. Democracy—which is also a good thing and which takes many forms, none of which TLF is apparently aware of—is the process by which these conflicts are resolved. The outcomes depend on the particulars of the conflict at hand. This means getting into technicalities.

Take the World Trade Organization, a pretty good example of what globalization is all about, though TLF seems to have overlooked it. The WTO treaties on trade in goods are, generally speaking, a good thing. The WTO treaties on intellectual property are, generally speaking, a bad thing. Both of them involve laws about markets. So, the democratic process should help us work this out, to know when laws should restrict markets and when markets should shape laws. That means more than cheerleading. It means asking what kind of globalization we want. There is really nothing inevitable about decisions that try to answer these questions: they involve complex weighing of interests and values. The more democratic this process, then the more different kinds of people you involve in it, the lower the LPP (Lexus per participant) ratio, the more interests and values are represented, and the more likely you are to come up with a balance that works. Macho ad-talk about MIDS and the One Big Thing doesn't get us very far in answering these questions.[3]

Now, TLF has his own way of getting around technicalities. When the going gets tough, TLF invents a new word. He's given the English language two real beauts with *globalution* and *glocalize* (pp. 142, 236; good names for a rock band and gargle formula, respectively). Globalution, in TLF's view, is the process by which globalization is going to force democratic revolutions on countries throughout the world. Globalution, and hence democracy, is forced upon countries through the workings of the electronic herd, the millions of investors in financial markets and foreign production that move their money around the world at dizzying speeds following the recommendations of admen who work on Wall Street. TLF compares the electronic herd to two Big Guys, the Lone Ranger and King Kong (p. 142). Now, we like the movies as much as the next gal, but we don't believe these two Big Guys penned any Bill of Rights.

As TLF points out, democracy requires community building, and community building doesn't happen by "overhear[ing admen's] conversations on their cellular phones with their offices all over the world. I really hate that. E-mail is not building a community—attending a PTA meeting is. A chat room is not building a community—working with your neighbors to petition city hall for a new road is" (p. 377). To our intense surprise we couldn't agree more with TLF on this point. But to attend PTA meetings or petition city hall, you need to be free from trampling by Friedman's electronic herd: to have relative job stability, health care, education, and especially time . . . maybe even a thirty-five-hour work week with four weeks of paid vacation guaranteed by law, as in that dying country known as France. How TLF expects Indonesians, Czechs, Senegalese—or Americans for that matter—to build community and hence democracy while being shot at and drooled on by two Big Guys is a mystery to us.

As usual, it's not a mystery for the penetrating mindlike substance of TLF. You just have to "express it more simply" (p. 143). For example, at one point in time, some "Indonesian reformer" on a cell phone told TLF that "he and his son got their revenge on Suharto once a week 'by eating at McDonald's'" (p. 143).[4] Now that is simple. We know 'cause we've tried. Though we didn't feel very democratized afterward, we did feel— to express it simply—fatter. But for TLF, none of this is a problem because, when push comes to shove, democracy is really about (watch out, readers, we're gonna hit below the belt) working harder, thoroughly indoctrinating oneself in one's employer's "culture," having downloaded upon oneself vast amounts of information for which employers used to be responsible, and then, at the end of the day or night, whichever, having the choice between Coke and Pepsi (and all of this can be found on p. 76).

"Glocalization," however, is another matter entirely. TLF defines "healthy glocalization" as "the ability of a culture, when it encounters other strong cultures, to absorb influences that naturally fit into and can enrich that culture, to resist those things that are truly alien and to compartmentalize those things that, while different, can nevertheless be enjoyed and celebrated as different (p. 236)." Along about now, we anthropologists (and yes, alert readers, there are more than two of us) begin really tearing our hair. For exactly one hundred years now, anthropologists like Franz Boas have argued that there is no such thing as a "strong" culture or a "weak" culture, that there is absolutely no way to say what things are "alien" to a culture and what things "naturally fit."[5] Very obviously, however, we have been using the wrong admen. Let's try again here.

Cultures just are, they aren't "strong" or "weak." And what they are is dynamic: that is, they change over time because of things like internal economic restructuring, immigration, cultural contact, markets, warfare, and colonialism. Native American culture wasn't "weak"; the societies where it flourished were attacked. Nigerian culture isn't "weak"; but the Nigerian government is being told by folks at the IMF, Shell Oil, and the diamond industry that it has to "restructure" or suffer the consequences they will impose. There's no selection of the fittest here; there's power— financial, legal, political, and military. There's nothing Darwinian about this picture.

But there is one thing you gotta hand to TLF—he loves his country. And why not? So do we. The difference is that TLF equates being employed by and able to consume the products of corporate America with American citizenship. But the majority of U.S. citizens—two of whom are writing this article—do not necessarily think of citizenship in this bizarre fashion. This mortal majority will be absolutely flabbergasted to learn that America's the ideal country because "the fifty states all hav[e] an incentive to compete and experiment in finding solutions to the intertwined problems of education, welfare and health care" (p. 301). Terrific. Twenty percent of the American population is functionally illiterate.[6] Two-thirds of the American workforce has lower wages today than it did in 1973.[7] And health care? Forty million people are without healthcare coverage in the leading country, that tiger-rider of the globalized world.[8]

Alert readers out there will have already noticed that TLF likes to have it both ways. When the responsibility for bad things might be ours, well, then, "there's no one at the controls" (pp. 93, 279). And when it's time to dish out the glory, lo and behold, "globalization is the tiger [and we Americans as] the people who are most adept at riding the tiger [are] now telling everybody to get on or get out of the way" (p 309) TLF has just emarmed his way out of the very difficult and important task of analyzing which decisions have effects and which effects are the unintended consequences of mechanisms (the stock market, the mass media, law reform) that no one fully controls. But instead of facing this question straight on, TLF in this little book actively promotes the inevitability syndrome: "hey!" (pp. 13, 14, 30, 49, 124, 130, 248, 360), nobody's in charge, and there's nothing we can do about it![9] We thought it was the Hindus, the Bantus, and the Whathaveyus who were fatalists. But this is fatalism American style.

ON TLF'S TECHNIQUES OF PERSUASION

In some ways, Friedman's writing reminds us of the rhetorical devices used by Ronald Reagan.[10] Reagan used obvious exaggerations, material omissions, contrived anecdotes, voodoo statistics, denial of unpleasant facts, and flat untruths. As Reagan did, Friedman shoehorns information to fit an ideological mold because he is out of touch with reality, spending his time with an equally isolated, like-minded elite. Such rhetorical reflexes are habit forming and indicate intellectual laziness. And then there is the amiability factor, that upbeat and positive tone. That one man happened to be a Republican and the other is a Democrat doesn't change much. With both we are confronted with the mind of a propagandist.

Dozens of academic and professional society journals have commented on Friedman's manipulative techniques, his oversimplifications, his ideological convictions, and so forth. Many of these reviewers identify the hidden techniques of persuasion at work: sound-bite rhetoric, unargued assertions, metaphorical reasoning, anecdotal evidence, insider jokes creating the sense of an elite of which he is a member, enthusiasm in the face of disaster, cooptation of the reader through "reasonable centrism," the collapsing of distinctions, the inevitability syndrome, mockery and verbal humiliation of those in opposite camps, and, of course, the belief in technological quick fixes. No one can accuse Friedman of understating his case.

Thomas Frank in particular stands out for his ability to identify Friedman's techniques of persuasion.[11] Frank pinpoints examples of Friedman's use of repetition and grandiloquent rhetoric. He describes Friedman's tactics as "hammering into our heads the notion that 'globalization' is the end object of human civilization and will undoubtedly make us rich, set us free, and elevate everything and everyone everywhere." He continues, "However familiar this incantation has become, one cannot help but be startled by the massive escalation of rhetoric in which this now official wisdom is expressed—grandiose is the tone of arrogance. . . . Much of Friedman's millennial enthusiasm arises from the mundane faith that capitalism is functionally identical to democracy." Frank spends a good number of pages recounting factual errors and sleights of hand of this sort. As Frank points out, "Democratization of Finance means we all get to invest in everything. The Internet becomes the model of perfect competition." What Friedman is really describing is an increasingly bifurcated world, a world where the haves have exponentially more, while the have-nots become ever more excluded from progress' march. How can financial markets democratize the United States, much less South Korea or Zimbabwe, when only an infinitesimally small elite has any idea of how they work and this elite does not communicate its knowledge to the general public? Yes, it is possible that financial markets might make people who do not understand them rich.

But since when is being rich being democratic? Mobutu was rich, but no one ever said he was democratic; the great trusts that ruled the American economic landscape at the turn of the nineteenth century made certain people very rich, but they were broken up in the name of democracy. If Friedman has any understanding of U.S. history, he has conveniently downsized it so as to make room for futuristic mantras.

Linguists could have a heyday with Friedman, for he repeatedly employs common categories of rhetorical manipulation, such as the following.

PARTIAL EVIDENCE

Substituting a part for the whole (unless the whole is Friedman, in which case every detail counts!), Friedman talks about globalization but leaves out a good deal of the globe. He frequently refers to Asia, mentions Latin America, and excludes Africa almost entirely. What about Europe? North America? What would Friedman's globe look like if the continents were physically sized in proportion to the attention he gives them?

REPETITION

Friedman's argument is entirely incantatory. He starts from the claim that technology created globalization (science marches on); he proceeds with the claim that globalization is good (the self-interested individual marches on); he notes that contradictory values exist and that they too are good ("the olive tree!"); he shows how these values will be trampled upon by the stampeding of the "electronic herd" (you can't stop progress); and he concludes by hoping that everything will work out all right nonetheless (American fatalism).

CLAIMS OF AUTHORITY

Friedman invokes "experts" in an entirely self-serving manner: when they do not agree with him, they simply aren't mentioned. Sentences such as "most economists/political scientists/international relations specialists agree that . . ." are simply hocus-pocus: none of these illustrious professions agree on anything, and it is a good thing they don't!

THE USE AND CREATION OF BUZZWORDS

Beyond those superb specimens already mentioned *(globalution, glocalization,* the *electronic herd,* and *microchip immune deficiency syndrome),* Friedman has provided the English language with *super-empowered individual* and made *turbo-charged* a word used to describe more than just cars. Buzzwords—snide little packages of almost-meaning—substitute for thinking.

THE EXCLUSION OF CONTRARY DATA OR OPINIONS

In Friedman's book, the only people ever to speak out against globalization happen to be dictators—a pretty damning association. Friedman never mentions other potential opponents of his idea of globalization, such as the French, the European Union, and progressive Third-World critics or activists. And how does Japan fit into this story, by the way?

UNSUPPORTED CLAIMS

Take a couple of winners: "With greater wealth comes more education, information and ultimately democracy" and "NAFTA [has] been a win/win arrangement" (p. 277). Or take the notion, discussed and dismissed in his introduction to *The Lexus and the Olive Tree,* that globalization wasn't invented in the last twenty years but has in fact been around for five hundred or more. But as Friedman says, "When everything is speeded up the world has a shorter memory."

FALSE ANALOGIES

Why is it that countries are like companies or like sports teams? Why is a dollar like a vote? Why is the Great Society equated with the Soviet Union? Perhaps Friedman never explains these analogies because the things being compared aren't comparable.

DEFLECTING COUNTERARGUMENTS WITH CHEAP SHOTS

Friedman likes to encapsulate his opponents in the same pithy little phrases that he uses to encapsulate his beliefs. For example, few knowledgeable environmentalists agree with Friedman's simplistic statement "If you want to save the Amazon, go to business school and learn how to do a deal" (p. 225). There are people with data, evidence, and arguments who strongly support private-sector-based programs for environmental protection, just as there are those with data, evidence, and arguments who support strong state intervention, and still others with data, evidence, and arguments who place their faith in "civil society"—nongovernmental organizations, activist movements, citizen resistance, and so on.[12] Does Friedman give us any clues about the data, evidence, and arguments justifying each of these positions? No, he puts in a plug for business school, of all things. Had he mentioned one by name, he might have received a commission.

FRIEDMAN FLAUNTS HIS OWN CREDENTIALS

Perhaps most manipulative of all is Thomas L. Friedman's use of Thomas L. Friedman. Not content (and rightly so) to rely on the strength of his own logic, he repeatedly reminds not-so-alert readers that he is a Pulitzer Prize winner and a foreign affairs columnist for the *New York Times* (a fact that seems to have unduly impressed an Albanian immigration official, pp. 123–24), that he travels internationally on a regular basis, that he sleeps in elegant hotels and eats fabulous foreign food, and most important, that he rubs shoulders with the high and mighty and even pities them occasionally, as with his gloating description of the rise and fall of George Soros (pp. 267–68).

ON THE EFFECTS OF FRIEDMISH

Of course, one reason why the Ronald Reagans and the Thomas Friedmans of the world operate in such a breezy manner is because it works. It worked with Ronald Reagan and, if the sales of Friedman's book are any indication, it works for Friedman. Thus our questions: why did people buy this book, and did they believe what they read in it? Undoubtedly some did believe it and some didn't. For those who uncritically accept Friedman's view of the world, there may be reasons—a yearning for optimism, pride in one's country, a wish to understand "the fast track," and, yes, comfort in simplistic answers to a bewilderingly complex set of questions. There are other reasons too: people are prejudiced, they do not want to consider the consequences of technology, they seek justifications for actions that may be regarded by future generations as less than noble. But whatever the reasons for Friedman's journalistic success, there are public costs to sloppy journalism, not the least of which is further loss of trust in major institutions of business and government. And trust is a social good, laboriously produced and easily contaminated, like the air we breathe and the water we drink.

We live in a time of psychosocial dislocations, a breakdown of familiar structures in part linked to the technological capacities that Friedman writes about. Under such conditions, some people go with the flow while others get a good grip on the familiar and hang on for dear life. Still others are skeptics. Aldous Huxley in *Brave New World* and George Orwell in *1984* saw this coming and imagined dystopias to warn people of the controlling processes used by centralized structures, processes that result in curbing or constricting critical thinking.[13] Orwell wrote about opinion manipulators; Huxley imagined a world where negative or restrictive feelings were contained through drugs and pleasure. Rereading such works in these times triggers an eerie feeling of déjà vu. What were supposed to be warning fables today read like partial descriptions of early-twenty-first-century reality.

Writers such as Huxley and Orwell show that the most effective kind of manipulation is subtle, indirect, and apparently reasonable. Yet, by incremental means, through hidden manipulations, we lose freedom and democracy just as surely as we would in totalitarian structures. This is why it is imperative that we maintain our capacity for critical thinking. With the loss of critical thinking comes indifference, a lack of engagement and accountability, a sense of anomie that is often a reflection of the indifference with which workers and citizens are treated by powerful institutions.[14] Thus, one major danger of the kind of distressingly incomplete writing we find in Friedman's work is that it narrows the reader's ability to think critically. A form of entertainment more than reflection, this style engenders crassness (as when Friedman describes the Rwandan tragedy as Tutsis and Hutus "downsizing" each other, p. 351) and a blasé attitude toward the growing inequalities in wealth and power in the United States and in the world. Sophisticated propaganda comes from all sides of the political spectrum. But as Paul Krugman writes, "What is convincing is not necessarily true."[15] Hence, our warning: Caveat lector!

WHAT ANTHROPOLOGY CAN TELL US ABOUT GLOBALIZATION

As globalization is not "One Big Thing," anthropologists cannot give a nutshell definition of how it works. But they have studied many of its various manifestations, and we recommend some of these studies. For starters, we suggest Janine Wedel's *Collision and Collusion*, whose account of the Russian financial disaster and its causes and consequences in the West is far richer than Friedman's extraordinarily simplistic story. Or, readers might enjoy Janet Abu-Lughod's *Before European Hegemony: The World System, A.D. 1250–1350*, which shows that global expansion and empire can occur without one overriding cultural hegemony. On the subject of marketing, the sociologist C. Wright Mills's description fits nicely with the kind of rhetoric we find at work in Friedman's book: "The salesman's world has now become everybody's world, and in some part, everybody has become a salesman . . . the bargaining manner, the huckstering animus. The memorized theology of pep . . . they are all around us." On democracy, Friedman readers might look at Julia Paley's book *Marketing Democracy* and her review of anthropological works on democracy. As she notes, "Social movements have often created programs and practices that call themselves democracy movements while intentionally posing alternatives to standard definitions of the terms." The meanings attributed to democracy in various contexts do not necessarily match U.S. normative ideals as embodied in our Bill of Rights and Constitution. Finally, for those seriously interested in understanding free market ideology, an article by the anthropologist Jack Bilmes, who studied the Federal Trade Commission before and after the advent of the Reagan administration, is insightful.[16]

Bilmes cites the economist Milton Friedman, who says, "To the free man, the country is the collection of individuals who compose it, not something over and above them." Bilmes points out that, for the economist, efficiency and gain are the measures of a system's effectiveness; for the anthropologist, however, the criteria for evaluating a social system center on survival, cohesion, and social regulation. As Bilmes puts it, "The anthropological model does not start with an assemblage of independent, interacting individuals and then add regulation as an unhappy but expedient solution to certain problems. The anthropologist has no ideal or theoretical vision of the unregulated person. To be social is to be regulated" (p. 132). Or, in the words of another anthropologist, Clifford Geertz, "Man is precisely the animal most desperately dependent on . . . control mechanisms . . . for ordering his behavior." Humans are cultural animals, as Geertz also notes, and "culture is best seen not as complexes of concrete behavior patterns . . . but as a set of control mechanisms— plans, recipes, rules, instructions . . . —for the governing of behavior."[17] Anthropologists tend to take a long-term view of social systems because of their emphasis on the survival of the human group.

The anthropologist and the free-market journalist thus provide us with two sets of parallel, but profoundly opposed, concepts significantly different in their implications. Along with Bilmes, we are deeply critical of the naive and simplistic "promotion of a purely economic form of reasoning" to the status of general explanation of what is happening in globalization. Were we journalists, we would want to reflect on the ways in which the profession of journalism is being degraded by propagandistic sloganeering of the sort Friedman engages in. Farce is what results when journalists repeatedly fail to inform people and promote instead political-economic propaganda. Critical readers should know the difference between analysis and hype, between information and infotainment. Besides, is skepticism not the intelligent journalist's (and scholar's) most effective stock in trade?

Friedman borrows a telling phrase from the economist Joseph Schumpeter: "creative destruction"—for example, "download or die!" (p. 334). He has warned us: his story is not about sweetness and light; it is about ramming it down your throat. This kind of deterministic thinking is not only propagandistic, it can also be depressing for the young people of today, who, even before the gene revolution, already showed tendencies toward thinking that life was just a blueprint, leaving them no room for dissent, initiative, or other creative endeavors. We are appalled to learn that some professors in reputable universities are using Friedman's book as a text, and doing so uncritically. Teaching the young to view the world through peculiarly rosy First-World glasses can be dangerous in a nuclear age. Teaching college students that those who disagree are savagelike and dispensable takes us intellectually back to nineteenth-century evolutionism, in which Western culture was presumed to be the pinnacle of civilization and progress. Perhaps that is what happens when a journalist relies so heavily on advertising copy for insights into worldwide phenomena. And, as with advertising, the risk is that some people may actually believe it.

EIGHT Extrastate Globalization of the Illicit

Carolyn Nordstrom

> Crime has been a silent partner in modernisation. Within
> a contracting world, crime and its traditional boundaries
> are transforming into predictable and active features of
> globalisation.
>
> Mark Findlay, *The Globalisation of Crime*

While doing fieldwork, I can watch people driving German-made cars talking on their Italian cell phones and taking a look at their Chinese-produced watches.[1] They pop Panadols from India for the headaches they get while negotiating military weapons procurement deals with Brazilian and British representatives, or while checking on shipments of laptop, satellite-linked communications computers from California. They oversee shipments of raw diamonds that will end up on the fingers of brides from Cincinnati to Calcutta, as they puff on cigarettes of Virginia tobacco. Their uniforms, whether military or business suits, are mass-produced in an urban center in Mexico, their underpants in Bulgaria, their socks in Russia, their glasses in Argentina. They sign multimillion-dollar timber export deals with Parker pens.

These observations are nothing new; why write about them? Because all the activities described involve unrecorded trade—variously called illegal, illicit, or informal.[2] In my experience, I am as likely to encounter these realities in the more remote parts of Africa as I am in Johannesburg, South Africa, or Europe. The example I began this piece with is set in Angola, a country whose infrastructure has been devastated by recent war. It is a scenario reproduced in many places, from central Angola to the financial centers of the planet's richest countries. Illicit economies play across the landscapes of the world's financial and political power grids in critical ways; they are becoming global in the same way formal markets are. So it is crucial to ask: what role do they play in economic analyses and the globalization debate?

In fact, they play a surprisingly small role in the debate, despite their real magnitude. Globalization, as described by prominent writers like Thomas Friedman, is presented as a legal, powerful, and positive force shaping the world. It heralds democratization, positive development, gainfully interlinked global economies, and a blossoming of transnational alliances. For good or bad   and this view holds that it is predominantly for the good—globalization is here to stay: it is the wave of the future.

Friedman is not oblivious to the profound complexities and contradictions that attend the new market and power systems unfolding along global lines; he writes in his popular book on globalization, *The Lexus and the Olive Tree*, "If there is a common denominator that runs through this book it is the notion that *globalization is everything and its opposite*. It can be incredibly empowering and incredibly coercive. It can democratize opportunity and democratize panic. It makes the whales bigger and the minnows stronger. It leaves you behind faster and faster, and it catches up to you faster and faster. . . . It makes us want to chase after the Lexus more intensely than ever and cling to our olive trees [stability and the security of homeland and tradition] more tightly than ever."[3]

Friedman addresses many of the key concerns raised in the globalization debate, but he fails to deal with the vast transnational nonlegal networks that move trillions in goods and services and millions of people around the globe. As Mark Findlay writes, "Crime is a feature of the transitional and the globalised society, and as such should be accepted as a common theme in globalisation. Why this is not so becomes an important

theme for analysis. Answers may lie in the relatively positive and pur-
poseful representations of globalisation and its 'legitimate' features, such
as development, when contrasted against the pathological representations of crime."[4] Because Friedman and his ilk see globalization as inherently good, when they look at the world's horizons they see the bright
shine of economic activity, not the shadows of the extralegal. "Things
whose existence is not morally possible cannot exist," Primo Levi writes,
exploring the question of why many German Jews failed to see the dangers they faced under Nazi oppression. Yet partial vision is as dangerous
in economics and politics as it is in engineering and medicine: building
whole policies on half-truths can have severe repercussions.

JUXTAPOSING FRIEDMAN AND ANGOLA

> The Roque [a vast unregulated market on the
> outskirts of Luanda, Angola] was born in a con-
> versation between two businesspeople expelled
> from the city. Two miserable marginalized people
> who[,] after many setbacks, met one another out-
> side the city, not far from the ocean, at a clandes-
> tine locale to sell and earn what they could so
> that they could help maintain their families. So
> began everything.
> Hendrik Vaal Neto, *O Roque: Romance
> de um mercado*

This chapter explores the increasing globalization of the unrecorded
trade (the trade that falls outside of formal legal accounting) that shapes
world financial markets. Of particular interest in this analysis are the
relationships of unrecorded commodity flows from resource-rich locales
in Africa to cosmopolitan industrial centers worldwide. Charting this
trade shows that Africa is not, as Friedman suggests, at the margins of
globalization but is profoundly implicated in the globalizing process.
Hundreds of billions, perhaps trillions, of extralegal dollars travel yearly
through the channels that connect Africa and the industrial centers of the

globe: within this circuit, raw resources are exchanged for hard currency and commodities. This circuit provides critical resources to centers of commerce, markets for their products, and control over larger processes of currency valuations and speculation, interest rates, and investment patterns in a way that challenges neoliberal assumptions about free-market internationalism and development. As we will see, places like Angola stand along a central corridor of global trade—but the extralegal nature of much of this trade means that globalization for such countries is often more exploitative than fair.

In a curious irony, the illicit is in part galvanized by the forces of globalization as defined by Friedman. For Friedman and the supporters of transstate commerce, global interlinkages are the vanguard of "democratic values"—equal opportunities, fair exchange, private property, heroic individualism, unfettered gain, and the advancement of human rights open to all who enter the playing field of cosmopolitan exchange. But for many outside the centers of financial empires, urban industry, and superpower politics, the playing field does not appear to be equal or to offer open access. In southern Africa, people talk of *capitalismo selvagem:* capitalism of the wilds, or jungle capitalism (dictionary definitions convey the harsher aspects of the term *selvagem:* savage, brutal, cruel). For less powerful countries, restricted global access, lopsided trade agreements, and a lack of political power to negotiate better deals with the more powerful economies of the world result in a situation whereby resource outflows benefit the cosmopolitan centers of the world far more than they do the host country. Resource-rich countries are four times more likely to be suffering political violence. Virtually all these resources go to cosmopolitan industrial locales around the globe; the proceeds benefit the host countries very little. The lack of legal, governmental, and international controls in war zones makes such profiteering easier. This is as much the face of globalization as the international manufacturing and trade agreements that Friedman focuses on.

Unable to break the ways in which the most powerful countries and the transnational corporations define global markets, some exploit activities outside state control to compete in global financial matters. Janet MacGaffey captures this:

Through their trade and other activities, the traders protest and struggle against exclusion. In their search for profitable opportunities, we find them contesting boundaries of various kinds: legal, spatial, and institutional, and also the bounds of co-operative behavior. They are individuals who refuse to abide by the constraints of the global power structure and its alliances between multinational capitalism, Western governments and African dictators. They contest the institutions and norms of both African and European society which frustrate their aspirations for wealth and status. They resist the hegemony and control of the large-scale entities dominating the global scene.[5]

Authors like Friedman suggest that nonindustrialized locales in Africa, Latin America, and Asia are outside the globalization loop and could greatly benefit from joining in the transnational associations. Many people in these locales, however, see a world where certain powers reap fortunes from their homelands—through both legal and illicit channels—while keeping these realities in the analytical shadows. If we look at total resource and monetary flows—not just the legal ones—many nonindustrialized states are in the center of important globalized networks.

THE SOURCE AND POWER OF THE ILLICIT: FACTS AND MYTHS

> Crime is as old as humankind. But global crime,
> the networking of powerful criminal organiza-
> tions, and their associates, in shared activities
> throughout the planet, is a new phenomenon
> that profoundly affects international and national
> economies, politics, security, and, ultimately,
> societies at large.
> Manuel Castells, *End of Millennium*

Leaving illegal economic activities out of the globalization debate is not something restricted to public scholars like Friedman. In fact, this is part of a much larger process. While there are excellent studies of extralegal activities in the world, none are incorporated into formal governmental and international organization economic indices. No formal government-generated document calculating gross national product (GNP) includes economic data and indices that fall outside the purely legal; no formal calculation of country economic indices by the United Nations, World Bank, or International Monetary Fund, or global summations of GNP, takes account of extralegal data. As accessible as indices on GNP are worldwide, figures on all levels of GNP—including all unrecorded economic activity (whether labeled illegal, illicit, informal)—do not exist. Senior economists I interviewed from Angola to Geneva all said the same thing: figures for the unrecorded economy are not formally collected or calculated; no one can give any semblance of an informed guess as to the size and nature of the "gross national unrecorded product." Deleting the illicit from formal economic analyses is not mere happenstance: it is linked to political and economic control. Such control, as this article shows, requires that the figures on the extrastate and the practices that underlie them are neither transparent nor accountable.

For public scholars, ignoring the unrecorded is possible only because of several widespread myths. A reigning myth is that the illegal and the informal constitute an insignificant portion of the world's economy and political power grids. In fact, the opposite is true: extralegal economies generate trillions of dollars a year and employ millions of people. In many of the world's countries, over half the entire GNP is generated extralegally. The following examples, which run from the tragically exploitative to the remarkably mundane, demonstrate how these figures add up: As much as 20 percent of the world's financial deposits are housed in unregulated banks and at offshore locations.[6] The UN estimates illicit drug earnings at $500 billion, and profits from the illicit arms industry to be of a similar size. Human trafficking, considered to be the third-largest illicit activity after arms and drugs, brings in hundreds of billions of unregulated dollars a year. Of comparable size is the empire of gain from the unregulated sex trade and pornography industries.[7] While analysts tend to focus on the dramatically criminal when looking at extralegal activities, estimates of costs of three categories of corporate crime in the United States alone—consumer fraud, corporate tax fraud, and corporate financial crime—range between $247 and $715 billion annually.[8] India's "black economy" in the early 1980s was estimated at more than $60 billion dollars, and has grown since then.[9] In Peru, 48 percent of the economically active population works in the "informal" sector; the figure is 58 percent in Kenya, and perhaps even higher in Russia.[10] Michel Camdessus, former managing director of the International Monetary Fund, estimates that $600,000 million is laundered annually in the world, representing between 2 and 5 percent of the world's gross domestic product.[11]

The myth that these figures are insignificant to the world's economy can gain purchase because of a tendency among analysts to look only at small segments of the illegal economy, not the total. For example, the $500 billion generated yearly by illegal weapons sales represents less than a fiftieth of the world's entire GNP, which amounted to $31 trillion in 2001, according to World Bank estimates.[12] Figures for illegal pornography, the illicit sex trade, and people-smuggling may run past a trillion dollars, but the myth that such activities stand apart from everyday life lends the impression that they stand apart from the kinds of economic powerhouses that shape global economic health. We know that illegal drugs capture a half trillion dollars a year in profit. But we tend not to consider the total effect of illicit weapons and drugs, human trafficking, illegal labor, "white collar" corporate crime, and a host of other unregulated goods and activities.

Moreover, mundane informal economies can generate as much as the dramatically illegal: a person in Miami can make as much money selling freon gas, forbidden by environmental laws, as selling narcotics, and gangs on the coast of South Africa have found that they can make more money smuggling protected species such as the Patagonian tooth fish than smuggling narcotics.[13] In South Africa, half of all cigarettes sold are sold on the black market, and 50 percent of all computer software used is illicit; in Vietnam and China, 98 percent of computer software used is illicit. The computer industry would be satisfied if these countries could achieve the "success rate" of the United States, with only 30 percent illicit software.[14] Food and oil smuggling can generate as much income as people-smuggling.[15] A brisk and highly profitable illegal trade exists in everything from endangered species and nuclear waste to human transplant organs.[16]

It might still be possible to ignore the extralegal if a second myth were true: that illegally generated monies flow outside of the world's formal markets and political systems. But this myth is as false as the first. Money, no matter what form it takes, is useless unless laundered so that it can enter legally recognized economies. Money laundering—the intersection of the illicit and the legal—has a far greater impact on global financial and political health than is generally admitted: "Unchecked, money laundering can erode the integrity of a nation's financial institutions. Due to the high integration of capital markets, money laundering can also adversely affect currencies and interest rates. Ultimately, laundered money flows into global financial systems, where it can undermine national economies and currencies."[17] The sum total: half a trillion here, a couple billion there, and a trillion there add up to a considerable proportion of the world's economy. These are not merely market concerns: economic force translates into political power.

The consequences of ignoring the illegal in considerations of globalization start to become more evident. If trillions of dollars a year are being laundered and incorporated into the legal economy, this influences everything from stock market prices to inflation. Calculations of financial stability, development viability, stock market trends, interest projections, economic projection calculations, and other core indices cannot be accurate with a significant chunk of the data missing. Yet that is precisely what is taking place.

If we understood the role that the trillions of unregulated dollars played in world markets, would we have been able to predict and avert the Asian market collapse? Would we be able to predict the next severe bear market in our home country? The development trajectory of a united Europe or the new Central Asian states? And just as important, would we have been able to forecast terrorist attacks, which rely heavily on extralegal channels for commodities, services, money transfers, and international travel? If the answer to any of these is yes, and clearly it is, why then do most economic discussions of globalization, from Thomas

Friedman's popular discussions to formal World Bank government financial indices, so frequently ignore the extralegal?

A SOURCE OF PROFITS

> The largest profits often come from unexpected arenas. In many places today, a chicken and a bag of tomatoes are often more scarce, and more precious, than automatic weapons.

The man speaking about the value of tomatoes knows the profits these can generate. But "informal economies" are not formally calculated in the economic indices generated by countries in assessing gross domestic product (GDP) or by formal United Nations and World Bank country reports documenting economic indices and performance. Alexander Aboagye, senior economist for the United Nations Development Program in Angola in 1998, tried to explain why calculations of the informal sector fell between the cracks of formal governmental accounting: "Everyone is thinking in terms of 'one person, one tomato.' But everyone here survives by trading informally like this, and that's eleven million 'tomatoes'—think in terms of all the commodities and services that circulate daily—moving around the country and across borders at any given time. Eleven million 'tomatoes' comprises a formidable economy; but the irony is, no one realizes the sum total of this vast market, its definition of the basic economy of the country."[18]

The answer to why this lack of accounting is pervasive in formal institutional indices might be evident in the Angolan field site I introduced in the first paragraph, where a person driving a German-made car spoke on an Italian cell phone while making a multibillion-dollar weapons purchase. Angola has lost a million of its citizens to the political violence wracking the country. It ranks at the very lowest end of the United Nations scale of development and quality-of-life indices. Globalization proponents such as Thomas Friedman say that countries such as Angola should develop cosmopolitan links to the global markets to survive and progress in the twenty-first century. Angola is one of the most resource-rich countries on earth—rich in everything from diamonds to oil, from precious timber to valuable seafood. And in Angola, 90 percent of the economy, by UN estimates, is based on exchanges made along extralegal lines.

Countries such as Angola, say the globalization pundits, lie at the backwaters of global crossroads. In fact, Angola is at the center of transnational exchange and power. It is just that a considerable portion of this exchange is nontransparent.

But nontransparent does not mean nonprofit. Every commodity sold represents a profit for a manufacturing company. If a weapon is sold illegally, it still represents a profit for the manufacturer, whether it be a Fortune 500 corporation in the United States or a small Bulgarian arms manufacturer. If a diamond is smuggled out of a country illegally, the merchant in Antwerp or Hong Kong who buys it and sets it in a gold ring to sell to a consumer half a world away still makes a profit. Fortunes are made on these illegal sales.

A trip to the center of Angola helps illuminate this process. War has defined the politics and the daily realities of Angola for decades. A peace accord in 2002 marked the end of four decades of war, first fought for independence from Portuguese colonial rule, and then fought internally upon independence in 1975. The cold war categories of Marxist (government forces) and capitalist (rebel forces) framed an internal war that had international dynamics: Western allies lined up to back the rebel forces of Jonas Savimbi, while the communist world stood behind the government. After the cold war fizzled out in the late 1980s, the war in Angola did not, giving the lie to assumptions that the war was predominantly about political ideology. It is also about international profits, resource extraction, and global power networks, as UN discussions of the links between diamonds, weapons profiteering, and the war in Angola indicate.

Angola, the Angolans themselves say, is both blessed and cursed. God, they say, made it one of the richest and most resource-endowed countries on the planet—and then bestowed greed on humankind. The resources of Angola are those critical to the industrial centers of the world. "Conflict diamonds" that buy weapons and prolong the suffering

of war have become household words internationally. Angola's diamonds are some of the finest in the world. Extensive offshore oil deposits
promise war-free extraction, and most of the major petroleum companies
have holdings: three offshore blocks recently received among the highest
signature bonuses in the industry: $900 million. Vast tracts of excellent
Angolan timber are shipped worldwide, and international trawlers har-
vest seafood in the nation's offshore waters. Except for the oil, much of
this passes across the borders of il/legality (however, an oil executive
recently explained to me that some 20 percent of the oil business may be
conducted outside the realm of the legal). The frontier qualities of countries, such as Angola, that are undergoing rapid political transitions and
economic hardships make them ripe for exploitation by large-scale, international organized crime syndicates interested in transit points for international shipments of drugs, weapons, and sanctioned goods; for money
laundering; and for human trafficking.

These observations capture the broad sweep of illicit activities in
Angola. How this is lived by average people—how gems get from a
mine through a well-developed illicit network of brokers to industrial
uses and luxury enjoyment from San Francisco to Tokyo is a critical part
of the story: it shows the deeply complex nature of the illicit and its inter-
sections with global economy. The following story was relayed to me in
conversation in an embattled region in central Angola in 2001:

> Marra lives by the river Kwanza—as do bits of diamonds. Her brother
> is doing some mining to make ends meet. One day he manages to find
> a good gem, and he keeps it. At this point there is a military attack, and
> Marra's brother is killed. Marra takes the gem and flees with her chil-
> dren and nothing else. Their crops and home are burned, and there is
> nowhere near enough food for all the deslocados arriving. It is a humani-
> tarian disaster: people literally dying in the streets daily. The deslocados
> know food and humanitarian aid is available in the provincial capital,
> and those who can, push on to make the several-day walk there.
>
> Marra comes into the capital with others of her village, and they
> go through registration for the displaced. There are guys in the city
> who have a bit of money: maybe they run the bar or a shop in town
> and have a lorry. They know when the deslocados come to town that
> some are likely to have gems and other valuables. Considering the fact

that about a third of the population [of Angola] is dislocated, this is a huge flow. So they make contact and provide a channel for the *deslocados* to sell their things. They give Marra maybe twenty dollars for the stone. Then they have to sell the stone. It's still not worth an awful lot yet: they get maybe a couple of hundred bucks. The stone has to be laundered to be worth anything . . . and that is done down the line. The stone goes up the chains, to the capital, Luanda.

So how does this stone get to European gem dealers? Well, what comes into this provincial capital? Food. This food comes in from Portugal. Portugal connections are stronger here in this area than other areas, where trade with South Africa is more developed. This is because of the enduring nature of the old trade routes forged in colonial times and still in place, not because these routes are better or more efficient or smarter or smoother, but because they are in place—habit. So, stones follow this old trade routing: central Angola   Luanda   Portugal — Europe.[19]

Factor in seafood: the Portuguese and Spanish fishing out Angolan waters, taking fish back to Spain and Portugal. Boats are coming this way anyway, paid for by the seafood business. So these merchants can bring [undeclared] goods in on the way to sell in Luanda and, perhaps, take [undeclared] gems out: Angolan colonials doing what they always did. As routes become affected by war and UN sanctions, the Portuguese have to keep their trade routes open, and they use all manner of personal and business contacts.

That's just one story, Marra's story. One person, one gem, one route. Multiply that.

Indeed, multiply that. When we refer to networks that make such diamond transfers possible, we are talking about thousands of people and many millions of dollars annually from a single locale such as Angola or Sierra Leone alone. If we extend this discussion to encompass the other gem-producing regions of the world and the armaments they purchase, the equation expands to incorporate millions of people and many billions of dollars. The number of people involved can rival the populations of states and even vastly exceed those of the smaller ones. The revenues generated can far surpass the GNP of smaller nations. The power that the leaders in these extrastate empires wield can rival that of state leaders. These vast networks shape the course of international affairs to as great a degree as the formal state apparatuses of some countries. When we enlarge our focus beyond gems and armaments to include all extrastate industries, the equation encompasses many millions of people and trillions of dollars. These are greater numbers of people and revenues than are found in many of the world's nations. These numbers represent a series of power grids that shape the fundamental econopolitical dynamics of the world today.

THE POWER (AND PROFITS) OF NONTRANSPARENCY

> The grass-roots [extralegal] war economy was
> more predictable and rational in many respects
> than the official one.
> Mark Chingono, *The State, Violence,*
> *and Development*

Wars are costly. Weapons manufacturers worldwide make approximately $700 billion a year on weapons sales.[20] Unrecorded weapons reap another $500 billion yearly. In addition, militaries need computers, uniforms, medicines, food, vehicles, petroleum, communications systems, systems analysts, maps, construction materials, boots, bridges, and bank accounts. Even legal armies gain a considerable portion of these goods through extralegal channels—as has been detailed in the Truth and Reconciliation Commission reports from South Africa documenting the actions of the apartheid South African Defense Forces. The sheer cost of modern weapons systems and cosmopolitan goods often forces militaries to turn to another level of extralegal activity: foreign currency to purchase these expensive commodities and services often comes from selling a country's resources, from minerals to narcotics to human labor, outside of legal channels. This allows governments to gain and control hard currencies and trade without formally accounting for these monies and actions; and it allows rebels, who do not have a legitimate tax base, to raise money and supplies outside of government (enemy) control. So from the cosmopolitan urban industrial centers of the world, high-technology weapons, communications systems, medical supplies, clothing, cigarettes, and jeans flow into the Angolas of the world along extralegal lines, while precious gems, valuable resources, and human labor flow back to the cosmopolitan urban industrial centers. Angola, it seems, is not a backwater on the global map, nor is it peripheral to the industrial centers of the world. It stands at the center of a web that provides critical resources to industrial centers. Angola's war is good for world business.

Yet this seems to be a dirty little secret. None of the world's transnational corporations or intergovernmental organizations formally monitoring global economies acknowledge in their financial fact sheets the illegal or illicit transactions and the economies they generate. If this were Colombia instead of Angola, the flow chart would have to add in Colombia's portion of an industry in illegal drugs that brings in $500 billion a year. If it were Congo, the chart would have to include gold, zinc, colombite-tantalite (a mineral used in making computer chips), and other precious minerals. If it were Burma, the chart would show the transnational oil pipeline, timber, opium, and the Thai cross-border sex industry.

The profit trail is extensive and equally nontransparent. Cars, trucks, trains, ships, and airplanes must transport nonlegal goods from the point of production to the final destination. Each is produced by industrial centers, fueled by petroleum products, and piloted by professionals. Each transverses controls and international borders, where complicit personnel assist nonlegal as well as legal transfers. Handlers transport the commodities, experts test them, accommodating financial institutions lend and launder money, and less-than-legitimate security forces take a cut to ignore the law. Each step in the considerable set of transfers that moves any commodity across time, space, international borders, and the boundaries of the law carries these nontransparent earnings into the markets of everyday life. "Inevitably, such fundamental changes in economic behavior and attitudes wrought indirectly and directly by the war had a strong impact on the organization of society," according to the Stockholm International Peace Research Institute. "In particular, they engendered shifts in the balance of power and political alliances at various levels of society."[21]

WHY LEAVE THE ILLICIT OUT OF FORMAL ANALYSES OF GLOBALIZATION?

> Globalisation is paradox. Primarily, it is a process
> reliant on crucial social relationships to defeat
> and deny time and space. Crime is one of these
> relationships. It is the natural consequence of
> modernization as well as sharing the consumerist
> and profit priorities which characterise the mod-
> ern. Like modernisation, crime can marginalise
> and re-integrate, unify and divide.
>
> Mark Findlay, *The Globalisation of Crime*

Just as multinational corporations and transnational companies overflow not only national borders but also international laws, so, too, do extrastate networks globalize and create new legal and political arrangements. The leading figures of the globalization debate are not purposely obfuscating economic realities by choosing to ignore that which falls outside the legal. But intent does not change the impact of this decision.

As scholars like Susan Strange and Manuel Castells observe, criminal systems not only are globalizing but also are reconfiguring the very meaning of *market* and the very viability of the state.[22] They write that diverse criminal networks are forging cross-group links, transnational associations, business partnerships, trade agreements, and foreign policy in unprecedented ways. Where before, different criminal groups controlled discrete "turfs," today they create associations that allow them to negotiate complex commodity systems and market control worldwide. And this, both Strange and Castells note, is changing the very character and foundation of the modern state. The state is not disintegrating, but it no longer holds the paramount power it once did: nonstate and nonlegal networks are overtaking some of the state's "turf," and the boundaries between state and nonlegal are more porous and difficult to define in a global market.[23]

To return to the core question: If extrastate activities comprise a power block within globalizing forces, why do globalization pundits ignore this? It might be argued that it is too dangerous to study the nonlegitimate: scholars might end up as little more than the statistics they gather. But if that were the case, why not discuss this fact and encourage others less reticent to conduct this important research? It might be argued that extralegal realities are too marginal to the world's economies to amount to a significant factor. But work on extralegal economies consistently indicates a considerable percentage of each state's economy takes place outside national and international law. I have noted that Angola's economy is 90 percent extrastate. But industrialized states and countries at peace do not overcome extralegal realities: one-half of Mozambique's economy is extrastate; the same is true of 58 percent of Kenya's, over half of Russia's, 50 percent of Italy's, 48 percent of Peru's, and up to 30 percent of the United States's.[24] Such figures are far from "marginal" to global markets.

Perhaps, then, the illegal and the illicit are too important to discuss. Perhaps ignoring them is not a simple oversight but the choice of the governments, industries, and people who build empires through less than legal means. As Castells notes, there is a "thin line between criminal traffic and government-inspired trade."[25] In this transitional era of globalization, who will be most effective at mobilizing economies and the force necessary to protect them remains as yet an unanswered question.

Thus, perhaps when people say it is too dangerous to study the illicit, the question that should be asked is: "Dangerous to whom?" If, as I have suggested, these networks of power, services, and goods rival formal state structures in important ways, extrastate economies are not merely market concerns but also sociopolitical powerhouses. Considerable fortunes are made and lost, and these fortunes intersect with formal states and economies in myriad, complex ways. In truth, the division between formal and nonformal, and between state and extrastate, is far less distinct than classical theory and popular discourse would have it. Thus the danger might be to our very conceptions of power and economy—to the theories we have so carefully crafted about the nature of the relationship between state, individual, and authority.

NINE

Class Politics and Scavenger
Anthropology in Dinesh D'Souza's
Virtue of Prosperity

Kath Weston

The argument is as old as the hills, or at least as old as capitalism: Those
who have money deserve money, and those who don't, well, it's a pity,
but too bad for them. This tired refrain echoes through *The Virtue of
Prosperity*, Dinesh D'Souza's entry into debates about how global capitalism is reshaping the distribution of wealth.[1] D'Souza builds upon John
Kenneth Galbraith's claim that the United States has produced the first
mass affluent class in history. Apparently the "haves" have never done
better, certainly not in such numbers. The rest, insists D'Souza, are
"losers" who lack entrepreneurial talent and have only themselves to
blame.

   If it were just a matter of offering an alibi for the affluent—where were
you when the chasm between rich and poor broke wide open?—
D'Souza's tract would scarcely merit the thorough debunking it invites.

The powerful will always have their apologists. Of greater concern is the extent to which *The Virtue of Prosperity* reinforces glib explanations for class tensions that have become widespread in the country that has led, prodded, some would say coerced, the current foray into globalization.

If *The Virtue of Prosperity* has a strength, it lies in D'Souza's ability to identify concerns that unite Right with Left. Parents both rich and poor, for example, worry about the effects of rampant marketing on the young. The book's most seductive weakness involves D'Souza's talent for recasting platitudes about class in the form of catchy one-liners: "How can we be sure of the triumph of the nouveau riche? Because nobody calls them 'nouveau riche' anymore" (10) and "Capitalism civilizes greed, just as marriage civilizes lust," a maxim so droll it appears not once but twice (126, 239). Such analogies may come as news to the high percentage of Americans who admit to having affairs, but why quibble.

To make his case for the virtues conferred by affluence, D'Souza enlists multiple rhetorics: the statistical-anecdotal (truth in stories about numbers), a commodity-based conception of class (you are what you can eat), denial of poverty (you aren't poor, you just think you're poor), and the anthropological (let's have a look at the natives). At their most insidious, these rhetorical moves recruit people who eke out a living at the bottom to share the view from the top—perhaps the only thing the masters of money are prepared to share freely.

IMPERIAL GALLONS OF FACTS: THE STATISTICAL-ANECDOTAL

What better way to introduce the contentious issues of wealth distribution and social justice than a debate? The problem is, in D'Souza's matchup ring, the opposing positions are contrived, the stories offered as evidence lack analysis, and the numbers don't add up. As the book opens, the pro-technology, pro-globalization "Party of Yeah" (a motley group of techies, futurists, and free marketeers) has arrived to take on the dream-smashing, caveat-raising "Party of Nah," an equally mixed lineup of environmentalists, social conservatives, and religious critics. But something is missing. Exiled from contention are the politics framed by human rights, globalization-from-below, indigenous, feminist, and labor movements.

Without these key participants in global discussions of resource distribution and shifting class relations, it is much easier to foster the impression that there are only two possible attitudes to take regarding mass affluence: You either love it and you want to move forward, or you hate it and you want to go back. Yet for many thoughtful social critics, the concentration of wealth in the hands of elites and "masses" that represent only a fraction of the planet's population offers more than an occasion to embrace or resist recent developments. These critics are more inclined to ask the difficult questions that D'Souza raises only in passing: Must your prosperity come at my expense? Are there other ways to conceive of affluence? What a different contest it would have been, had they been invited.

How, then, does this downsized debate proceed? First D'Souza cites a statistic or quotes an anecdote from someone he assigns to the Party of Yeah, such as the physicist Freeman Dyson, who celebrates the short work that the Internet has made of poor people's alleged "cultural isolation." Then Studs Terkel is trotted on with a few choice words in rebuttal, his eighty-some years a metaphor for an aging Left: "Saving the world, my ass. These rich guys are trying to convince the rest of us that everyone is better off because *they're* better off" (39–40). Nothing here about the feminization of poverty, or the color of the women most likely to be raising children on high-starch diets in high-rent rooms. Despite a formal commitment to balancing the views of his two contending teams, D'Souza is the referee who knows the outcome of the game, maintaining a strong grip on his whistle and every inclination to blow.

A critic less convinced than D'Souza of the pervasiveness of affluence, or its virtues, might point to other voices heard not at all in this book: the poor and once-poor speaking for themselves. James Baldwin's description of his youth on the streets of Harlem remains disastrously contemporary. To live poor and black meant, and can still mean, a life attuned to "every disastrous bulletin: a cousin, mother of six, suddenly gone mad, the children parceled out here and there; an indestructible aunt rewarded for years of hard labor by a slow, agonizing death in a terrible small room; someone's bright son blown into eternity by his own hand; another turned robber and carried off to jail."[2]

Ah, but give Mr. Baldwin a word, and you will find yourself called upon to deal with the ways that class relations in North America cannot be understood apart from their gendered and raced inflections. D'Souza himself scarcely attends to race, except implicitly via throwaway comments about immigrant labor and a heartwarming reference to tech-sector cafeterias in which Gujaratis, Bengalis, and Keralites gather at their own tables. So many languages, so many cuisines! How could racial discrimination possibly play a meaningful role in entrepreneurial failure or success?

What happens if we retrieve this throwaway question long enough to look for an answer? Leave aside for a moment D'Souza's dubious characterization of corporate employment as "entrepreneurial." Forget, if you can, those workaday encounters in which supervisors interpret culturally appropriate displays of respect as "lack of assertiveness," and in which racism masquerades as impartial judgments about "lack of fit." Set aside, as well, the enduring legacies of slavery and a tattered history of public policy initiatives intended to destroy the entrepreneurial endeavors of Native peoples. In *The Varieties of Ethnic Experience*, the anthropologist Micaela di Leonardo demonstrates that the timing of immigration with regard to economic booms and state subsidies has everything to do with patterns of accomplishment that Americans tend to construe as individual success.[3] D'Souza's cafeteria scene borders on caricature, not only because it ignores such factors, but also because segregation in school cafeterias has become symbolic in public discourse of continuing race/class conflict.[4]

The statistical-anecdotal evidence D'Souza marshals to demonstrate that today's poor are stragglers who warrant their lot and, even so, are not too badly off, is easily refuted. He offers measures that are not comparable, traffics in unsupported assertions ("I believe that," "I have no problem with"), sparks the inevitable romance with numbers, then hopes against hope that love is blind. Like the children in Mr. Gradgrind's classroom in Charles Dickens's *Hard Times*, his ideal readers sit waiting for "imperial gallons of facts" to be poured into our little heads. D'Souza's critics tend to engage him on his own ground, which is the ground of much contemporary social critique, fighting numbers with numbers and truisms with reason. An obvious tactic, if an unreliable one, yet always worth a try.

One passage from D'Souza's book is worth quoting at length because it is telling. "Some people may be surprised to learn that 50 percent of Americans defined by the government as 'poor' have air-conditioning," D'Souza notes. And that is only the beginning: "60 percent have micro-wave ovens and VCRs, 70 percent have one or more cars, 72 percent have washing machines, 77 percent have telephones, 93 percent have at least one color television, and 98 percent have a refrigerator" (75). Suppose, for a moment, that "some people" concede the point, despite the availability of other sets of statistics. What do these numbers say about a topsy-turvy economy in which it becomes possible to scrape together the money for household appliances that look like luxuries, yet inconceivable to cover the basic necessities that sustain life? Better enjoy that microwave dinner, because if it doesn't contain the nutrients you need, you may very well not be able to afford health care.

Similarly, D'Souza's references to the increasing size of homes sold in the United States since the 1950s connote prosperity only when there is no mention of the concurrent decline in affordable housing for a large proportion of its residents. The mobility of the U.S. workforce may not look so much like progress when it is understood to include migration in search of jobs and less expensive places to live. The wonders of new building materials fade a bit when carpenters maintain that "they don't build houses like they used to," a grassroots critique of resource allocation, quality, and environmental decline.

There are so many points on which D'Souza is just plain wrong. He unilaterally dismisses "all the humbug about 'the overworked Ameri-can'" with the assertion that Americans spend fewer hours than ever at work (81). Not so: In the year 2000, Americans worked an average of just under 49 1/2 weeks a year, substantially more than they worked in 1990 and *hundreds* of hours longer annually than their counterparts in Ger-many, Britain, and Japan.[5] The much-vaunted increases in life expectancy for poor people that D'Souza cites are distributed very unevenly with respect to region and race/ethnicity; the figures for Native peoples, which he does not cite, are extraordinarily low, even by global standards. Because much of the growth in overall life-expectancy numbers proceeds from improvements in infant mortality figures, the impression that people in the United States have more years of retirement in the offing due to unprecedented affluence may not hold. Assuming, that is, they can afford to retire. Many Americans must continue to work into their golden years, and many more will be required to do so if productivity gains continue to derive from compelling people to work longer and harder.

Let's not romanticize poverty, but let's not romanticize the affluent either. To say, as D'Souza does, based on arrest and incarceration statistics, that poor people "indulge far more than the rich in [certain] social pathologies" such as drug abuse (128–29) is to beg the question of who is most likely to get arrested and what counts as pathological to whom. Few would dispute the benefits that accompany high-priced legal representation, or the link between access to money and class/race disparities in sentencing and conviction. Crimes typically committed by the poor are more likely to carry harsh mandatory sentences. Wealthier perpetrators are more likely to talk or buy their way out of arrest. When the latter do go to jail, they often benefit from the relatively light penalties associated with white-collar crimes.[6]

When D'Souza resurrects nineteenth-century characterizations of poor people as the ones most often "found" abusing alcohol and beating up their spouses, he similarly begs the question of which cases of abuse governments direct state agencies to find. In *Welfare Racism*, Kenneth Neubeck and Noel Cazenave call attention to the punitive aspects of state-sponsored welfare policies, which historically have included innumerable pretexts for inspecting and disciplining the lives of the poor.[7] All the evidence indicates that alcoholism and domestic violence cut right across class lines.[8] Such class-based differences as there are, are more likely to be artifacts of reporting than incidence: a matter of who is more likely to come under surveillance and who has the clout to keep things quiet.

D'Souza is no more careful with his liberal application of statistics to the wealthy. The glowing figure he cites for the historic average of stock market returns, which derives from the Dow Jones Industrial Average, would be considerably lower if calculated on the basis of global markets or averaged for the twenty-five years following the Great Depression.[9] D'Souza's claim that most well-off people today earned their money, rather than inheriting it (233), ignores the advantage that even a small amount of inherited wealth can bring.[10] Chuck Collins and Felice Yeskel aptly capture the character of the majority on the Forbes 400 list of wealthy Americans with their subtitle "Born on Third Base—Claimed They Hit Triples."[11] D'Souza's declaration that the rich are more likely to be pro-environment and socially conscious than the poor ignores the flourishing movement against environmental racism, which opposes selective dumping and burning of toxic materials in poor neighborhoods. And what of the need for such a movement? At last glance, "the poor" were not sitting on the boards of major corporate polluters or shipping banned pesticides overseas to make a buck.

D'Souza acknowledges some worries accompanying mass affluence, but he discards most of them along the way. He rightly surmises that some readers will wonder whether hard work still pays in a society where boy millionaires can order their elders to process their e-mails and wipe up their floors. What entitles the affluent to so much when their servants, as he puts it, toil for so little (44)? D'Souza's answer: Inequality is here to stay, but only for the short term. Besides, the winners in the game of wealth deserve what they have because they have something special going for them: an "entrepreneurial IQ" (93).[12] Concerned about environmental degradation, the seemingly inevitable by-product of the proliferation of affluence's gizmos and gadgets? For D'Souza, that's an easy one: Just bring back the "conserve" in conservatism (46). Or perhaps you've wondered whether the chairman of the Federal Reserve Board should be heeded when he warns of the danger of social unrest if this stubborn gap between poor and rich keeps expanding. D'Souza's response: Surely the poor won't mind so long as social policy keeps them moving forward, albeit at a slower pace than their betters (71). The underemphasized words here: *so long as*. Finally, might North Americans

be becoming just a tad too materialistic, dreaming of family entertainment centers instead of minding their manners and valuing spiritual pur-
suits? Tough question, but D'Souza does not find it insurmountable. For
him, there is a morality to acquisition, because he believes that having
more resources gives the wealthy the means to do more good in the
world (130–31). Left unexplored is the matter of whether the affluent do
indeed use their riches for good, however that might be defined. Nor
does it occur to D'Souza that people with few material resources might
prefer the opportunity to embark upon more do-gooding ventures of
their own, rather than being subjected to the well-meaning interventions
of the rich.

What is most disturbing about D'Souza's cavalier approach to numbers and anecdote, rebuttal and repartee, is not merely the glibness, the
omission, the overstatement, or the errors that occur when he appeals to
the statistical-anecdotal but also the sense that he so often *sounds* right.
His claims do whatever convincing they can manage because they bring
into play pervasive cultural narratives about class and modernization.
Because two other rhetorics that he employs, discussed below, resonate
with what many people in the United States already think they know, the
narratives of class they convey may be more important to the persua-
siveness of his arguments than any mountain of figures and facts. For
D'Souza, as for many North Americans, class appears closely linked to
the consumption of commodities, what might be called the shopping cart
conception of capitalism. After this rhetorical move comes the vanishing
trick in which poverty disappears: D'Souza's contention that poor people
in a rich country aren't really poor, since their shopping carts are relatively full.

Or are they?

SHOPPING CART CAPITALISM:
YOU ARE WHAT YOU CAN EAT

Now then, how much merchandise do you have in your basket?
Everyone from the government to the guy next door wants to know. This

is the rhetoric of shopping cart capitalism, which perpetuates the notion that prosperity can best be gauged by consumption. With his focus on air conditioners and microwave ovens as indicators of affluence, D'Souza, too, falls prey to a commodity-based conception of class. In this rhetoric, class relations have more to do with what you can afford to eat than whether you have to work to eat or whom you have to answer to. Significantly, the official definition of the poverty line also uses commodities to evaluate economic hardship.

In the early 1960s Mollie Orshansky (aka"Miss Poverty"), a research analyst with the Social Security Administration, developed the concept of the poverty line in order to draw attention to problems faced by low-income families. Her original calculations, only slightly revised since, begin with the assumption that the average household spends one-third of its income on food. Peg that fraction to the cost of the most meager adequate diet proposed by the U.S. Department of Agriculture and multiply by three. The equation yields a cutoff number below which making ends meet is government-certified to be a struggle.

Many now consider the concept of the poverty line to have outlived its usefulness. Alternatives, such as the living wage, propose to take account of historical changes in the economy. Not only have living standards risen in the United States—this is D'Souza's point, after all—but the production of food, clothing, housing, and transportation has been reorganized, industrialized, and globalized in ways unimaginable in the 1960s. Food today accounts for only about one-sixth, not one-third, of household expenditures. Childcare, in contrast, has become a major expenditure as more women have entered the workforce, in part to compensate for falling real wages.[13]

Gordon Fisher explains that "Orshansky's 'multiplier' methodology for deriving the [poverty] thresholds was normative, not empirical, that is, it was based on a normative assumption involving [1955] consumption patterns of the population as a whole, and not on the empirical consumption behavior of lower income groups."[14] The same can be said for modified versions of a poverty line adopted by countries such as India, which originally tied its income threshold to calorie intake.[15] Changes in the assumptions built into this model produce major shifts in the numbers below or above the line, without anyone's daily circumstances actually improving. If analysts were to build in a normative assumption of access to sanitary drinking water (in the case of India) or health care (in the case of the United States), the numbers of poor would escalate dramatically.

By making deprivation quantifiable in a society that reveres numbers, Orshansky's invention helped codify *poverty*, a term that entered public policy debate only in the mid–twentieth century.[16] Commodity-based understandings of class such as the poverty line help reduce dynamic class relations to fixed classes: "the rich" and "the poor." The effect is to draw attention away from the operations of power by isolating the actions of those who control resources from the suffering and inequality perpetuated by that control. Your "poverty" may be related to my "affluence," but putting our relationship in terms of rich and poor allows me to downplay the ways in which some of my gains may rest upon your back.

Poverty and prosperity, however debilitating, however exhilarating, cannot be gauged directly. Living standards must be defined. What counts as affluence is one eminently anthropological question that D'Souza never asks. To broach the matter would be to treat poverty and prosperity as meaningful, politicized concepts rather than objectively given states.

What does it mean to construe abundance in terms of high and low? What symbolizes wealth? In the United States, for progressives and conservatives alike, the master symbol has become a shopping cart filled with foodstuffs, a basket of goods. Once the groceries have been accounted for, a limited range of electronic consumer products provides an index of affluence: televisions, air conditioners, cars. Add to these a few oft-cited examples of luxury services that have allegedly trickled down to the masses, such as plane travel and elective plastic surgery, and you have a neat package of items that lend themselves to counting.

It does not require a critique of materialism or consumer culture to understand why the basket-of-goods narrative about class is so problematic. In and of themselves, commodities are not affluence. They are *symbols* of affluence that give some indication of material resources but tell very little about the contexts in which people use them, or about the credit systems that give temporary access to goods without control. Does it matter that poor people tend to pay more than rich people for the same basket of commodities, or that they often end up with goods of inferior quality? Does it matter that some Americans hold clear title to the entire basket and more, while others have to duck and dodge the repossessors? That the only way for a sizeable number of Americans to furnish their homes is to sign a contract with rent-to-own merchants who charge 100 percent to 200 percent annual interest on household goods, thus setting themselves up in a kind of debt bondage?[17]

Should it matter that public discourse about well-being in the United States generally subordinates a discussion of working conditions to a discussion of the "choices" available on store shelves? Or that a few privileged shoppers can afford to hire someone else to push the cart? What about the nationalism and histories of conquest built into the shopping cart conception of class? "Most Americans find it hard to believe that anyone would not want their way of life because of their wealth of material possessions," writes Charmaine White Face in *Indian Country Today*.[18] "From a Lakota perspective, it is very difficult to like something if it is forced on you." There are needs that cannot be satisfied with a shelf of canned goods and a remote control.

Of course, capitalism is in the business of generating needs, not satisfying them. Although not everyone in the United States accepts the basket-of-goods class narrative, it is kept alive through repetition. In a 2001 *New York Times* article by Eric Schmitt titled "Census Data Show a Sharp Increase in Living Standard," the *Times* asks readers to adopt the point of view of the always and already affluent.[19] Cheerfully reporting that more than 90 percent of households now own a car, the story offers no information on whether making payments on a car is the price of getting to work in order to get the money to make payments on the car. This way of measuring living standards cannot hope to gauge the impact on car ownership of deteriorating public transportation systems or the movement of jobs away from areas with affordable housing, both of which necessitate an automobile commute. Buried in Schmitt's article is a warning that "many characteristics [of the census], like income and poverty statistics, are not directly comparable to similar data from the 1999 or 2000 counts."

Translation: The reported increases in prosperity are based on possession—not even ownership—of a collection of commodities that have become symbolic of prosperity, such as automobiles, floor space, and televisions. What do these measurements mean in the absence of data on evictions, mortgage foreclosures, the abolition of rent control, and the decline in government subsidies for shelter? Filings for personal bankruptcies doubled in the ten short years between 1990 and 1999, giving "boom" another meaning altogether for hundreds of thousands in the United States.[20]

Imagine an alternative census of the best that the boom years had to offer, scripted from the bottom up. This context-of-living approach to class relations would offer data on rental costs, trailer ownership, and indigenous land claims. How many hours of overtime were people in the United States forced to work? How many have had to use a charge card to pay for treatment at a hospital emergency room? How many could not seek treatment because they had been turned down for credit? Or because the neighborhood hospital, in a cost-cutting move, had shut down its emergency room? How many were compelled by rising housing costs to move? How many lost a job because childcare arrangements failed or cars broke down? How many jobs do you have to work at a time? Are they unionized? After the last round of layoffs, are you doing the work of two? How many hours a night do you get to sleep? How far does the pay for a day's labor go in the United States, compared to back home in the Philippines or Senegal? Why is it that economists exhort consumers to keep the economy afloat on a sea of confidence and spending, then chastise them for a low savings rate and propensity to go into debt? These are things that Americans need to know in order to understand the meaning of affluence and want: not just the price of a basket of goods.

The financing of American dreams has a history, in which the invention of consumer credit constitutes a late-breaking yet utterly pivotal installment.[21] The lack of any ceiling on the interest charged by finance companies is the product of politics, not a natural fact. On a household basis, middle-income families have borrowed more and worked more to keep those shopping cart wheels rolling, while their poorer neighbors have had to work multiple jobs and devise ingenious living arrangements to get by. Air travel might no longer constitute a luxury for the middle class, as D'Souza notes, but how much is that due to a combination of family diaspora in search of jobs and the miserly allotment of vacation days in the United States, which lags all wealthy nations in paid time off? A train or automobile trip across the continent is out of the question when you have to report back to work in a week.

THE DENIAL OF POVERTY: YOU AREN'T POOR, YOU JUST THINK YOU'RE POOR

Within a year after the publication of *The Virtue of Prosperity*, hard times had begun to be more equitably distributed. The New Economy, that perpetual money machine, had started to look like a late-twentieth-century version of the fantastical perpetual motion machine of Renaissance times. Fascination with the imperial wonders that flow from technology had given way to a bit of soul-searching. Could it be that abundance depends less on technology and more on social relations that influence how technologies will be employed? Is globalization really an inevitable, inexorable process? Do most North Americans have anything they could call prosperity, or do some just have it on loan? To the extent that they live a "postindustrial" life, what do they owe to people abroad who assemble the goods that appear on their shores? And if wealth belongs to the wealth creator, as D'Souza surmises, who would that be: the person with the capital to transfer into an investment account? The manager who implemented the transfer? The people who soldered together the circuits on which banking now depends? These are questions that link class to power and social relations rather than commodities alone.

Even before these events, D'Souza had articulated a narrative about class intended to head off such nagging concerns, couched in a rhetoric that denies the existence of destitution in "rich" nations. Poverty, he alleged, has been eradicated in countries as phenomenally wealthy as the United States. Since few would argue that there is no class divide in the United States, where the top 1 percent of households controls nearly half of all financial wealth, the argument turns on whether those who come up short are genuinely poor. For this purpose D'Souza wants to distinguish between poverty and relative poverty, and by implication, between relative affluence and the real article.

What D'Souza's argument comes down to is this: North Americans living below the poverty line are not really poor; they just think they are poor. If they were to spend a week as pavement dwellers on the streets of Mumbai (Bombay), they might come to understand just how well off they are. However poor they might seem in relation to the unprecedented levels of affluence enjoyed by North American elites, they would be considered spendthrifts and wastrels in places where ten U.S. dollars per day is a fantasy wage.

Critics on the Left often accept the premise but urge people to take relative poverty seriously nonetheless, because it turns out that differentials, rather than hardship per se, may do the most damage. High rates of infant mortality, malnutrition, and disease, as well as less tangible ills such as resentment, correlate with significant divides in wealth, whether those divisions occur within a "rich" country or a "poor" country.[22] Nor is this merely a perspective grounded in wealth. In India, the Expert Group on Estimation of Proportion and Number of Poor, set up by the government's Planning Commission, concluded in 1993 that "the notion of 'absolute poverty' is inadequate because 'relative poverty' is also an equally important aspect of poverty and is, in fact, a determinant of absolute poverty at a given level of national income."[23] Inequality, indigence, and riches are entangled. Mumbai pavement dwellers and New York street dwellers, unite.

Clearly this is not to say that the experiences of living poor in a rich country and in an impoverished country are identical, or that access to resources does not vary according to place. The working poor with their yard sales in the United States discard as junk countless items that would be considered precious by any beggars who have survived the latest "Clean Up Mumbai" campaigns. But D'Souza's insistence that securing food, clothing, and shelter no longer represents a significant problem in the United States (75) would come as something of a shock to the many people standing in line at food banks, the undercounted numbers sleeping in the parks, the reinvented ragpickers who make a living collecting cans, and the many children for whom classrooms with holes in the roof are supposed to count as shelter.

Part of the problem is that D'Souza and others who sustain the triumph-over-need narrative of life in the affluent society have not incorporated any critique of cultural relativism into their critique of relative poverty. If they had, they would not continue to treat societies as self-contained entities that, while they may occasionally bump in the night, remain distinct for the purposes of comparison. Societies are hardly separate in a global economy where the affluence of some is predicated upon the exploitation of others elsewhere on the planet. The jacket that serves to mark someone's affluence may be sewn by a woman in a sweatshop in Brownsville, Texas, or in a maquiladora across the Mexican border. Any neat division between rich countries and poor countries, implicit in D'Souza's observation that "this is not India or Rwanda" (232), sets up a rhetorical cordon that relies upon border controls, immigration police, investment policies, and coercive trade agreements to foster inequalities *both* domestically and abroad.

The factories of the borderlands adjoin the trophy homes of D'Souza's new entrepreneurs in all senses but the geographic. Suppose everyone everywhere were to follow the D'Souza work-study plan for upward mobility, getting an education on the way to becoming self-made women and men. Who then would wait tables? On the outside chance that restaurants happen to undergo the self-service makeover already applied to gasoline pumps, who would be left to clean the offices abandoned for an evening meal? Who would sort out the discarded product-packaging that many of us, united in the false equality of consumerism, now endeavor to recycle? Who will convincingly explain the promise of upward mobility to the highly educated but unemployed on the streets of Kinshasa?

D'Souza's presumption that affluence will inexorably spread, albeit on a different time line for an unfortunate few, flies in the face of history and recent experience. Nothing could be less likely under current economic arrangements. Someone has to make commodities for destitution wages in order for them to be cheap enough for any emerging middle class to buy. The voyeur, not the analyst, has the luxury to believe in an economy that secretes its poverty in scattered "pockets," rather than in a poverty that supplies the foundation upon which the edifice of this global economy rests.

So it is an unwarranted faith that D'Souza invests in entrepreneurship and education when he selects the poor graduate student with a good idea to illustrate his theme of techno-capitalism as a world without limits. One good idea, he contends, can parley itself into a fortune in an economic system in which "it does not matter who you are or where you come from" and the only responsibility for misery is one's own (1–3). Why such an intelligent fellow as D'Souza's apocryphal graduate student would willingly undertake what the novelist Margaret Drabble has called the pain of upward mobility (imperceptible only to those who have never climbed) is not quite clear, since his poverty, we are later assured, is also only relative.[24] In any case, what matters *most* is what D'Souza would have the reader overlook: where this student comes from. One look at a set of statistics that D'Souza fails to consult—the demographics of people accepted into U.S. graduate schools—reveals that the support (financial and otherwise) required to make it through these programs is not at all equitably distributed. High school dropout rates for Latinos and Native Americans are astronomical. The fantasy of a highly material world in which only the idea matters begins to dissolve in the face of this simple reminder that the winnowing machinery has been in operation long before a graduate student enrolls in her first course. Class, race, and gender privilege is already built into the story.

All this means that poor graduate students backed by family wealth stand in a very different relationship to poverty than students without such resources or peers who never made it to college. Although the economic struggles of students from affluent backgrounds can be real enough, these young people are much more likely to be passing through poverty's neighborhood. Four years, one good idea, and four hundred microwave burrito dinners later, most will have the advantage of connections and resources that will give them a much better chance of grasping the brass ring than all the lottery drawings in the world. Yet it is to the lottery, not the campus, that many people of limited means turn to sustain the hope that anything is possible, once they come to understand the odds of working their way out.[25]

Not surprisingly, considering his politics and his own class location,

D'Souza's most intriguing observations concern the denizens of wealthier haunts. He is on to something when he notes the significance of the trend toward treating managers like casual labor. He is right to comment upon the emergence of new linguistic categories such as "affluenza," a dis-ease afflicting children whose relatives control more than their proportionate share of the wealth. The unexpected turn to spirituality that he observes among the newly affluent—corporate Zen practitioners and the like—does seem to require explanation. And when chief executive officers appear on camera in jeans next to presidents in polo shirts, while their lawyers and accountants don ties and suits, one is tempted to agree that the meaning of class/gender/race markers in fashion deserves another look. These are just the sort of telling cultural indicators that beg for analysis. If D'Souza hadn't already decided to play the part, one might consider calling in an anthropologist.

SCAVENGER ANTHROPOLOGY: "LET'S HAVE A LOOK AT THE NATIVES"

With the publication of *The Virtue of Prosperity*, D'Souza joined a coterie of intellectual scavengers who have picked and torn at the bones of anthropology to bolster their positions as knowledgeable authorities on "cultural" matters. By and large, they come away with scraps of meat and a fair amount of gristle, rather than the corpus of a discipline that is very much alive. In D'Souza's case, this final rhetorical strategy, a claim to ethnographic authority, develops initially through a parody of ethnographic writing. Subtitled "Anthropologist in a Strange Land," the book's introduction allows readers a glimpse through the keyhole at an exclusive Silicon Valley party, where "virtual" describes the guests (virtually all white) and the "alpha males" are out in force.

Analogies soon proliferate between California body piercing and body decoration in New Guinea. It is a party, after all, and all in good fun, so at first it seems that it might be of little consequence if D'Souza lacks a critique of primitivism or mixes up the gorillas with the chimps. But there are serious implications that follow from D'Souza's lighthearted attempts to equate West Coast peninsulars with Pacific islanders by situating both as "tribal inhabitants" who occupy different regions of the Pacific Rim.

For these analogies to work, New Guinea and the United States have to be imagined as distinct and parallel spaces, with New Guinea the pristine, isolated, left-behind location that anchors the contrast with the motherland of nanotechnology and chips. Otherwise there would be no humor, no sense of paradox, when the chief financial officers of Internet start-up companies arrive to show off the latest in "tribal" accessories. If New Guinea were not pictured as outside the reach of trade and satellite communications (in a way that no place on earth now is), it could not stand in for all things superseded by modernity. To accomplish this magic, D'Souza relies upon the old, discredited anthropologist's trick of writing in the ethnographic present, taking observations out of time and circumstance to present them as enduring "custom" or "practice." Body art, sun worship, wild play . . . context melts away, making it easy to forget that a Silicon Valley social gathering bears little resemblance in purpose or practice to an initiation ritual in the islands. To collapse the two is to lose any critical perspective on the power differentials that allow capitalism to claim everything for itself, including fantasies of "the primitive."

Chimeras from ostensibly more savage times haunt more than the book's opening pages. In order to lionize techno-capitalism as "self-interest ennobled by filial attachment and responsibility," D'Souza contrasts it with the period before industrialization, a time of conquest when, he says, "if the people in your tribe wanted more possessions, you simply seized them" (239). This conglomeration of radically different historical periods and ways of life into the politically motivated term *tribe* would be just plain silly if it were not used to whitewash the present and rewrite history. In even the most nationalist versions of colonial conquest, Native peoples are not the ones doing the seizing. For its part, techno-capitalism has no need to seize outright what it accrues under cover of law.

Would that all this were only a matter of anthropologies good and bad, of jokes in poor taste, of D'Souza sometimes getting the practice of anthropology right but more often getting it wrong. There are reasons why the subtitle "Anthropologist in a Familiar Land" would not pack the same rhetorical punch as D'Souza's "Anthropologist in a Strange Land." There is much in anthropology's colonial legacy to contribute to the ongoing attraction of such a pitch.

Nor is the colonial critique within anthropology old business, long since dispatched. Fantasies of class isolation passed off as description have colonial roots, not just in neoconservative but also in left-liberal social science critique. Commentators across the political spectrum regularly allege that the affluent live isolated lives. They also commonly portray the coercively "safe" space of gated communities and clubs as insulated from contact with less privileged Others. Indeed, it could be and has been argued that such spaces, along with full-service airports that allow you to visit a city without ever seeing it, and Las Vegas hotels that offer cleaned-up capsule versions of Venice or New York, are part of the process of producing certain groups of people *as* Other.[26] But these are not and will not be spaces apart, at least until airplane passengers bus out their own mess and golfers return at dusk to manicure the greens. Contact across class lines is pervasive, the neat lines of separation a fantasy. Those old colonists were ever-conscious of the "prying eyes" of servants and paranoid about slave revolt, even as they endeavored to treat people they regarded as their inferiors as never wholly there. If social science bolsters fantasies of class isolation by rendering the waiter at the table invisible, it is more than a problem. It offers the waiter no analytic alternative to looking down on others from a class location she or he may never occupy.

D'Souza himself has little inclination to use anthropological methodologies such as participant observation in order to understand the lives of those whom prosperity has eluded. The closest this self-described "anthropologist in a strange land" comes to fieldwork with the poor is playing chess with a "bum" on Market Street in San Francisco who scams him for a five-dollar bet. This might be considered the rough equivalent of the sub rosa journalistic practice of using taxi drivers as sources had D'Souza sat down with a mind to ask questions. Instead, after his opponent runs off with the cash before finishing the game, D'Souza begins to speculate. The incident provides an entrée for him to compile a litany of offenses that poor people commit because they are "captives to necessity" (128). Unfortunately this vignette is, in a sense, typical of his entire procedure for conducting research: Interview and observe the affluent, especially their pundits, then condescend to ventriloquize the poor.

How else could D'Souza propose that the real issue in the digital (class) divide involves an understanding of how to use computers, rather than computer access? An hour of participant-observation at the "inner city" library branch in my neighborhood would indicate otherwise to anyone who cared to inquire. There is almost always a line of neighborhood children waiting to use computers in the limited time that the library has funds to remain open. While the librarians sometimes disapprove of where the kids use the Internet to take them, even games sharpen reading skills in this place that has replaced the street as a refuge. Talk to the children and they will tell you that most do not have computers at home. Talk some more and you will hear about check day and payday, when the stomach will be full and a request for candy, a toy, or a treat is most likely to be honored. One in five children in the United States today is poor, even by the outmoded poverty line definition. Access very much remains the issue.

Apparently D'Souza does not have to measure his own month in job hunts or pay periods, because he takes as a sign of North American prosperity the "fact" that even the help are well off. His call to a Southern California placement agency for housekeepers and nannies turns up the startling information that "the servants" earn as much as eighty dollars per day (74)! But suppose we were to add another fieldwork experiment to assist in D'Souza's anthropological education. Send him off with the social critic Barbara Ehrenreich , who worked for a housecleaning company in order to find out what it would be like to live on such a wage.[27] How far will eighty dollars a day—a fabulous sum in many regions of the world, no doubt—stretch in a major U.S. metropolitan area such as Los Angeles? Like Ehrenreich, who could not make ends meet short of sleeping in a car, D'Souza would soon hang up his apron. Any "bum" would bet on it.

Of course, D'Souza has one more claim to ethnographic authority at his disposal, the very move his right-wing promoters breathlessly await, and that is to turn Native Informant. Baldly stated in the way that rhetorical moves seldom are, his message goes something like this: Don't talk to me about struggling to get by. I'm from India. I know real poverty. But D'Souza does not come from the poorest classes in India, a country with its own deep class fractures, and so once again readers are treated to the sleight of text that allows a view from above to represent the entire nation.

A school friend of D'Souza's from Bombay jokes about wanting to move to the United States because it's a country where the poor people are fat. D'Souza uses the joke to imply that being poor in North America is not really about lacking basic necessities such as groceries (75). By focusing on food, the price of which is heavily subsidized in North America, he can downplay the skyrocketing cost of other necessities such as housing. Let either chap make the switch, especially on a restricted budget, from pulses and roti to a North American diet filled with processed ingredients, and watch all cultural equations between health, weight, and prosperity begin to dissolve.

D'Souza stakes his claim to native authority on growing up middle class in Mumbai. Forget about automobiles, he says: his family had no television, no hot running water, no shower (10). Such analogies between living working-class in the United States and living middle-class in most "Third World" countries have become a staple of discussions about class. But sweeping comparisons should not be made on the cheap. This is not to say that there are no hardships associated with middle-class living on the subcontinent, or that the segment of the poor in the United States who have a roof over their heads would give up their water heaters without a fight. No one mistakes Ahmadabad for Peoria. It is simply that most "How poor is poor?" competitions lead back to a question already shown to be inadequate: How many consumer goods did your family have in the basket?

Not all middle-class families in Bombay, then or now, have water heaters, but then not many middle-class North American families have servants to heat the water for a bucket bath. Until fairly recently, the middle class in Bombay had to pay extra for the privilege of having chemicals and packaging added to their foods, while the middle class in the States worked extra hours so that they could "go organic" and pay a premium for keeping the chemicals and additives out. In the nonaligned years when D'Souza was growing up, both poor and middle-class Indians had

better access to health care than many of their North American counterparts. When it comes to assessing affluence across a border that is at once
historical, cultural, political, and economic, it can quickly become a matter of comparing apples with oranges or *chikoo* with mangos. A far cry
from comparing a land with poverty that is relative to a land with
poverty that is absolute.

You might be interested to know, then, that according to D'Souza, in
contrast to the perpetually dissatisfied American-born poor who seem to
be obsessed with material things, slum dwellers in India accept their lot
(127). In place of happy slaves we have happy tenement dwellers, who
are nothing if not resigned. This would certainly come as news to Kiran
Nagarkar, the Sahitya Akademi Award winner who grew up poor in the
Mazgaon neighborhood of D'Souza's city, Mumbai, and whose novel of
chawl (tenement) life, *Ravan and Eddie*, is rich with humor, critique, and
ambition.[28]

While there may indeed be less "fawning and toadying" by those in
"menial jobs" in the United States than in some other countries, as
D'Souza claims (109), this is a hard-won right, not some automatic outcome of affluence. African Americans and Latinas in domestic service
had to fight the demands of white employers that they scrub floors on
their hands and knees when mops were freely available.[29] Nor does the
North American habit of calling waiters "sir" provide any reliable indicator of class equality, as D'Souza suggests (109). Not at $2.15 an hour
plus tips. Exaggerated deference is one way to mark superior status in
this ostensibly egalitarian society.

And what of D'Souza's life in the United States as writer, researcher,
man about the house? Is it too much to say that anyone who considers
cruise ships the "Greyhound of transport" hasn't ridden the Greyhound
buses lately? In D'Souza's neighborhood, he says, only one mother
works—hardly the median, or even the mean, in a nation where
multiple-earner households prevail. Shifting the ground of personal tes-
timonial to the United States, D'Souza points to the happenings on his
uncommon block in support of the assertion that "affluence has made the
traditional family viable again" (156). Leaving aside the issue of whose
tradition he has in mind, circa what date—there seem to be no grand-
parents in the picture, so this would not be a return to, say, a joint family

household—one has to ask "viable for whom?" A 1999 study by the Council of Economic Advisors found that parents at the height of U.S. prosperity had on average twenty-two *fewer* hours each week to spend at home than they did in 1969.[30] D'Souza's freedom to work from home using new technology is hardly the same as the freedom enjoyed by women near Silicon Valley who assemble circuit boards in their homes at low piece rates because they cannot afford childcare.

Many recent studies suggest that the latest versions of capitalism have served less as a remedy for poverty than as a generator of even greater inequalities.[31] Careful social analysts disagree less about the expansion of inequality than about whether entire areas of the globe have been abandoned to sweatshops and the scrap heap. As corporations use technologies to deskill some forms of work and render others superfluous, will a reserve army of labor remain important to capitalist accumulation, or will entire populations languish as the reserve army is decommissioned?

D'Souza attempts to get around inconvenient observations about the persistence of inequality by cloaking class/race/gender tensions with the flag, arguing that the United States in its current form is the best society ever known. Perhaps he might like to consider an eastern European adage that deals more candidly with power. "We don't know yet what our past is going to be," people say. Will techno-capitalism prevail, or will the latest version of capitalism look like the last gasp of an unsustainable economic system? Will class conflict one day appear to have been named as everything but? Will the proud owners of refrigerators with water dispensers and electronic message boards write the history of those who had to make do with handouts, or even with a couple of plastic vegetable bins and no self-defrost? To the victor often belongs the most widely circulated narrative, as well as the spoils. Nor will my past necessarily be your past, for though we might share a nation or a world, we are not one.

LEARNING TO LOOK DOWN FROM THE BOTTOM

Poverty has no more monopoly over virtue than prosperity. Oppression does no wonders for those who survive it. The woman spare-changing on the corner lays no greater claim to wisdom than the steely-faced fellow who feels for his wallet, then looks away. Not everyone who lives hand to mouth has the discernment of, or can wield the pen of, a James Baldwin. All the more so because the poor in a wealthy country are encouraged by every broadcast, store window, and lottery drawing to look below, not above, as though they, too, peered down from a great height at the fate of those who cannot afford to dream of more "stuff." But of course anyone can dream, and in that respect no one lives down below. There are endless mechanisms in place to seduce the poor into yoking desires that only a member of the moneyed classes can fulfill to the apprehension that there is always somewhere farther to fall. Dreams are free, and yet they are no longer free in a society that ties aspiration so closely to the ability to buy.

This ability to look down on others from the bottom is not a given but an ingenious social product, a skill acquired through habit and assiduous practice. How many times a day are rich and poor alike hailed with the leveling language of consumerism? It is as though your bottle of Taittinger and my can of Colt 45 were simply a matter of preference, rather than also a matter of the funds in our pockets. What a lovely fiction that we can meet not as owner and worker, not as white male manager and Filipina American employee, but as consumers united in our propensity to shop.

There are many venues that operate to produce similar impressions of class equality and class differences based solely upon merit. The stock market simulations that have become commonplace in U.S. classrooms, for example, require students to adopt the point of view of a stockholder to play the game.[32] Traces of different social locations marked by class, race, nation, age, and gender can be detected in the stocks that students select to track. The ones who choose Intel are not necessarily the same as those who pick McDonald's, Nike, and L'Oréal. But as the economist Mark Maier points out, "In a typical classroom, the stock market's random fluctuations will ensure that a handful of students will do well, tallying high profits and winning prizes put up at commercial web sites. Pride in such gains is misplaced" (30). Misplaced though that pride be, these increasingly popular exercises, cosponsored by business and the state, teach D'Souza's misbegotten lesson: If you got it, you did something to earn it, while those other guys just lost out. No wonder, says Maier, that one crucial difference between investment simulations in the classroom and investment through a broker goes unremarked. In the simulated world, everyone starts out rich.

Imagine what might happen if the poorer of these students were taught to look up, not with aspirations of mobility—for what is mobility but a projection that allows a person at the bottom to fantasize looking down from above?—but with a critique of inequality instead. They might start by identifying some of the fault lines and discrepancies within neoconservative accounts of class difference. Take the owner of the bill collection agency who is thrilled with the affluent society, D'Souza reports, because he can drive a different car to work each day (15). This man may indeed be representative of a kind of excess that was new to the late twentieth century, if only in its availability to the merely well off, as opposed to the richest of the rich. But he is an owner, after all, and his daily ride owes everything to the legions of bill defaulters who are less well served by the affluent society yet who, ironically, pay his bills.

Is there, in the end, any virtue in prosperity, as D'Souza claims? It is important to seek affluence, he intones, because "the income[s] of the poor are so measly that most poor people are simply incapable of doing much social good" (130). (Since they are, according to him, only relatively poor, should they not be able to accomplish a little something?) Look closely at what passes for reasoning here: If you are poor you cannot contribute to society because contributing to society takes money. The sentiment only holds if social good equals material good, if showing up to comfort a widow in her grief constitutes no good at all. Even then, why assume that entrepreneurship is the answer and that, as Pierre Bourdieu puts it, "one could only be enterprising within an enterprise"?[33] This could just as easily be a call for the redistribution of wealth and social justice.

It is true that money isn't everything; on that most people can agree. Neither is prosperity, whatever its virtues. Still, this remains an easier sentiment to voice looking down from above than looking up from a widening bottom. Class politics have as much to do with power and a decolonized imagination as possessions. To have a say over how you will greet the sun; to have something material to offer each child and each guest; to learn what deprivation teaches without romanticizing its damage; to join together in the face of suffering; to fix the one who reaches for an extra piece with a hard stare until the pie has made its rounds; to distinguish between the pleasures of commodities and a juggernaut of endless growth: these, too, are North American dreams. Taking a stand on my own best native authority, I might say that many of us who grew up working-class in the United States quote the adage another way. Money isn't everything, but it helps.

TEN Sex on the Brain

A NATURAL HISTORY OF RAPE AND THE DUBIOUS
DOCTRINES OF EVOLUTIONARY PSYCHOLOGY

Stefan Helmreich and Heather Paxson

Recent best-selling books with such pastoral titles as *A Natural History of Love* and *A Natural History of Parenting* promise a collection of educational stories about the birds and the bees, sung in the key of the scientifically informed nature program.[1] Into this celebration of the kinship between human habits of the heart and animal and plant reproductive customs, however, has lately entered *A Natural History of Rape,* offering a stern baritone reprimand to the gentle lullabies of more bucolic accounts of the nature of sex.

Rape is natural: this is the central claim made by the biologist Randy Thornhill and biological anthropologist Craig T. Palmer in *A Natural History of Rape: Biological Bases of Sexual Coercion.*[2] Thornhill and Palmer do not mean by this that rape is therefore good or inevitable; they write that "to assume a connection [between what is biological and what is

180

morally right] is to commit what is called the *naturalistic fallacy.*"[3] What they *do* mean is that males may have evolved a predisposition toward raping females that will express itself when circumstances permit. They maintain that an evolutionary perspective can aid in reconstructing the natural history that could have led to the existence of rape, which they define as forced copulation. The data they present derive from studies of the sexual behavior of insects such as scorpionflies—Thornhill's specialty—as well as from a review of psychological experiments and sociological surveys conducted among humans.

Rape is a highly political subject. Indeed, Thornhill and Palmer articulate their own political aim: the elimination of rape among humans. Feminist social science analyses, first advanced in Susan Brownmiller's 1975 book *Against Our Will,* posited that rape is not only a sexual assault but also an act of coercive social power.[4] Such social explanations have formed the basis for many present-day rape prevention and crisis counseling programs. Thornhill and Palmer challenge these, arguing that their evolutionary view will be more effective than social science approaches in understanding and preventing human rape.

A Natural History of Rape has been described as controversial. Advance publicity based on excerpts in *The Sciences* inspired MIT Press to double the print run from ten thousand to twenty thousand.[5] These are huge figures for an academic book. Thornhill and Palmer have also made appearances in such high-profile venues as the studios of ABC and CNN.

What might be the allure of the argument that rape is natural? More important, has it any merit? In this chapter, as cultural anthropologists of science and of gender, we critically examine Thornhill and Palmer's case. The two write that "scientific critiques . . . must focus on the very heart of the perceived difficulty with an idea or body of research. To show that a tangential or trivial part of some work is wrong and then argue that the work is fundamentally flawed is not valid scientific criticism."[6] We agree. We thus offer a critique of the core, essential claims of *A Natural History of Rape* and identify conceptual difficulties with the data as well as logical problems with the explanations offered by Thornhill and Palmer from the field of evolutionary psychology, the study of how human mental capacities may have evolved.[7]

We first ask what it means to write a "natural history" of rape instead of a social history. Next, we examine each of the elements suggested by the title, *A Natural History of Rape:* we challenge Thornhill and Palmer's accounts of what is *natural* and what being "natural" entails, pointing out problems with their framework of evolutionary psychology. We question their neglect of social *history* and historical context. And we point out how their definitions of *rape* are distorted by their failure to account for what rape means to those upon whom it has been inflicted—upon those who see rape from what anthropologists have called "the native's point of view." We argue that, far from offering a more scientific explanation, their analysis is based on faith and speculation, not on empirical evidence. An explanation of rape that declares itself to be more useful than social science interpretations, yet can offer only unsubstantiated scientific hypotheses coupled with prescriptions for social change that sound curiously naive, does not warrant serious attention.

WHY WRITE A "NATURAL HISTORY" OF RAPE?

Why do Thornhill and Palmer offer us a "natural" history of rape as an alternative to a social account? It is because they believe that "when one is considering any feature of living things, whether evolution applies is never a question. The only legitimate question is how to apply evolutionary principles. This is the case for all human behaviors—even for such by-products as cosmetic surgery, the content of movies, legal systems, and fashion trends."[8] Having thus assumed the broad applicability of evolutionary principles to any human behavior, Thornhill and Palmer's argument proceeds directly to how rape can be so explained.

The two authors begin with the tenets of evolutionary psychology, a field that views human behaviors and minds, no less than bodies, as products of evolutionary forces such as *natural selection* and *sexual selection.*[9] Natural selection is the process whereby inherited variation among individuals of a population leads to differential reproductive success, shaping future patterns of variation in later generations. Sexual selection is the process whereby secondary sex characteristics such as the dramatic tail feathers of the male peacock emerge as the result of males and females acting as selective forces on one another, through mate selection. Evolutionary psychology attempts to articulate the steps through which features of the human psyche may have been shaped by such selective forces. Like its intellectual ancestor, sociobiology, evolutionary psychology is concerned with postulating the existence of hereditary triggers for evolved behaviors, especially those that find expression in what researchers term *psychological mechanisms.* As Thornhill and Palmer explain it, "The brain must be composed of many specialized, domain-specific adaptations."[10] Adaptations are traits that have endured because they have been conducive to an organism's survival and reproduction. Those adaptations residing within us today constitute the fundamental nature in which Thornhill and Palmer seek the origins of rape.

Why would rape have evolved? What might have facilitated the development of male inclination to forced copulation? To begin, Thornhill and Palmer take up theories of sexual selection and parental investment.[11] Females and males, they claim, have different stakes in the game of getting their genes into the next generation. In humans, females must gestate and bring into being an entire organism to assure that their genes survive. Males, by contrast, need only make sure they disseminate their sperm widely. These different levels of investment result in different strategies in mating: females will be choosy, males indiscriminate. Rape, then, *could* have evolved among less desirable males as a tactic for dealing with choosy females who did not favor them as mates. Thornhill and Palmer suggest, based on the economic logic of cost-benefit analysis, that, if there is little penalty for rape, males will more often attempt to force an opportunity to make a genetic contribution to the next generation. They suggest implications in the present day: "Men's greater eagerness to copulate and their greater interest in and satisfaction with casual sex evolved because those traits promoted high sex-partner number in evolutionary historical settings."[12]

But rape's natural history, they argue, need not entail that rape is a usefully adaptive response to present-day circumstance: "Today, most humans live in environments that have evolutionarily novel components. . . . Therefore, human behavior is sometimes poorly adapted (in the evolutionary sense of the word) to current conditions."[13] The book entertains both the hypothesis that rape could have been adaptive in our evolutionary history and the hypothesis that rape—like masturbation or bestiality—might be merely a *by-product* of other psychological adaptations related to male sexual desires. In other words, while rape may have evolved, the jury is out on whether it was ever adaptive. It is as evolutionary by-products, side effects, that Thornhill and Palmer explain such nonreproductively advantageous practices as male-male rape and child-rape.

On the face of it, Thornhill and Palmer seem to suggest that, as a hereditary behavior passed down from generation to generation, a tendency to rape is genetically determined, regardless of the natural or social environment of persons involved. However, they distance themselves from this strict deterministic view by defining biology broadly: "In reality, every aspect of a living thing is, by definition, biological. . . . The interaction of genes and environment in development is too intimate to be separated into 'genes' and 'environment.' Not only is it meaningless to suggest that any trait of an individual is environmentally or genetically 'determined'; it is not even valid to talk of a trait as 'primarily' genetic or environmental. However, since 'biological' actually means 'of or pertaining to life,' it is quite valid to claim that any phenotypic trait of an organism is biologically, or evolutionarily, determined."[14] Leaving aside the fuzziness of a such a generalized, out-of-focus, definition of biology— "every aspect of a living thing"—let us zero in on what we take to be the heart of Thornhill and Palmer's contention: They argue that *evolution* is a determinative force that can provide the *ultimate* explanation of rape. Explanations of rape that refer to social causes, such as social conditioning, they maintain, provide only *proximate* explanations. These may tell us how behaviors are prompted, but not why they exist in the first place. That first place—that ultimate nature—is what their evolutionary psychology aims to elucidate.

Their framing of the issue may have some logical force, but as Thornhill and Palmer concede, theirs is an untested hypothesis: "When evolutionary psychologists speak of evolved 'psychological mechanisms,' they are actually postulating physiological mechanisms in the nervous system that, at the present stage of scientific knowledge, can only be inferred from patterns of behavior."[15] It is important not to lose sight of the fact that the arguments presented in *The Natural History of Rape* about biological bases of rape among humans are hypotheses, *not* research findings. To make their postulated mechanisms convincing would require persuasive inferences and evidence, but these Thornhill and Palmer do not offer.

"NATURE" OR FUNCTIONALIST FALLACY?

Thornhill and Palmer acknowledge that evidence to demonstrate how evolution shaped rape behavior is lacking. They write that the point of their book, rather, is to "describe the evidence that may be garnered in the future to settle the question."[16] Settling it incontrovertibly, of course, would require an extended molecular, physiological, and ecological analysis of how a set of genes, interacting with the environment, codes for a set of proteins that can enter into metabolic processes linked up with, say, hormonal dynamics in ways that can produce rape behaviors in specific reproductive environments. Absent such evidence, we are left with a series of tales about how evolution *could* have led to particular traits. But just because stories can be told about how particular functions *could* have been favored by natural selection does not amount to proving that these functions have in fact been so favored. We argue that Thornhill and Palmer are in the grips not so much of a naturalistic fallacy—the assumption that what is biological is moral—as of a *functionalist* fallacy.

Key to Thornhill and Palmer's approach is their claim that "selective pressure will be apparent in the functional design of [an] adaptation."[17] As scientists, they say, we should start by observing behaviors, like rape, and the ends to which behaviors appear to be aimed. This presents the first conundrum. How does one identify the behavior called rape, let alone its function? Why, to begin with, should we use the word *rape* to describe dynamics in nonhumans, as Thornhill and Palmer suggest when they ask, "Why does rape exist in many, but not all, species?"[18] The question broadens the definition of rape to the degree that it loses specific meaning. When "scientists apply the word to fruit flies, bedbugs, ducks, or monkeys," biologist Anne Fausto-Sterling points out, this conflates different phenomena: "Yet the 'instinct' of a female bedbug to avoid forced intercourse certainly holds nothing in common with the set of emotions experienced by a woman who has been raped. Using the word *rape* to describe animal behavior robs it of the notion of will, and when the word, so robbed, once again is applied to humans, women find their rights of consent and refusal missing. Rape becomes just one more phenomenon in the natural world, a world in which natural and scientific, rather than human, laws prevail."[19] Thornhill and Palmer dismiss the distinction between what we can call "rape" in humans and what they call "rape" in scorpionflies, one of their central examples.[20] They offer, "Asserting that rape is by definition unique to humans excludes the behavior of non-human animals as a potential source of information about the causes of human rape."[21] While this may sound reasonable, it is not really an argument, since it assumes precisely what it wishes to affirm.

Thornhill and Palmer do not hold that rape exists in all species. They do, however, maintain that rape is universal among humans. The assumption is implicit in their question "Why does rape occur in all known cultures?"[22] They explain this generalization in expansive terms: "Human males in all societies so far examined in the ethnographic record possess genes that can lead, by way of ontogeny [development or physical expression of a gene], to raping behavior when the necessary environmental factors are present, and the necessary environmental factors are sometimes present in all societies studied to date."[23] This explanation assumes the universal presence of the very genes for rape behavior that their argument must demonstrate. How do they know the genes are present, and what do they look like? One might wonder whether Thornhill and Palmer really believe that anthropologists have extracted DNA from all the people with whom they have worked and then proceeded to sequence those genes to identify ones that code for rape. Any such research would be well ahead of work done by scientists in the Human Genome Project.

If, however, we take Thornhill and Palmer to mean that rape is merely widespread in humans and the animal world, they still must explain why evolution offers a compelling explanatory model for rape's existence. Thornhill and Palmer begin by drawing a number of inferences from present-day mammal and human behaviors about the selective pressures on ancestral populations. They infer that, because human males have, on average, greater upper-body strength than females, prehistoric males fought with one another and from this evolved psychological mechanisms to favor competitiveness. They infer from the existence of breasts that human females have evolved emotional mechanisms that aid in infant care. They infer from the popularity of pornography among human males that males have evolved to wish to spend their sperm at every opportunity. They assert, "It is not surprising that female sexual infidelity is a major cause of divorce in the United States."[24] And they announce, without citing any sources, that "rape [is] often treated as a crime against the victim's husband."[25] From this presumed aspect of present-day marriage patterns, they infer that early hominids were concerned (if unconsciously) about "paternity reliability."[26] This could all be true. But none of these inferences are evidence; they are further hypotheses. As Hamish Spencer and Judith Masters point out in *Keywords in Evolutionary Biology*, sexual selection is "easily bent to the generation of fascinating stories rather than useful explanations of observable phenomena."[27]

Thornhill and Palmer move next to analogies between humans and other animals. They explain that analogous traits—wings in bats and wings in flies, for example—are similar not due to shared descent but because they may have been produced by similar selective pressures.

Scorpionflies, Thornhill and Palmer suggest, have adaptations that facilitate forced copulations and might therefore provide analogies for similar human adaptations. Male scorpionflies possess "a clamp located on the top of the abdomen, behind the wings," that they use to retain a female "in copulation for the period needed for full insemination." This clamp, say the two authors, is "designed specifically for rape."[28] The two postulate that, since humans do not have such obvious physical mechanisms facilitating rape, we "must look to the male psyche for candidates for rape adaptations."[29] But one might as persuasively suggest that, since cows have four-chambered stomachs, we must look to the human psyche for an equivalent! Having made the adventitious suggestion that we leap from scorpionfly rape clamps to human psychology, Thornhill and Palmer assert that, "if found, such adaptations would be analogous to those in the male insects."[30] Maybe. But we would do well to keep in mind that, as the evolutionary biologist Richard Lewontin has written, "analogy is in the eye of the observer."[31] Not only does Thornhill and Palmer's line of argument here seem farfetched, it directly contradicts their earlier caution against analogical reasoning: "A human psychological adaptation such as that responsible for rape must be studied in humans, and a chimp or orangutan psychological adaptation must be studied in chimps or orangutans."[32]

In spite of the paucity of their evidence and in the face of blatant inconsistency with their own rules, Thornhill and Palmer hypothesize possible human psychological rape adaptations: perhaps the ability to discern the vulnerability of a victim, or a " 'beauty-detection' mechanism, designed specifically for rape," or a mechanism that causes men to rape their wives if they suspect they have been unfaithful, or a male capacity to "unconsciously adjust the size of . . . ejaculate" "in a manner conducive to high probability of fertilization during rape."[33] Thornhill and Palmer also postulate that the spermatozoa of different males will compete with one another if a woman is inseminated by more than one partner, mimicking at the cellular level the competition that the two authors describe at the level of the organism. Again, these are inferred mechanisms—hypotheses—and the genes that could lead to them are conjectural. But in calling these traits "mechanisms," Thornhill and Palmer imply function a priori, suggesting *before* an explanation has even been advanced that there *is* a goal-directed design to be discovered. This is simply speculation.

Thornhill and Palmer prove themselves able to make up a story, based on genes, for almost any trait. They offer, for example, this evolutionary explanation for feminism: "The idea that women have evolved to avoid rape also may help explain certain aspects of the feminist movement, since opposition to sexual coercion of all forms—but especially rape—is a major concern of that movement. . . . We suggest that the combination of greater mobility and less protection by mates and male kin results in women perceiving an enhanced risk of sexual coercion. This perception (probably accurate) may have fueled the feminist movement's promotion of the kind of female-female alliances against male coercion that are seen in many other mammalian species."[34] If feminism and female solidarity, across species, are to be viewed as evolutionary strategies in the face of male aggression, would this mean that, if we accept Thornhill and Palmer's definition of rape, we should also speak of resistance to forced copulation among scorpionflies as "insect feminism"? The silliness of this suggestion points up the sloppiness of their logic.

Thornhill and Palmer even offer an evolutionary explanation for the "paradox" of the popularity of one of their most prominent adversaries, the biologist Stephen Jay Gould.[35] Readers find his arguments appealing, Thornhill and Palmer say, because humans have evolved to present themselves as moral and benevolent (a claim advanced without evidence); Gould's argument that not all traits are aimed at competition is congenial to these beliefs. Thornhill and Palmer's use of their evolutionary argument to make a case against one of their academic rivals illustrates the elasticity of their framework.

This flexibility also renders Thornhill and Palmer's distinction between ultimate and proximate causes—between explanations of why and how—problematic. How does one know when one has reached the bedrock of ultimate evolutionary explanation? Is it when describing traits humans have shared since they first became humans, or those they share with primate relatives? Is it traits they share with other animals, even insects? With plants? With bacteria? The level of ultimate causation is elusive; its designation depends on the questions asked. One can always conjure up an ultimate rationale and categorize everything else as "proximate." This arbitrariness permits Thornhill and Palmer to slip between evolutionary time scales and from human to primate to mammalian and insect bodies and back again. And their use of the word *why* to describe evolutionary causes smuggles in *meaning*, even though Thornhill and Palmer vigorously argue that traits that are natural have no implicit significance.

Thornhill and Palmer are in the grips of a functionalist fallacy, the idea that traits exist because they have been adaptive, if not in the present, then earlier. Gould diagnoses the difficulty. He notes that evolutionary psychologists have argued that "many universal traits of human behavior and cognition need not be viewed as current adaptations, but may rather be judged as misfits, or even maladaptive, to the current complexities of human culture. But most evolutionary psychologists have coupled this acknowledgment with a belief that the origins of such features must be sought in their adaptive value to our hunter-gatherer African ancestors."[36]

The theater of early human evolution is a central court of appeal for Thornhill and Palmer's ultimate causes, and this is an environment to which we have no empirical access. We have no reason to believe that early humans were not also burdened with inheritances that made no sense in *their* contemporary world: we face the problem of where in our evolutionary past to draw explanatory boundaries.

The explanations in *A Natural History of Rape* follow the three-step recipe decoded by Lewontin for spurious sociobiological argument.[37] This goes as follows: First, describe some aspect of universal "human nature"—here, that men have a tendency to rape women—and offer analogies from animals to suggest these traits are seated in shared nature. Second, claim that what is universal must be so because it emanates from biology. Third, since the evidence is not available, claim that traits in question arose through natural or sexual selection, and construct a logical tale for how whatever is universal was favored by evolution and may therefore have a strong hereditary, indeed genetic, component. Note that this tale need bear no relation to what actually occurred. Thornhill and Palmer's account, like much evolutionary psychology, is no more than a "just-so" story.[38]

Thornhill and Palmer's book is replete with the rhetorical slipperiness such a lax standard of argumentation allows. Again and again they offer hypotheses and later refer to them as if they had been proven. For example, in chapter 2 (p. 37), they write, "In mammals with a history of greater sexual selection on females, evolutionary theory *predicts* the following [nine predictions about sex differences in mammals; our emphasis]." On page 84, they write of "the sexual *adaptations that exist* in women and men, described in chapter 2" (our emphasis). The adaptations hypothesized for mammals (a group that subsumes a lot of diversity) are now said simply to "exist." On pages 59–60, Thornhill and Palmer write that rape *"may be an adaptation* that was directly favored by selection because it increased male reproductive success by way of increasing mate number" or that it *"may be only a by-product* of other psychological adaptations" (our emphasis).[39] On pages 64–65, they argue that we "must look to the male psyche for candidates for rape adaptations."[40] This slide from *may* to *must* would require many more steps to make a sound argument.

Thus Thornhill and Palmer's warning against the naturalistic fallacy—that "what is, ought to be"—obscures functionalist fallacies at the center of their work. It also hides their persistent suggestion that "what may be, must be." The individualized, unconscious cost-benefit evolutionary explanations they offer—that men will rape when costs are low—sidestep any explicit moral charge for the nature they discuss. But their arguments are meant to anchor rape in nature, through arguments about why evolution might rationally have favored or supported rape behavior. The nature in which Palmer and Thornhill site rape is ordered and predictable because every behavioral trait is explicable through recourse to a functionalist story about an adaptation or its by-products. We are not persuaded that rape can be so easily explained through recourse to cost-benefit reasoning, nor that it is useful to exclude from an explanation of rape the dynamics of a social world in which behavior is often arbitrary and far too complex to be explained by a single story.[41]

"HISTORY": NATURAL OR SOCIAL?

What is rape? Most anthropologists would describe rape as a social behavior, the experience and meaning of which depend on where and when it happens and to whom.[42] Three examples of human behaviors that have been called rape—wartime rape, rape of slaves, and fraternity gang rape—each of which takes a different form and requires a different understanding, demonstrate that social histories of rape cannot be replaced or improved upon by a "natural history of rape" that appeals in the last instance to conjectural reproductive success stories.

Rape in the Context of War

For Thornhill and Palmer, the fact that a rape takes place in war tells us only what the proximate cause might be, evolution being the ultimate cause. But why women are raped in the course of war depends very much upon the specifics of the war. Soldiers have raped women because their bodies are seen as additional "booty" to be looted along with household possessions. Thousands of German women were raped by Allied soldiers at the end of World War II in an act of celebratory revenge. Militarized mass rape is viewed by both aggressors and victims not just as a crime against a woman's person, not just as an expression of male sexual proclivities, but as a calculated act of aggression against an enemy people.[43]

The anthropologists and Balkans specialists Susan Gal and Gail Kligman argue that in contexts of ethnic nationalism, mass rape has been a particularly effective weapon.[44] Ethnic nationalism may be contrasted with civic nationalism, in which, as in the United States and France, the nation comprises people who subscribe to shared beliefs and political commitments. Under ethnic nationalism, "a nation" is bound together through shared culture, language, and history believed to cohere as a kind of inheritance, symbolically passed down through "blood." Women, through reproducing and socializing future citizens, may be regarded as the symbolic bearers of a cultural and national identity fathered by men; rape thus disrupts the symbolic unity of the nation. In such a context, "sexual violation of women erodes the fabric of a community in a way that few [technological] weapons can."[45]

In the 1990s, ethnic nationalism drove the war in Bosnia-Herzegovina; in 1992, more than twenty thousand women reportedly were raped. Bosnian Serb soldiers imprisoned Muslim Croat women in makeshift "rape camps" for the express purpose of sexually violating them for days or months. This was so well documented that it prompted a 1996 United Nations criminal tribunal to define rape for the first time as a war crime against humanity.[46]

To understand why this happened in Bosnia, it is important to consider how the twentieth-century history of the region made it a cauldron for ethnic nationalism. Skipping back all the way to our hominid ancestors, as Thornhill and Palmer would have us do, cannot substitute for this social history. For hundreds of years, the Ottoman Empire ruled the area through local religious leaders without carving up the Balkans into administrative districts. Serb-speaking Orthodox Christians lived side by side with, if independently from, Serbo-Croat-speaking Muslims. Religious and, later, ethnic identification was encouraged. Following World War II, however, as the new state of Yugoslavia was formed, Josip Tito unified the disparate peoples of the region into a multiethnic socialist federation. After Tito's death, the federated republic began to dissolve as different groups broke off and proclaimed themselves nations. Seeking autonomy, Serbs and Croats fought bitterly over cities and territories they had been sharing as neighbors for generations (see Tone Bringa, chap. 4 this volume). In this context, rape was used "as a weapon of war in 'ethnic cleansing.'"[47] Women impregnated by Serbian solders were often held for seven or eight months before being released, too late to seek an abortion.[48] Muslim Croat girls and women who had been raped were forced to give birth to what were viewed as non-Muslim children, thereby diluting claims of Croatian nationhood where people identify ethnic identity with parenthood. Here, cultural ideas about gender shape kin-based metaphors of national and ethnic belonging (see Keith Brown, chap. 3 this volume). In such a setting, the meaning of and motivation for rape exceeds the physically sexual to become a highly orchestrated strategic instrument of war. It is *not* paternity that is being maximized here; it is a focused collective effort to terrorize, and destroy the cultural integrity of, the vanquished group.

Rape is not inevitable in or limited to ethnic nationalist war, nor is it an inevitable feature of human life—it is not useful to view militarized mass rape as a logical outcome of evolutionarily driven competition between males to impregnate women. Rather, its presence in different places requires examination of social history in specific contexts. The anthropologist Veena Das, for example, has written about the rape of tens of thousands of women by both Muslim and Hindu factions after the partition that led to the creation of India and Pakistan. She argues that "the idea of appropriating a territory as nation and appropriating the body of the women as territory" was powerfully informed by British imperial images of the nation and of the role of women within it.[49] We must look at the history of the British Empire to evaluate the case she makes.

In 1994, during Rwanda's civil war, armed Hutus raped thousands of Tutsi women. Many of these women were raped with machetes and spears and were then killed; even Thornhill and Palmer would have difficulty arguing that this is the "by-product" of some kind of reproductive strategy. In other instances, "the government was bringing AIDS patients out of the hospitals specifically to form battalions of rapists."[50] Rape was thus used intentionally to kill; it was a weapon not of ethnocide, but genocide. Mass rape commanded from above, as in Rwanda, cannot be usefully understood as the act of a lone individual whose deepest instincts are finally able to express themselves without being checked by social disapproval. It cannot be explained in the same terms as individualized incidences, such as rape by an acquaintance in an unlit parking lot. Thornhill and Palmer might reply that rape using objects hijacks for nonreproductive ends a previously evolved rape mechanism, but such a response so generalizes the mechanism that it becomes meaningless, very far indeed from one of the "specialized, domain-specific adaptations" that the two authors describe.[51] Militarized rape is meant to further the strategic ends of those who orchestrate it.

Rape under Plantation Slavery in the Antebellum United States

Rape was also a documented and frequent occurrence under plantation slavery in the southern United States before the Civil War. Here the reigning ideology was not ethnic nationalism but private property within a system of chattel slavery. When white slave owners raped and impregnated their African slave women, they thereby increased their property, but *not*, as they saw it, their progeny: "Legally, and in contrast with the patriarchal reckoning of descent for the non-slave population, the children of interracial unions between slave owners and enslaved women were themselves slaves. Although one may assume that slave owners used rape as a means of wielding power and obtaining sexual pleasure, the economic dimension of the prohibition on miscegenation was also evident: sexual intercourse with enslaved women—in the context of matrilineal descent laws for enslaved people—produced more slaves."[52] While these were certainly reproductive events, understanding who was targeted and why requires understanding the politics and economics of race under American slavery.[53] Here, again, a "natural" history of rape fails to explain very much. Angela Davis writes, "Excessive sex urges, whether they existed among individual white men or not, had nothing to do with this virtual institutionalization of rape. Sexual coercion was, rather, an essential dimension of the social relations between slave master and slave. . . . The right claimed by slave owners and their agents over the bodies of female slaves was a direct expression of their presumed property rights over Black people as a whole. The license to rape emanated from and facilitated the ruthless economic domination that was the gruesome hallmark of slavery."[54] In this context, rape was about property ownership and economic advantage, not an evolutionarily selected drive to ensure males' genetic contribution to the next generation.

With the end of slavery and the failure of Reconstruction, black women continued to be targets of white rape, but this period also saw a huge rise in false accusations of rape against black men (a striking shift, as no black men had been accused of rape during the Civil War). Angela Davis has argued that, as the institutionalized subordination of blacks under slavery ended, some whites began to use the myth of the black rapist and the threat of retaliatory lynching as a terror tactic to prevent blacks from achieving full citizenship and economic equality. When black men continue today to be disproportionately accused and convicted of rape, Davis further argues that this myth has had enduring consequences for writing on rape well into the twentieth century. In perpetuating the notion that black men are more prone to rape than white men—owing to a "culture of poverty" argument or to racist stereotypes of blacks as sexually voracious—some antirape work, Davis suggests, has failed to push for full investigation of unsolved rape cases.[55] The prosecution and prevention of rape in the United States requires attention to how racism distorts the identification of men who rape. An evolutionary view, even if it demonstrates the bankruptcy of race as a biological category, cannot do this kind of work.

Fraternity Gang Rape

A book by the anthropologist Peggy Sanday, *Fraternity Gang Rape*, was written in response to a high-profile rape on the university campus where Sanday teaches. She explains how serial rapes of women at fraternity house parties are committed by fraternity brothers as a form of male bonding.[56] Sanday interviewed women and men who witnessed or participated in these events. In the practice of "pulling train," young men have sequential intercourse with a woman who may be drunk or unconscious (which would make this rape under U.S. legal standards, based on lack of consent). This activity, Sanday concludes, bonds the young men through pleasure, excitement, and secrecy. This is a rite of male camaraderie, not male competition (although Thornhill and Palmer might argue a case for sperm competition inside the body of the raped). It can also be described as a ritualized way by which some young men learn— through example, peer pressure, and positive reinforcement—to sexualize and objectify women and to use women to demonstrate heterosexual masculinity in a homosocial environment. In other words, they learn to rape.

Why do Thornhill and Palmer nevertheless insist that a "natural" or evolutionary psychological explanation is somehow better, more plausible, or more useful than one that examines social and historical context? Cultural anthropology can suggest some answers. The two authors' assumption that males are concerned with "paternity reliability" is based on convictions derived from a social context where inheritance is traced through the father's line, a cultural practice that, as anthropologists remind us, is far from a human universal. Thornhill and Palmer project this identification of fatherhood with sperm onto sperm itself, focusing on the role of sperm competition in acts, including rape, that are "about sex." Anthropologists have long recognized, however, that not all peoples are obsessed with knowledge of paternity.[57] Bronislaw Malinowski famously found that Trobriand Islanders did not have a concept that linked fatherhood to biology. Trobrianders believed that, in order to become pregnant, a woman had to have intercourse more than once, and perhaps with more than one man; intercourse was thought to "open" a woman to enable a spirit or soul to enter her womb, and sperm was viewed as nourishment, not a quickening substance. Thornhill and Palmer might respond that, while these people may have been "ignorant" of paternity, deep down their genes told them to safeguard it, and, unbeknownst to them, sperm were battling for supremacy in women's bodies. But as the anthropologist Emily Martin has argued, culturally shaped views of sperm as active and eggs as passive often powerfully— and *erroneously*—guide how these entities are described even in scientific literature.[58] Spermatozoa, even though they have tails, do not "race." Sperm are *not* little competitive men; ova are *not* itsy-bitsy coy females. For Thornhill and Palmer, the egg appears to be the same inert stuff it was for Aristotle, waiting to be animated by the magic of sperm. They project onto sperm and egg their stereotypical cultural visions of active male and passive female relations, distorting the much more complicated biology of the matter.

Thornhill and Palmer also work from a definition of sex that warrants attention. They argue that American feminists, beginning with Susan Brownmiller, have redefined rape as an act of patriarchal power, and not an act of sex. But to assert this—either rape is about power *or* it is about sex—is to assume that "sex" among humans is fully separable from social and political power, that "sex" is essentially a biological phenomenon aimed always at reproduction and having more in common with copulating scorpionflies than with a civil marriage ceremony, notions of romance, or acts of military conquest. This is where many social scientists today differ most fundamentally with evolutionary psychologists.[59] We agree that rape is sexual, or "about sex," as Thornhill and Palmer insist. It is clear that in human societies, sex and power, pleasure and danger, may be very much related.[60] Where we part company begins with our understandings of what "sex" is. The feminist social scientists dismissed by Thornhill and Palmer make the argument that "sex" is not one single thing: the myriad acts, motivations, emotions, attitudes, reactions, and potential repercussions that together produce "sexual encounters" are not reducible to one definitive event that may or may not lead to reproduction. It is for this reason that "rape"—coerced sex—also cannot be explained through one underlying unifying theory. Stranger rape, date rape, male rape, homosexual prison rape, rape within slavery, forced impregnation during gang rape as a prisoner of war: all of these might involve forced copulation, but there is no reason to suggest these are all ultimately caused by some hypothetical evolutionary mechanism in males.[61]

We have no reason to doubt Sanday's cross-cultural finding that rape—which she defines, similarly to Thornhill and Palmer, as sexual "coercion"—occurs more frequently in societies where men and women's daily activities are largely segregated, where gender roles are fairly rigid, and where men have more economic and political power than women.[62] Thornhill and Palmer would argue that this is because the "social costs" of rape would be lower in such societies; it seems far more plausible, and useful, to note that in these societies boys and men are trained to view themselves as both different from and superior to women. Nor does this mean that rape only happens when rapists have learned to rape in ways as explicit and ritualistic as those evidenced by fraternity "trains" or genocidal programs in Rwanda. But it does suggest that culture plays a more immediate and relevant role in producing rape behavior than does, say, human sexual dimorphism. Biology unquestionably enables human behavior; however, cultural belief, coercive power, moral values, and historical legacy together exert a stronger pressure than the highly conjectural biology of Thornhill and Palmer when it comes to shaping particular instances of individual human action.[63]

"RAPE": WHOSE PERSPECTIVES TELL THE TRUTH?

As we have seen, Thornhill and Palmer do not begin their analysis from the experience of those who have been raped, but rather from what they see as the more objective view of evolutionary biology, a view they believe will be more useful for rape prevention and crisis counseling. One of the key commitments of cultural anthropology, in contrast, has been to understand "the native's point of view"—that is, not to impose on others' experiences one's own assumptions. Thornhill and Palmer's refusal to take into consideration the native's point of view—the rape survivor's or, for that matter, the rapist's—alongside their resolute insistence on attributing possible evolutionary causes of rape to the neglect of immediate social conditions, leads to some rather odd, even Victorian, policy suggestions for rape prevention:

> We envision an evolutionarily informed educational program for young men that focuses on increasing their ability to restrain their sexual behavior. Completion of such a course might be required, say, before a young man is granted a driver's license. Such a program might start by getting the young men to acknowledge the power of their sexual impulses and then explaining why human males have evolved to be that way. . . . It should be emphasized that the reason a young man should know these things is so that he can be on guard against certain effects of past Darwinian selection.[64]

It does not sound to us like a particularly good or useful idea for teachers to inform adolescent boys that they have evolved to dominate women sexually. But apparently for Thornhill and Palmer, as the historian of biology Howard Kaye suggests, evolved traits are much like sins in Calvinist theology: they can be overcome with hard work.[65] Boys learning the gospel in driver's education can join Thornhill and Palmer in their moral clarity: "We are not evolved to understand that our striving reflects past differences in the reproduction of individuals. Such knowledge can come only from a committed study of evolutionary biology."[66]

When it comes to the girls, Thornhill and Palmer are similarly simplistic:

> The educational program for young women should . . . address how . . . elements of attractiveness (including health, symmetry, and hormone markers such as waist size), and clothing and makeup that enhance them, may influence the likelihood of rape. This is not to say that young women should constantly attempt to look ill and infertile; it is simply to say that they should be made aware of the costs associated with attractiveness. . . . It should be made clear that although sexy clothing and promises of sexual access may be a means of attracting desired males, they may also attract undesirable ones.[67]

Barbara Ehrenreich assesses this prescription tartly: "As for the girls, Thornhill and Palmer want them to realize that since rape is really 'about sex,' it very much matters how they dress. But where is the evidence that women in mini-skirts are more likely to be raped than women in dirndls? Women were raped by the thousands in Bosnia, for example, and few if any of them were wearing bikinis or bustiers."[68] Could tragedy in Rwanda have been averted if Tutsi women had paid closer attention to their attire? It is hard to imagine that Thornhill and Palmer were unaware of such empirical data that destabilize their assumptions and make their recommendations seem woefully naive. Had they taken seriously the possibility that even local stereotypes of "attractiveness" frequently have no influence on the selection of targets for rape, they might have presented a stronger case.

Their policy suggestions make one wonder about Thornhill and Palmer's concept of human will. Why do they insist that women must respond to the threat of rape through their fashion choices rather than through verbal protest? Thornhill and Palmer deny women the voice that feminists have worked to have heard and respected. This voice is recognized by such legal institutions as the State of Texas Commission on Law Enforcement, which has begun to train its officers to be aware of "social rules" that "may be exploited by a potential rapist"—for instance, that women are often taught "not to make a scene."[69] Instead, Thornhill and Palmer seem to suggest that "No" really cannot be heard by men as "No." They write, "Women need to realize that, because selection favored males who had many mates, men tend to read signals of acceptance into a female's actions even when no such signals are intended."[70] Men seem, to Thornhill and Palmer, able to control their fate, while women cannot.

Thornhill and Palmer's policy suggestions demonstrate a striking lack of knowledge about rape as it occurs among real people. Brownmiller notes that *A Natural History of Rape* "misrepresented my position. I didn't say rape was only about power. I also say it's about humiliation and degradation. When women started to talk about this in the early 70s, the women who had experienced rape said they felt it had been an act of humiliation. They didn't see it as a sex act. But obviously we didn't think this had nothing to do with the sex act; of course it is, sexual organs are used."[71] Brownmiller points out that she and others writing in the 1970s were primarily concerned to give a voice to women's experiences of rape. Thornhill and Palmer conflate "what feminists say"—an analytic position—with what feminists and others report women victims as saying about rape: that they experienced it as an act of violence and violation, rather than as what they think of as "sex" (a consensual intimacy with another person). Thornhill and Palmer thus override what many rape survivors have reported about rape ("rape is not about sex") with their own dispassionate view of what motivates men to rape. Their critique of feminist analyses of rape, then, is based on comparing women's firsthand reports about the actual experience to their own speculations as to men's unconscious motivations for raping. It is not a persuasive comparison.

Even more arrogantly, they ask, "Why is rape a horrendous experience for the victim?" and declare that "evolutionary theory can help us understand the ultimate reasons why rape is as distressing as it is."[72] Again, their analysis entirely ignores rape survivors' firsthand experiences: "Mate choice was a fundamental means of reproductive success for females in human evolutionary history. Thus, rapists' circumvention of mate choice has had extremely negative consequences for female reproductive success throughout human evolutionary history. The psychological pain that rape victims experience appears to be an evolved defense against rape."[73] Along these same lines, they propose that "women have a special-purpose psychological adaptation that processes information about events that, over evolutionary history, would have resulted in reduced reproductive success."[74] In other words, when women fight off would-be attackers, it is due to a special inborn antirape mechanism that is looking after the well-being of their genetic legacy, rather than, say, their will to avoid suffering the physical and emotional trauma of sexual assault. And indeed, offering us their interpretation of published self-reports about violent rape, Thornhill and Palmer state that "reproductive-age married women [appear to be less] psychologically traumatized when the rape includes violence, thus providing clear evidence to their husbands that copulation was not nonconsensual."[75] This leap from appearance to evidence is purely speculative.

The evidence Thornhill and Palmer do offer is sparse indeed: their only direct example of how women are affected by rape is "an instance in which a woman was raped by a male orangutan."[76] The two authors quote a primatologist, the victim's boss, recalling the victim's husband as saying of the attack, "Why should my wife or I be concerned? It was not a man." The authors argue, "Her husband reasoned that since the rapist was not human, the rape should not provoke shame or rage."[77] This story—about a man's response to the rape of his wife, and hearsay at that—is meant to illustrate the thesis that a female will be more bothered by rape when there is a chance that she will become pregnant by someone besides her husband. What we hear from Thornhill and Palmer about women's experience is filtered through the presumed views of male rapists and the women's chosen mates.

From this vantage point, they propose a definition for rape as follows: "copulation resisted to the best of the victim's ability unless such resistance would probably result in death or serious injury to the victim or in the death [of] or injury to individuals the victim commonly protects."[78] Contrast the assumptions of this definition with a passage written by psychologist Rebecca Campbell, director of the Sexual Assault and Rape Prevention Evaluation Project, Michigan Public Health Institute. Campbell has studied rape and its emotional effects on survivors: "It is the debris, the skin, and the semen that is rubbed into you and all over you, again and again. It is spilled on you, dumped on you, and into you. It is the bacteria and the viruses that could be being mixed into you. It is the diseases, curable and incurable, that might be forced into you. . . . That is what rape is."[79] The two incidences of human rape described in Thornhill and Palmer's book do not come close to demonstrating awareness of this kind of perspective on being raped. The first, an anonymous description of a date rape, comes from "a friend of ours."[80] The second is the orangutan story, in which we never hear a word from the woman in question.

Thornhill and Palmer's Victorian suggestions for rape crisis counseling, based on their claim that they can get to the truth of rape in a way rape survivors cannot, are weak. A more effective means of reducing the incidence of rape might be instead to work toward a society in which men are not viewed as dominant and not trained to feel superior and entitled, and women are not routinely depicted as vulnerable and voiceless. Insofar as rape is often "about sex," we argue that encouraging boys to respect women, to see beyond a woman's appearance or relative sexiness, and to appreciate her personality, intellect, and humanity will have an impact on rates of rape and attempted rape. We believe too that international politics committed to reconciling differences through diplomatic rather than military means will reduce the numbers of women made to suffer rape worldwide. Without war there is no militarized mass rape.

CONCLUSION: SCIENCE OR FAITH-BASED SPECULATION?

In *The Natural History of Nonsense*, Bergen Evans examines the reasons people believe unreasonable things, arguing, "We see what we want to see, and observation conforms to hypothesis."[81] His book did not forward an evolutionary explanation for nonsense, but rather invoked the genre of natural history ironically, in the spirit of humorous reflections on human gullibility. It would be nonsense to seek a natural explanation for the wide variety of things that count as nonsense. And so too with rape. But Thornhill and Palmer's nonsensical analysis uses the frame of natural history seriously. We do not think Thornhill and Palmer are ill meaning; we do take them at their word that they find theirs a compelling explanation. But we suggest that this is precisely because their convictions are based more on faith than on science.

In 1996, the Catholic Church held a conference at the Vatican on evolutionary and molecular biology.[82] Catholic theologians are not creationists, nor do they promote fundamentalist readings of the Bible; rather, the theologians at this meeting were interested in reconciling ideas about the creation of human souls by God with the latest findings in evolutionary biology, the adaptationist premises of which these theologians accepted. One contributor to the conference proceedings pointed out that the evolutionary models of sociobiologists were too metaphysical—dependent on premises that could not be proven—to satisfy the condition of being proper science.[83] He wrote that Richard Dawkins, E. O. Wilson, and others "present something akin to a scientific religion in that they purport to give an overall world-view, sometimes including ethical or pseudo-ethical statements. . . . A hidden metaphysical agenda underlies what is presented to the public as a pure and neutral scientific rendition of nature."[84] Sociobiologists and evolutionary psychologists, the author continued, were too faith based, too unaware of their own metaphysical claims—about the design capacities of natural selection, for example.[85] The Catholic Church, many conferees felt, should not compete with another faith. Ironically, the blindness of the practitioners of sociobiology and evolutionary psychology to their own practices of interpretation leave them in a curiously fundamentalist position, believing their interpretations of genetic code to be the literal truth. Stephen Jay Gould makes exactly this argument about evolutionary psychology: so committed to the adaptationist program is this field that nothing can escape functionalist interpretation, a real problem when inquiring into dynamics from the past that we cannot entirely retrieve and that have many possible shapes.[86] We might say that *A Natural History of Rape* has something in common with Michael Corey's *Natural History of Creation,* a publication that argues that the book of Genesis is "fundamentally identical to the modern evolutionary account."[87]

An unquestioning faith in the adaptationist program is behind the doctrine of this evolutionary psychology. In the family of "natural history" books—their sheer proliferation a sign that marketing and not science might be behind such titles—*A Natural History of Rape* stands out as a particularly stubborn entry. Why have Thornhill and Palmer's arguments been so marketable? The authoritative language of science is often quite persuasive, even if it is deployed in the service of an argument that is logically flawed and supported by dubious evidence. According to Caryl Rivers and Rosalind Barnett, "The blitz of media coverage that accompanied the advance publicity on the book was too often misleading. Reporters quoted well-meaning but scientifically unsophisticated sources such as rape counselors who said things like, 'Well, it may be in our genes but we have to fight against it.' That accepts the premise that, because this notion was presented as 'science' it must be right. Unintentionally, they gave credence to very speculative science, helping to cement it in the public mind."[88]

More important, however, the stories Thornhill and Palmer tell about women and men align with and confirm stereotypes of masculinity and femininity scripted in Western popular culture, from fairy tales to pornography. For all the controversy it generated, this book offers nothing we have not heard before. But, with its logical slipperiness, social naïveté, and disregard of women, this book is potentially hazardous. Brownmiller is concerned that the book "will be used as a defense by lawyers in rape cases. . . . The ones who will benefit will be high-profile rapists who can afford to hire [such lawyers]."[89] No matter how much the authors try to hedge in subsequent interviews and articles, their book does argue that male humans have developed an evolutionary propensity to rape women.

But it does so on the basis of faith, not evidence. Perhaps we could take a page from Daniel Cohen's *Natural History of Unnatural Things* and argue that Thornhill and Palmer's book is an occult artifact,[90] divining the true purpose of nature through recourse to the kinds of self-fulfilling prophesies that characterize the psychic hotline, not the logical, evidentially based protocols that make a coherent evolutionary or psychological study.

ELEVEN Anthropology and *The Bell Curve*

Jonathan Marks

I can measure a rod one foot long and add another foot in
length, but I can not add two amounts of intelligence and
make it a double intelligence.

Franz Boas, "Recent Anthropology"

The Bell Curve was one of the most talked-about books of 1994–1995.[1] In
rehashing many old scientific and pseudoscientific fads, it capitalized on
the notoriously short memory of the American public. Mercifully, that
same feature has worked against it: a few years later, when I ask under-
graduates about *The Bell Curve*, they have some vague idea of it as a pon-
derous and frightening old piece of literature that they'd rather not read,
like *The Brothers Karamazov* or *Martin Chuzzlewit*.

On the other hand, it may have had a real impact on public policy.
Those of us who value scientific work in the formation of policy must be
embarrassed at that prospect, for it represents far from the best of what
science has to offer, and in some ways it demonstrates the worst.

Its central argument was that (1) intelligence is an organic property, set
largely genetically, and accurately assessable by testing; (2) some people

have more of it than others; (3) social status and income are consequences of it; (4) disparities among groups in social status and income are consequences of innate intellectual shortcomings; and therefore, (5) social programs designed to ameliorate inequality are futile and should be dismantled. The first author, Richard Herrnstein, was a longtime professional advocate of the first point; the second author, Charles Murray, has long been a professional advocate of the last point.

None of this was a novelty to anyone familiar with the course of ostensibly scientific arguments about human diversity over the last century or so. Thus, in this chapter, I review *The Bell Curve* from the standpoints of science, history, anthropology, and genetics and demonstrate the scholarly poverty of the work.

THE BELL CURVE COMES DRESSED AS SCIENCE

Anthropologists in recent years have come to subject their own cultural practices and discourses to the same kind of scrutiny and analysis as those of residents of Samoa or the Trobriand Islands. Recognizing that science often plays a cultural role as authority—"nine out of ten doctors smoke Lucky Strikes," or some such, as advertisers used to tell us—one can ask, "Where does that authority come from? What does science look like? How do I know it when I see it?"

Science has familiar features, which are naturally the very features exploited by works attempting to masquerade as science. They are not only common features of science but also effective symbols of science.

The most familiar feature of science is "white men in white coats": science is a classically and stereotypically gendered, raced, and uniformed activity. While *The Bell Curve* is not laboratory science and thus lacks the uniforms, it fits the stereotype in other ways quite nicely: it is the joint product of a distinguished-looking Harvard professor of psychology and a scholarly writer from a think tank. *It looks like it is by people who know what they're talking about.*

The next stereotypical feature of science is the generation and presentation of new data. This feature is so thoroughly ingrained—science as novelty!—that it affects self-perceptions of science as well. New findings and discoveries are fundable; critique and debate are not. This creates pressure to collect more and more data, however useless they may be, and pressure to make everything seem newer than it really is.

More important, science frequently progresses more through (unfunded) critique and reanalysis than through the initial discovery and presentation. Consider, for example, paleoanthropology, in which the initial interpretation of a fossil is rarely the one ultimately settled upon. Nevertheless, the achievement is ascribed to the finder (or describer, since frequently the literal finder is an invisible employee of the scientist), rather than to the reviser, who has often made better sense of the fossil's real biological meaning.

Thus, although critique and debate are vital to the production of knowledge, there is nevertheless a popular image that holds them to be the province of poseurs and troublemakers, and the generation of new discoveries and findings to be the province of "real" scientists. This attitude makes it easier for incompetent or even falsified data to be accepted, because, as new data, it looks more "real" than the reanalysis, revision, or reinterpretation of old data. *The Bell Curve looks like a new discovery, and places its critics on the defensive.*

Finally, statistical analysis is a popularly perceived signature of science. On the one hand, statistical analysis can legitimately be said to have marked the transformation of premodern descriptive to modern analytic natural science. On the other hand, we all know what Benjamin Disraeli meant when he grouped statistics along with "lies" and "damned lies." *The Bell Curve* utilizes data transformations and graphic treatments ranging from the mundane to the esoteric, and presents simple results ostensibly derived from them that necessitate considerable faith on the part of the reader. *The Bell Curve looks like a sophisticated analysis.*

The Bell Curve is thus carefully crafted to look like traditional science, to claim the authority of science and the high ground as novelty over and against any critics and detractors. It effectively mobilizes the symbols of science—the stature of the authors, new data, statistics—to evoke the respectful reaction properly accorded to a scholarly scientific work.

However, as Alan Ryan notes, "There is a good deal of genuine science in *The Bell Curve;* there is also an awful lot of science fiction and not much care to make sure the reader knows which is which."[2]

There are very few reasons why a piece of ostensibly scientific literature would not wish to distinguish itself fully and explicitly from a non-science doppelgänger. The most obvious is that it is not to the advantage of the work to have the reader view it through too critical eyes. As Jesus is reputed to have said, "Why light a candle, just to cover it up or put it under the bed?" (e.g., Luke 8:16)—to which the answer, obviously, is that you really don't want *too much* illumination.

THE BELL CURVE HAS NOTORIOUS CONNECTIONS

The Bell Curve does a poor job of discussing the historical antecedents for its views.[3] This, of course, helps to create the strategic illusion of originality. Ultimately, the use of science to inform and direct social policy can arguably be laid at the foot of Plato. In its modern form, however, the most direct antecedent of *The Bell Curve* is a loose confederacy of ideas collectively known as social Darwinism, popular in America in the latter portion of the nineteenth century. Its core was the justification of social hierarchy as the expression of an underlying natural hierarchy: people were where they deserved to be. Any attempt to alter this—from unionization to child labor laws to welfare—would be a subversion of the natural order.[4]

Social Darwinism's leading American exponent was a Yale professor named William Graham Sumner, who saw unfettered competition and Puritan morality as the keys to social progress: "Let every man be sober, industrious, prudent, and wise, and bring up his children to be so likewise, and poverty will be abolished in a few generations." And the cream, it was argued, rose naturally to the top: "The millionaires are a product of natural selection. . . . They may fairly be regarded as the naturally selected agents of society for certain work. They get high wages and live in luxury, but the bargain is a good one for society."[5]

Needless to say, such views were popular among the industrialists, monopolists, tycoons, and robber barons of the age, who saw in these views not only a vindication of their own successes but also an absolution for the poverty and misery they were accused of inflicting upon others. Their successes were fated by the strength of their own resolve and mettle—whether inborn or acquired. The destitution of the masses was their own damn fault. But those views were unpopular with most other listeners, who saw the merciless exploitation of impoverished laborers as evil, the causes of wealth and poverty as more historically and socially complex, and the invocation of natural law as a vulgarly self-serving justification for the status quo and, especially, for the infliction of poverty and misery upon the workers. Consequently, social Darwinism did not last far into the twentieth century.

Ultimately social Darwinism was a theory about destiny and about rugged individualism: people were the masters of their own fates, either through their constitutional endowments or the sweat of their brow—it didn't much matter; the rich were entitled to theirs, while the poor had simply gotten what they deserved. At some level, however, the existing social hierarchy was almost ordained, simply nature taking its course. The fact that some people lived in opulence and many in squalor was just a fact of life. To try to alter it, therefore, was not only vain but also tantamount to a crime against nature.

Anthropology arose in the late nineteenth century as "essentially a reformer's science," in the words of its first academic professional, Edward Tylor. In Tylor's hands, the central concept of the field became culture (or civilization). Culture was conceptually distinct from the endowments of nature and was achieved by all peoples, to greater or lesser degrees, although all were potentially equal participants. Independently invented in America from the German concept, "culture" became, in the hands of Franz Boas, something more localized, a mental tincture that suffuses every aspect of human thought and behavior with localized and distinct meaning.

The Boasian paradigm, however, also had a more subversive element. It successfully showed that many group differences commonly ascribed to differences in nature were actually differences of culture, that is, ascribable to the history and circumstances of life. Not only were stereotypical behavioral features of populations highly mutable but so were many physical features, such as head form and body proportions. More important, this view undercut the traditional explanation that associated the degree of civilization with the innate intellectual capacity of its members. Wrote Boas in his classic explication *The Mind of Primitive Man*, "In short, historical events seem to have been much more potent in leading races to civilization than their faculty, and it follows that achievements of races do not warrant us in assuming that one race is more highly gifted than the other."[6]

The subversion lies in appreciating that the accumulation of economic, political, or social power lies in the vagaries of history, and not in the innate qualities of those who happen to be the most civilized, most powerful, or most wealthy at any point in time. It is not biological kismet or karma that creates cultural differences and social or economic hierarchies.

Modern anthropology thus cast itself in opposition to older, deterministic theories of social forms, most notably social Darwinism and eugenics.[7] Both, it is important to note, carried political implications: social Darwinism justified bellicose colonialism, and eugenics justified immigration restriction and involuntary sterilization of the poor.[8] Boas was at the forefront of scholarly critique of eugenics, because he studied and appreciated the historically ephemeral aspects of the phenomena the movement ascribed to biology, in postulating genes for "feeblemindedness" to be the root cause of poverty and crime.

The political, social, and economic history of the twentieth century seems to bear out the Boasian position quite well. The upward mobility of immigrants and shifting of geopolitical power certainly testifies to the awkwardness of using transcendent natural difference to explain social hierarchies narrowly localized in time and space. Such hierarchies are notably precarious: dynasts beget dolts, peasants beget moguls, the strong overtake the smart and are in turn overthrown by the stronger or smarter—and all in spite of their gene pools. In other words, it is impossible to explain a variable with a constant.

And yet there have been periodic attempts to return to the old determinist perspective. In 1962, the anthropologist Carleton Coon proposed that whites and blacks had evolved separately from *Homo erectus* into *Homo sapiens,* whites having attained that goal two hundred thousand years before blacks. Thus, "it is a fair inference," Coon declared, that whites "have evolved the most, and that the obvious correlation between the length of time a subspecies has been in the *sapiens* state and the levels of civilization attained by some of its populations may be related phenomena."[9]

Segregationists such as the psychologist Henry Garrett of Columbia University; the anatomist Wesley Critz George of the University of North Carolina, Chapel Hill; and Carleton Putnam seized upon the anthropological work to support their position, with Coon's blessings.[10] At the end of the decade, the Berkeley psychologist Arthur Jensen asked famously, "How much can we boost IQ and scholastic achievement?" and concluded, infamously, that genetic limitations would prevent much boosting, and that, consequently, the well-known gap in IQ scores between blacks and whites reflected an irremediable deficit in the native intellectual abilities of blacks.[11] Jensen's claim, while published in a mainstream forum, has not held up well, as I detail below.[12]

By the second half of the twentieth century, these scholars had been marginalized by the postwar orthodoxy that group differences in intelligence were effectively negligible. They nevertheless found an outlet: a journal founded in 1960 called the *Mankind Quarterly,* which congealed around a few unrepentant hereditarians. Paramount among them were the journal's two associate editors. One was a botanical geneticist named R. R. Ruggles Gates, who was effectively the last formal polygenist, arguing that the human races were actually distinct species.[13] Gates was such a vile figure to the geneticist and lifelong socialist J. B. S. Haldane, that the latter, living in India, resigned from the Indian Statistical Institute rather than host a visit from Gates.[14] The other associate editor was the psychologist and segregationist Henry Garrett, who maintained that "the equalitarian dogma" was the nefarious work of anthropologists, Jews, and communists.[15]

Shortly after the journal began publication, it was savaged comprehensively in a major review for *Current Anthropology* by Juan Comas.[16] Some anthropologists who had innocently accepted an association with the journal were scandalized by it.[17] A letter to *Science*, the magazine published by the American Association for the Advancement of Science (AAAS), declared that, because "*The Mankind Quarterly*'s attitude is so harmful . . . I hope the AAAS takes some action."[18] The Oxford anthropologist G. A. Harrison wrote in the British journal *Man*, "Few of the contributions have any merit whatsoever, and many are no more than incompetent attempts to rationalize irrational opinions. . . . It is earnestly hoped that *The Mankind Quarterly* will succumb before it can further discredit anthropology and do more damage to mankind."[19]

The *Mankind Quarterly* remained intact and in print, however, because it was subsidized by a foundation called the Pioneer Fund. The fund maintained a rather shadowy philanthropic existence until being "outed" by articles in *Rolling Stone*, *GQ*, and the *New York Review of Books* in the wake of the notoriety of *The Bell Curve*.[20] The Pioneer Fund, it turned out, was a goose laying golden eggs for academicians interested in advancing the notion that innate factors determine one's life course. Begun in 1937, its first president was the eugenicist Harry Laughlin (who had stunned even other eugenicists by accepting an honorary doctorate from the Nazi-controlled Heidelberg University a year earlier). It has since supported many of the most famous hereditarian scholars, paramount among them Arthur Jensen (to the tune of over a million dollars).

Charles Lane's scrutiny of *The Bell Curve*'s references turned up citations to five articles published in the *Mankind Quarterly* and seventeen researchers who have published there. The *Mankind Quarterly* is not, however, a mainstream scholarly outlet, and publishing within it constitutes a statement of identity. Perhaps the most interesting aspect of *The Bell Curve*'s bibliography is the citation of eleven articles by the Canadian psychologist J. Philippe Rushton, and a preemptive coda to appendix 5 defending Rushton's work as "not that of a crackpot or a bigot" and "plainly science" (p. 643).

So it is worth asking why *The Bell Curve* is so defensive about J. Philippe Rushton. What are his ideas? The answer is that Rushton's ideas are weird and scandalous: that Africans have been the subjects of natural selection for high fertility and low intelligence, Asians for low fertility and high intelligence, and that Europeans are a happy medium; and, moreover, that these traits can be read in surrogate variables, such as brain size, degree of cultural advancement, crime rate, and penis size.[21] Said Rushton to an interviewer, "It's a trade-off; more brains or more penis. You can't have everything."[22] Sensitive to the possibility that Rushton's work might give sociobiology a bad name (as if such a thing were possible!) David Barash reviewed it in *Animal Behaviour* in the most uncompromising terms: "[Aggregating unreliable and incomparable data sets, Rushton's work holds out] the pious hope that by combining little turds of variously tainted data, one can obtain a valuable result; but in fact, the outcome is merely a larger than average pile of shit." And, lest his feelings be misconstrued, he says, "Bad science and virulent racial prejudice drip like pus from nearly every page of this despicable book."[23] Rushton's work is never cited favorably by mainstream scholars.

In 2000, Rushton's publisher purchased mailing lists from the American Anthropological Association, American Sociological Association, and American Psychological Association and sent their memberships unsolicited copies of an abridgement of Rushton's book, an unprecedented act more like that of a propagandist than a scientist and precipitating much controversy in, for example, *Anthropology News.* This printing and mailing was underwritten by the Pioneer Fund.[24]

With friends like these, suffice it to say, *The Bell Curve* hardly needs enemies. The book's associations with a source of funding rooted in archaic ideologies and its screwy contemporary outlet, and the extensive citation and defense of the bizarre work of Rushton, make it clear that this is no ordinary work of scholarship.[25] It is, rather, a radically partisan work, a work of advocacy in the manner of a lawyer's brief, not a scientist's ratiocination. It fails to make the crucial distinction between possibly credible support for its position and that of the lunatic fringe. It thus requires an adversarial approach modeled on the judicial system to be understood properly, rather than the approach reserved for more familiar scientific work.[26]

To say, then, that *The Bell Curve* was controversial is to miss the point. It was an adversarial argument framed in a nonadversarial venue, a prosecutor without a defense attorney. No wonder it might have seemed reasonable at first glance!

IQ IS NOT AN INNATE BRAIN FORCE

Central to *The Bell Curve*'s argument is the possibility of assessing intelligence with some degree of accuracy. Two assumptions enter into it: (1) that intelligence is a property that can be linearized—reduced to a single scale on which everyone can be placed and then compared meaningfully; and (2) that it can be discerned in pencil-and-paper tests.

Once again, some history is valuable. A French psychologist named Alfred Binet developed the idea of posing standardized problems to French schoolchildren in the early 1900s in order to identify those who required extra attention. He did not intend his test to represent anybody's basic mental capacity; rather, he intended it simply to help teachers discern who was progressing faster or slower than others in school.

The score soon became a "quotient" by dividing the result by the subject's age, creating a ratio of the subject's "mental" age and chronological age. In other words, it asked whether the child was doing things done mostly by older children. The IQ concept was imported into the United States by Herbert Goddard, Lewis Terman, and Robert Yerkes and transformed into a measure supposed to assess someone's innate brain power.

This American twist on IQ was augmented by the British psychologist Charles Spearman, who found that children's performance on different kinds of tests was often correlated: a child who did well on one kind of test generally did well on another. He developed a statistical tool called "factor analysis" to analyze the correlations among data sets, and ultimately concluded that the correlated test scores indicated the presence of a general factor underlying intelligence, which he called "g."[27]

Early tests given to recruits during World War I and to immigrants entering America often quizzed them on knowledge of popular culture or urban American society. Giving tests to illiterates posed only minor problems, as a parallel test was devised that required no reading or writing. Not surprisingly, the best scores were consistently obtained by well-educated and acculturated urban whites.

Even as the tests were redesigned, however, their results came under fire because they were promoted by their administrators as evaluating something more than the degree of formal and informal Euro-American education obtained up to that point by the subject. As early as the 1920s, researchers giving IQ tests to non-Westerners realized that any test of intelligence is strongly, if subtly, imbued with cultural biases. In an appendix to *Coming of Age in Samoa,* Margaret Mead relates that Samoans, when given a test requiring them to trace a route from point A to point B, often chose not the most direct route (the "correct" answer), but rather the most aesthetically pleasing one.[28] Australian aborigines found it difficult to understand why a friend would ask them to solve a difficult puzzle and not help them with it.[29] Indeed, the assumption that one must provide answers alone, without assistance from those who are older and wiser, is a statement about the culture-bound view of intelligence.[30] Certainly the smartest thing to do, when faced with a difficult problem, is to seek the advice of more experienced relatives and friends!

Other ethnographic examples abound.[31] Among the Yakima of the Pacific Northwest, the charge to complete the intelligence test as rapidly as possible was senseless; they wanted to do it correctly and saw no need to hurry about it. Among the Dakota, to answer a question that someone else could not answer would be considered arrogant.

Thus if the subjects do not share the same assumptions as the researchers, and are not motivated in precisely the same manner as the designers of the tests and the initial subjects, they will not score as well. Seeing middle-class white American values such as haste, directness, and individualism rewarded disproportionately as if they were transcendent measures of innate cerebral power, one can only marvel at such naïveté. Moreover, it is hard to imagine that the ability to participate successfully in a buffalo hunt, say, is in any way measured by pencil-and-paper tests.

Nevertheless, the tests measure something. What they measure well is exactly what they were originally designed to measure: performance in school. Children with high IQs often do well in school, and since children who do well in school often go on to higher education and better-paying jobs, it should come as no surprise that one can readily find correlations among the variables of IQ, school performance, and income.

One of the basic mantras of science education is that correlation does not imply causation. What this means is that, although two measures may vary together, so that knowing one permits you a better-than-random estimate of the other, that simple pattern does not tell you whether A causes B, B causes A, or both are caused by something else. Simply by *observing* the relationship between two variables, we are not in a position to *explain* that relationship.

The Bell Curve is chock-full of correlations, the kind that anyone can get out of a basic sociology database. Yes, people who go to college tend to have higher IQs than those that do not. Yes, people who go to college tend to earn more than people who do not. Yes, blacks in America tend to earn less, go to college less frequently, and have a lower average IQ score than whites. *The Bell Curve*'s interpretation, however, is that blacks go to college less often and earn less *because* their average IQ is lower. Whether the truth lies in correlation ("*and* their average IQ is lower") or causation ("*because* their average IQ is lower"), the next question is the important one: What can be done about it? This was the question posed by Arthur Jensen, the most cited researcher in *The Bell Curve*, and the recipient of the greatest amount of the Pioneer Fund's largesse. *The Bell Curve* argues that, because IQ is a set, genetic trait, we simply cannot boost IQ or scholastic achievement much.

THE ENVIRONMENT IS SUBTLE AND COMPLEX

It has become axiomatic in the social sciences that the more social variables you control, the more similar two populations become in their IQs. Herrnstein and Murray recognize this and acknowledge that their own data—the National Longitudinal Survey of Youth, part of which included an IQ-like Armed Forces Qualifying Test—show it too. The raw difference in IQ by race in their database is reduced by over 35 percent when they compare blacks and whites of roughly the same socioeconomic status.

Their socioeconomic status measure is rather crude, however: it consists of a combination of parental education, parental occupation, and family income, with the latter constituting "by far the most common missing variable" in over one-fifth of the data (p. 574). If the gap is reduced by over one-third with such a measure of "environment," one could imagine that the remaining 65 percent—nine points or so—must be due to heredity.

Alternatively—and perhaps more scientifically—one might imagine that if controlling in such a facile way reduces the gap by over one-third, then perhaps the rest of the gap can be accounted for by controlling for other, more subtle social variables. That is exactly what other studies have attempted and demonstrated, and what *The Bell Curve* either ignores or actually *criticizes:* notably, J. R. Mercer's 1988 study which found that IQs of Latino and non-Latino students converged once eight variables were controlled: (1) "mother's participation in formal organizations, (2) living in a segregated neighborhood, (3) home language level, (4) socioeconomic status based on occupation and education of head of household, (5) urbanization, (6) mother's achievement values, (7) home ownership, and (8) intact biological family."[32] Put another way, *The Bell Curve* itself controls grossly and inadequately for social and cultural differences, and it minimizes work that did so more comprehensively and came to the opposite conclusion. This is surely as great a perversion of ordinary scientific standards as any creationist could devise!

In fact, a reanalysis of the database actually used by Herrnstein and Murray showed that more subtle social variables did have a major impact on the difference in scores. Factoring in community context, urbanism, and family size reduced the gap dramatically. Indeed, the very way in which *The Bell Curve* created an "index" for socioeconomic status diluted the strong effect of family income on IQ score.[33] In their own data, "the black-white gap in math and reading scores could be totally accounted for by the following differences between black and white children: family income, size of household, proportion of students in the school the mother attended who were poor, the age the child was weaned, whether the child was read to, and, most important, how much the home was emotionally supportive and cognitively stimulating. Black and white children similar to one another in these conditions performed similarly on the tests."[34]

It would be extraordinarily naive to suppose that simply controlling for income could make two racialized samples comparable.[35] Black people making $60,000 and white people making $60,000 do not lead identical lives; the experience of growing up black in America is simply different from the experience of growing up white in America. A banal observation, I should think (yet apparently lost on the authors of *The Bell Curve*), and demonstrated nicely in a recent study of birth weight.

Black mothers are at considerably higher risk for low birth-weight babies than white mothers, a fact duly noted even in *The Bell Curve* (pp. 332–33). A large difference remains even when you compare white mothers and black mothers at the same income levels. Biological? Yes. Birth weight is certainly a biological attribute. Racial? Yes. The sample is contrasted on the basis of race. Innate? Possibly. But what R. J. David and J. W. Collins Jr. did was to introduce a third group of mothers as a control—African-born women who had immigrated to the United States. This group clustered not with the African American mothers, but with the *white* mothers.[36] The obvious conclusion, drawn by the authors, is that the higher probability of having a low birth weight baby is biological and "racial"—but is a consequence of the experience of growing up black in America, not a feature of the African gene pool.

We may note that low birth weight also correlates with reduced IQ; so once again, this is a subtle feature emphasizing the difference between growing up black and growing up white in America. Parsing a data set so that the only nongenetic variables you control for are parental occupation, education, and income hardly scratches the surface of the differences in the circumstances of life between black and white people in America. No wonder *The Bell Curve*'s analysis found it couldn't account for the entire IQ gap!

HERITABILITY IS A RED HERRING

In fact, it is well known that minorities commonly fare poorly on IQ tests, in rough proportion to the degree of oppression and social prejudice they are obliged to endure. Historically, eastern European Jews did so poorly on IQ tests that the tests "would rather disprove the popular belief that the Jew is highly intelligent."[37] In 1924 these Jews would be specifically targeted by the Johnson Immigration Restriction Act, on account of their bad "germ-plasm," but seventy years later they comprise Herrnstein and Murray's "cognitive elite"!

Likewise, Koreans in Japan, where there is strong prejudice against them, do significantly worse on IQ tests than Japanese. In America, Koreans and Japanese are on a par in IQ , and both are among Herrnstein and Murray's "cognitive elite." In South Africa, whites of Dutch ancestry consistently fared worse than whites of English ancestry (whose ancestors beat them in the Boer War)—but they reached parity in the 1970s, after a few decades of Afrikaner political dominance. In many cases, the socially inferior group is necessarily bilingual, and the children take the test in what is in effect their second language.[38] As the anthropologist John Ogbu has noted, there is a widespread tendency to interpret such differences in naturalistic terms—it relieves the dominant classes of responsibility for the disparities in social and economic circumstances.[39] But the historical ephemerality of those very group differences in IQ makes it difficult to sustain the "biological" explanation in any of those cases.

The most compelling argument invoked for the innateness of IQ is the fact that it has a significant "heritability." This was raised by Arthur Jensen in 1969 and provoked a considerable amount of discussion; and it is still raised by Richard Lynn—another favorite source in *The Bell Curve,* regular contributor to the *Mankind Quarterly,* and beneficiary of the Pioneer Fund.[40] Consequently, the term requires a bit of exegesis.

Heritability is technically the amount of variation associated with genetic factors divided by the total observable variation for a particular trait. I say "associated with genetic factors" rather than "caused by genetic factors" because there is no mechanistic argument involved—no genes isolated and transcribing messenger RNA in this analysis; the measure is correlational.[41] Consequently, heritability is *not* an estimate of the genetic contribution to a trait. If this sounds paradoxical and confusing, it is. This is a term whose ambiguity has been exploited to great effect. Since the denominator—the total observable variation—incorporates environmental factors, it follows that by changing the environment you can change the measured heritability. Thus, the measure can have only local and specific relevance, since the environment is local and specific.[42]

This in turn means that heritability estimates cannot be applied across populations: an estimate of heritability is specific to the population and situation in which it was measured, for the simple reason that it incorporates variation due to environmental factors, which must be population specific and situation specific.

Heritability, then, is a contextualized description of a population, not a property of the trait.[43]

In Richard Lewontin's famous example from the Jensen years, imagine two identical plots of soil.[44] A handful of seed is sown in each; the seeds are genetically different from one another. One plot of soil receives sunlight, water, and fertilizer; the other does not. In the first plot, the plants vary in size, and that variation is largely associated with (and presumably due to) their genetic differences. Plant height in that plot has a very high heritability. In the other plot, the plants also vary in height, also on account of their genetic differences, and so plant height also has a high heritability there. But these plants are all somewhat stunted due to their environmental deprivation. Thus the two populations of plants both have high heritabilities for height, but the large difference between the two populations is entirely due to environmental factors. Lewontin also did the opposite mental experiment: Seed drawn from two different inbred lines will yield plants that vary in size across the plots because of the genetic differences between the strains; yet the heritability will be zero for both plots, for there is no genetic variation in either. *Heritability is not a measure of the innateness of a trait.*

Coming at it from the other side, consider the number of digits a human being has, strongly determined genetically to be exactly twenty, an inheritance from a remote aquatic pentadactyl ancestor.[45] Yet the heritability of digit number in a modern population is quite low. Why? Because although some rare people have a genetic condition of polydactyly, the leading causes of deviations from twenty are physical accidents (i.e., loss of fingers or toes). Very little of the observable variation is associated with genetic variation; nevertheless the trait is very strongly genetically programmed. Among the Pennsylvania Amish (in whom Ellis–van Creveld Syndrome is found, which includes a phenotype of polydactyly, and in whom there are presumably fewer industrial accidents), we would expect the heritability of digit number to be higher. Again: *heritability is not a measure of the innateness of a trait*.

You can measure heritabilities of anything in any population. N. Block notes that "wearing earrings" had a high heritability in America prior to about 1980, when it was strongly negatively associated with a Y-chromosome; since that time the heritability has decreased.[46] Any gendered activity would have a significant heritability, since it would be associated with the genetic distinctions of sex: thus, the heritability of "baby-sitting" has been measured to be about .4! The result, he notes, can be "*intelligible, but it does show that heritability is a strange statistic*."[47]

Another example that may be illustrative of the absence of causality is the heritability statistic. Imagine a society in which people with a particular genetic trait—say, blue eyes—are routinely shunted off to deprived, intellectually unstimulating sites. Someone with blue eyes will thus tend to have a low measured IQ, and variation in IQ will tend to have a strong association with genetic difference, since a genetically rooted feature is forming the basis of this imaginary segregation. Blue eyes may thus be considered a significant cause of the low IQs, but only in an indirect sense. The real cause is the action of this odious social program upon the relatively innocuous natural variation. But the measurement of heritability will not permit that crucial inference to be drawn.

Let us return, then, to the extensive arguments by Herrnstein and Murray that IQ has a heritability of .6–.8. Whether that is true, or whether the heritability of IQ is substantially lower, as others have argued, the calculation is irrelevant to the issue at hand.[48] The issue was supposedly the observed difference between populations on standardized tests, and what can be done about it.

Given that the genetic-statistical argument of the innateness of the black-white difference in IQ is spurious, we are then in a position to ask, "What other kinds of evidence are there?" And, as in earlier debates about innateness, we can turn for powerful data to the historical changes between generations of the same population.

Here we encounter a phenomenon that Herrnstein and Murray acknowledge as troubling. It is simply that, as intelligence tests have remained stable over the last few decades, various modernized populations have increased substantially in IQ.[49] People today do better on the same tests than their parents did. Describing a seven-point increase in IQ over the course of a generation for the Japanese, A. Anderson properly classifies it along with the changes in height, body proportions, health, urbanism, and education that have occurred over the same period.[50] In Holland, the mean IQ rose twenty-one points in thirty years; in America the change is closer to fifteen points. As Douglas Wahlsten puts it bluntly, "More recently born children exceed the raw intelligence of their own parents at a comparable age by almost the same average amount as Americans of European ancestry exceed Americans of African ancestry."[51]

Could any reasonable person then deny the sensitivity of IQ to the conditions of life and the obvious possibility of blacks and whites ultimately equilibrating? Herrnstein and Murray could, and do (pp. 308–9).

Apart from the evidences of secular trends in IQ, there is of course a considerable body of data on the importance of the circumstances of life for determining the IQ. The researchers C. Capron and M. Duyme found a major difference in IQ between French children adopted by wealthy parents and those adopted by poor parents, and a difference between children born to wealthy parents and those born to poor parents, which they attributed to prenatal conditions.[52] C. Jencks and M. Phillips summarize the effects of race and parenting: "Black children adopted by white parents had IQ scores 13.5 points higher than black children adopted by black parents. . . . Mixed-race children who lived with a white mother scored 11 points higher than mixed-race children who lived with a black mother."[53]

THE CONTRIBUTION OF ANTHROPOLOGICAL SCIENCE

The Bell Curve is an ideological treatise that selectively reviews and selectively criticizes existing literature and tortures a new database to defend the proposition that American social policy should be predicated on the inability of social conditions to ameliorate economic and academic disparities between the nation's black and white populations.[54]

The relationship between the observed disparities and the inferred differences in "cognitive ability" recalls a dispute in early-twentieth-century anthropology. Does the fact that someone does not do something mean they cannot? When Franz Boas distinguished formally between race and culture (or biology and history) in *The Mind of Primitive Man,* he was arguing specifically against the proposition that it was possible to infer properties of individual mental capacity from observing the achievements of groups.[55] Lurking always in the shadows was the ghost of Count Arthur de Gobineau, who had asked rhetorically, "So the brain of a Huron Indian contains in an undeveloped form an intellect which is absolutely the same as that of the Englishman or Frenchman! Why, then, in the course of ages, has he not invented printing or steam power? I should be quite justified in asking our Huron why, if he is equal to our European peoples, his tribe has never produced a Caesar or a Charlemagne among its warriors, and why his bards and sorcerers have, in some inexplicable way, neglected to become Homers and Galens."[56]

What Gobineau took for granted is that "did not" means "could not." What the inhabitants of a country do not accomplish is a poor guide to their abilities: Europeans did not build the pyramids, but thousands of years later they do build skyscrapers. The fact that Gobineau could not name a Huron poet or healer says something about the bias provided by written records and, of course, about Gobineau's own ignorance. The fact that Gutenberg and Fulton were not Hurons does not mean much, considering that they weren't French either, so Gobineau's claim to their inventions lies merely in sharing the continent of their origin—a tenuous (if democratizing) connection, to be sure. The Hurons shared their continent with many peoples who did some pretty impressive things too, after all, like the Maya, Anasazi, and Incas. And of course, cultural history is contingent on its precedents: it took several thousand years of European history before Fulton could perfect the steamship. If the Hurons had known they were in a race, they might have worked harder at it!

Thus, there is a basic asymmetry between "didn't" and "couldn't." The fact that someone does something means that they could do it; the fact that they did not do it *does not* mean that they *could not* do it.

This can be more readily expressed as an epistemological dilemma: the difference between ability and performance. On the one hand, we have a cultural notion of ability, a set of potentials with an existence independent of the contexts that make them manifest. It is a transcendent property, a reality that underlies any particular example of a subject's life and achievements. On the other hand, we have no way to measure it, or to perceive it. All that is accessible to us is performance, what real people do, either in the course of their lives or simply in an afternoon. And performances are predicated on many things, only one of which is ability. Thus, the asymmetry: if you score 160 on an intelligence test, it means you had the ability to do so; but if you don't score 160, it doesn't mean you did not have the ability.

The very vocabulary used by Herrnstein and Murray, and by psychometricians widely and unfortunately, is telling: they claim that tests measure "cognitive ability."

But they do not.

They cannot.

Nothing can. Cognitive ability is a metaphysical concept; *any* ability is a metaphysical concept if it is taken to be decontextualized and separate from the conditions of life. Any measured attribute of a human being is already partly determined by the life that has already been lived, and shaped by its experiences. In more concrete terms, consider that the tests used by Herrnstein and Murray, the Armed Forces Qualifying Test, had a component of vocabulary. One does not have to be much of a philosopher to recognize that it must be testing, in part, *the words you have been exposed to,* or the degree of sophistication of speech you have already experienced. There is no sense in which it could possibly be measuring innate cranial potential, for that potential, if it ever existed, has been molded and given expression by the conditions of life.

It is, however, possible to make sense of the relationships among genetics, IQ tests, and intelligence if we begin by considering the pattern or structure of the variation. Human behavior differs principally from group to group. Its variants constitute what we mean by "culture"— *between-group* variation in thought and deed. Genetic variation, on the other hand, has a very different structure. Paradigmatic is the ABO blood group, in which all populations have all three variants in varying proportions. That pattern seems to account for over 80 percent of the detectable genetic variation in the human species: it is *within-group* variation. In addition to the different patterns of variation, immigrant studies make it quite clear that the between-group variation in behavior that we call "cultural" is, as Boas noted, historical in origin, not biological. This creates an a priori difficulty in seeing how genetic variation could be a major component of behavioral variation. All of which is not to deny a genetic component to human behavior, of course: it is simply that most human behavior varies from group to group and is nongenetic (it is cultural-historical in origin); yet within a group, people may differ from one another for reasons ranging from family experiences and ethnic tradition to genetics. However, from the patterns detectable in the human gene pool now, it is most likely that any such genetic variation would have a much larger within-group component than between-group component; thus, any average differences in the distribution of such alleles are very likely to be tiny and overwhelmed by other factors. Consequently, the existence of IQ alleles should not be particularly threatening, given what we already know of real-world genes and their effects. No such discussion, of course, is to be found in *The Bell Curve*, which relies heavily on more archaic concepts, such as innateness, immutability, and constitutional differences.[57]

CONCLUSION

The most basic lesson in the human sciences is that statements about human biology are invariably political, particularly at the level of group comparisons, where one is looking for ostensibly innate features. *The Bell Curve* leads its reader from scientific-looking data and arguments to an endpoint about social policy, concluding that programs of social intervention are effective only for a very small number of people and, by implication, should be scaled back (pp. 549–50). Social diversity reflects a diversity of endowments, and unequal endowments, it tells us, are just a fact of life (p. 551). And to the extent that a civil society strives to maximize the quality of life for all, that responsibility should be borne by the neighborhood, not by the government (p. 540).

One of the instructive lessons of the controversy over Carleton Coon's 1962 *Origin of Races* is that scholars on the political left and scholars on the political right recognized the political import of the work. Only the author himself—perhaps disingenuously, but certainly it was his public stance—denied it.[58] It is, of course, a self-serving stance to deny all responsibility for one's scientific writings. But ultimately such a position calls into question the very nature and validity of science itself.

At the dawn of the modern era, Francis Bacon articulated the value of science to an intellectual community that was, at best, suspicious of it.[59] Bacon's ultimate justification for supporting the new scientific philosophy was that it would improve people's lives. But four centuries later we are faced with an inversion of the Baconian promise for science: some science actually exists with the goal of increasing the level of *misery* in the world. Given its scholarship, citations, and associations, it is hard to see the goal of *The Bell Curve* as other than to rationalize economic inequality, to perpetuate injustice, and to justify social oppression. Such science gives the rest of the field a bad name. Moreover, it is tempting to speculate upon the ultimate fate of science (and subsequent European history) if works like *The Bell Curve* had been known in the seventeenth century, when early advocates were risking their fortunes and reputations to convince their readers that this new thing, science, was both benign and oriented toward human betterment.

CODA

J. Philippe Rushton became president of the Pioneer Fund in 2002, upon the death of Harry F. Weyher. Weyher's recollections, published in 2001, included vacationing with the segregationist activist Henry Garrett ("a fun person") and polygenist Ruggles Gates ("also a good companion").[60] Upon succeeding to the presidency, Rushton embarked upon a perfervid defense of the Pioneer Fund in response to extensively documented critiques by W. H. Tucker and P. A. Lombardo.[61] Rushton's own work, ostensibly showing that the average IQ of indigenous Africans is set at seventy, is invoked favorably by V. Sarich and F. Miele, whose problematic book on race comes adorned with jacket blurbs by Arthur Jensen and Charles Murray.[62]

Notes

1. INTRODUCTION

1. www.word-detective.com/020798.html, accessed on May 10, 2004.

2. Edward Said, "Clash of Definitions," in *Reflections on Exile and Other Essays* (Cambridge: Harvard University Press, 2000), pp. 569–90; quote is on p. 573.

3. We are not implying that there is something uniquely American about mythmaking, punditry, or the views espoused by some of the pundits targeted here. But because of America's power and global dominance, the ideas propagated by America's pundits have a radically disproportionate influence in the world.

4. Marjorie Shostak, *Nisa: The Life and Words of a !Kung Bushwoman* (Cambridge: Harvard University Press, 2000); and Theodora Kroeber, *Ishi in Two Worlds: A Biography of the Last Wild Indian in North America* (Berkeley: University of California Press, 2002).

5. Robert D. Kaplan, *The Coming Anarchy: Shattering the Dreams of the Post Cold War* (New York: Random House, 2000), book jacket.

6. Ibid., p. 30.

7. Ibid., pp. 45, 49.

8. Samuel Huntington, *The Clash of Civilizations* (New York: Touchstone Books, 1996), pp. 138, 258.

9. Thomas Friedman, *The Lexus and the Olive Tree* (New York: Farrar, Straus, and Giroux, 1999), p. 270.

10. Dinesh D'Souza, *The Virtue of Prosperity: Finding Values in an Age of Techno-Affluence* (New York: Free Press, 2000), p. xi.

11. Ibid., p. 76.

12. Ibid., p. 126.

13. Ibid., pp. 182–83.

14. Barbara Ehrenreich, *Nickel and Dimed: On (Not) Getting By in America* (New York: Metropolitan Books, 2001).

15. James Baldwin, *The Fire Next Time* (New York: Dial Press, 1963), p. 34.

2. THE SEVEN DEADLY SINS OF SAMUEL HUNTINGTON

Epigraphs: Alfred Kroeber, "The Delimitation of Civilization," *Journal of the History of Ideas* 14 (1953): 264–75; my thanks to Barney Bate for drawing my attention to this quotation. Edward Said, "Clash of Definitions," in *Reflections on Exile and Other Essays* (Cambridge: Harvard University Press, 2000), pp. 569–90; quote is on p. 585.

1. Samuel Huntington, "The Clash of Civilizations?" *Foreign Affairs* 72, no. 3 (1993): 22–49; and Huntington, *The Clash of Civilizations and the Remaking of World Order* (New York: Touchstone Books, 1996).

2. After the September 11, 2001, attacks on the Pentagon and the World Trade Center, a number of conservative commentators, citing Huntington, pointed to the terrorist attacks as evidence of the aggressiveness of Muslims and of an impending "clash of civilizations" between Islam and the West. Interestingly, Thomas Friedman, one of the other figures critiqued in this volume, himself attacks this argument, saying, "The real clash today is actually not *between* civilizations but *within* them." He goes on, echoing the argument developed in *The Lexus and the Olive Tree* (New York: Farrar, Straus, and Giroux, 1999), to characterize the "real" clash as "between those Muslims, Christians, Hindus, Buddhists and Jews with a modern and progressive outlook and those with a medieval one"; "Smoking or Non-Smoking?" *New York Times*, September 14, 2001, p. A27.

3. This is actually a quotation from Pierre Lellouche, cited in Huntington, *The Clash of Civilizations*, pp. 203–4. See also Robert Kaplan, *The Coming Anarchy: Shattering the Dreams of the Post Cold War* (New York: Random House, 2000).

4. Ulf Hannerz, "Borders," *International Social Science Journal* 154 (1997):

537–48. The Nuer are in Africa; the Tikopia, in Melanesia; and the Kwakiutl, in North America.

5. Huntington, *The Clash of Civilizations*, p. 158.

6. Ibid., p. 158.

7. Ibid., p. 160.

8. To muddy the water still further, in *Black Athena: The Afroasiatic Roots of Classical Civilization* (New Brunswick, N.J.: Rutgers University Press, 1989), Martin Bernal argues that classical Greek civilization was strongly influenced by the Africans Huntington is unsure about crediting with civilization. Bernal argues that the African influence on ancient Greek culture has been systematically erased in Western educational genealogies. See Said, "Clash of Definitions," for a discussion of the implications of this for Huntington's argument.

9. Aihwa Ong, *Flexible Citizenship: The Cultural Logics of Transnationality* (Durham, N.C.: Duke University Press, 1999), p. 188.

10. Huntington is here quoting from Adda Bozeman, "Civilizations under Stress," *Virginia Quarterly Review* 51 (winter 1975): 1–18; quote is on p. 1.

11. Said, "Clash of Definitions," p. 581.

12. See Margaret Mead, *Coming of Age in Samoa: A Psychological Study of Primitive Youth for Western Civilization* (New York: Blue Ribbon Books, 1928); and Ruth Benedict, *Patterns of Culture* (Boston: Houghton Mifflin, 1934).

13. James Clifford, *The Predicament of Culture: Twentieth Century Ethnography, Literature, and Art* (Cambridge: Harvard University Press, 1988); Renato Rosaldo, *Culture and Truth: The Remaking of Social Analysis* (Cambridge, Mass.: Beacon Press, 1989). Rosaldo says that "the garage sale . . . provides a precise image for the postcolonial situation where cultural artifacts flow between unlikely places, and nothing is sacred, permanent, or sealed off" (p. 44).

14. Hannerz, "Borders," pp. 537–48.

15. The words are quoted from Fouad Ajami, "The Impossible Life of Muslim Liberalism," *New Republic* 2 (June 1986): 27.

16. On the Ilongot, see Renato Rosaldo, *Ilongot Headhunting* (Stanford: Stanford University Press, 1984); on the Semai, see Clayton Robarchek, "Ghosts and Witches: The Psychocultural Dynamics of Semai Peacefulness," in *The Anthropology of Peace and Nonviolence*, ed. Leslie Sponsel and Thomas Gregor (Boulder, Colo.: Lynne Rienner, 1994), pp. 183–96.

17. John Dower, *Embracing Defeat: Japan in the Wake of World War II* (New York: W. W. Norton, 1999).

18. At the time of writing, for example, there is considerable speculation in the American media about the connection between Halliburton's ability to win huge contracts for the postwar reconstruction of Iraq without competitive bidding and the fact that the company's former chief executive officer, Dick Cheney, is vice president of the United States. In the world of defense contracting more

generally, it is well known that the revolving personnel door between the Pentagon and leading defense contractors is vital to those contractors' strategies for winning government contracts. For a glimpse behind the curtain of this world, see Dan Briody, *The Iron Triangle: Inside the Secret World of the Carlyle Group* (Hoboken, N.J.: John Wiley and Sons, 2003).

19. Anthropological readers will recognize here an allusion to Mary Douglas, *Purity and Danger: An Analysis of the Concepts of Pollution and Taboo* (New York: Ark Books, 1984). Douglas argues that we often experience things as dirty or dangerous not because they are intrinsically so but because they confuse categories and thereby destabilize our sense of cognitive order.

20. Said, "Clash of Definitions," p. 583.

21. Ong, *Flexible Citizenship*, p. 188.

22. Ibid.

23. Clifford Geertz, *The Interpretation of Cultures* (New York: Basic Books, 1973).

24. The phrase is Tahsin Bashir's, cited in Huntington, *The Clash of Civilizations*, p. 174.

25. One cannot help but notice that certain features of Huntington's thought are—there is no other word for it—fascist. His use of the language of disease to describe cultural mixing is one example; his sense that population growth is a reliable index of civilizational vigor is another.

26. Clifford Geertz, *Islam Observed* (New Haven: Yale University Press, 1968).

27. Huntington, *The Clash of Civilizations*, p. 258. The final quotation is from James Payne, *Why Nations Arm* (Oxford: Basil Blackwell, 1989), p. 124.

3. SAMUEL HUNTINGTON, MEET THE NUER

1. Samuel Huntington, "The Clash of Civilizations?" *Foreign Affairs* 72, no. 3 (1993): 22–49.

2. This chapter focuses on Huntington's extended restatement of his 1993 argument in *The Clash of Civilizations and the Remaking of World Order* (New York: Simon and Schuster, 1996). His book also contains a new strand of argument not present in the article, dealing with the importance of demographic pressures, especially in the Muslim world. At some length, Huntington traces out the phenomenon of the "youth-bulge," when the age cohort between the ages of fifteen and twenty-five reaches a certain critical percentage of the total population of a country. This age group provides the main personnel for violent action: their numbers make a state, or a civilization, "aggressive," until birthrates decline. For reasons of space, and because Huntington himself does not fully integrate the different arguments, this chapter does not discuss this compelling dimension of the book.

3. Huntington, *Clash of Civilizations*, p. 40.

4. Huntington acknowledges Mead and Benedict in his preface to a subsequent work he coedited, *Culture Matters: How Values Shape Human Progress*, ed. Lawrence E. Harrison and Samuel P. Huntington (New York: Basic Books, 2000), p. xiv. References to works by Alfred Kroeber, along with Clyde Kluckhohn, Emile Durkheim, and Marcel Mauss, are tucked away in the footnotes in *Clash of Civilizations*, p. 325.

5. Clifford Geertz, *Local Knowledge: Further Essays in Interpretive Anthropology* (New York: Basic Books, 1983).

6. For examples of this kind of work, particularly focused on the culture concept, see Lila Abu-Lughod, "Writing against Culture," in *Recapturing Anthropology: Working in the Present*, ed. Richard G. Fox (Santa Fe, N.M.: SAR Press, 1991), pp. 137–62; Robert Hayden, "The Triumph of Chauvinistic Nationalisms in Yugoslavia: Bleak Implications for Anthropology," *Anthropology of East Europe Review* 11, no. 1–2 (1993): 73–79; John Borneman, "Anthropology as Foreign Policy," *American Anthropologist* 97, no. 4 (1995): 663–71.

7. Huntington, *Clash of Civilizations*, p. 289. For a critical assessment of Huntington's theory and its applicability to the war in Bosnia, see also Florian Bieber, "The Conflict in Former Yugoslavia as a 'Fault-Line War'? Testing the Validity of Samuel Huntington's 'Clash of Civilizations,'" *Balkanologie* 3, no. 1 (1999): 33–48.

8. David Schneider, "Some Muddles in the Models: Or, How the System Really Works," in *The Relevance of Models for Social Anthropology*, ed. Michael Banton (London: Tavistock Press, 1965), pp. 25–86.

9. In this regard, the thrust of this chapter is rather different from other anthropological responses to Huntington's article. For an example of work that urges anthropologists to balance their focus on their own turf—culture—with work in the traditional preserves of political science, see Aihwa Ong, "Clash of Civilizations or Asian Liberalism? An Anthropology of the State and Citizenship," in *Anthropological Theory Today*, ed. Henrietta L. Moore (London: Polity Press, 1999), pp. 48–72.

10. Huntington, *Clash of Civilizations*, p. 20.

11. Ibid., p. 28.

12. Ibid., p. 126. Huntington used the same example again in 1999, in an address at Colorado College, after Austria, Finland, and Sweden had become members of the European Union—or "rejoined their cultural kin."

13. Ibid., p. 156.

14. Ibid., p. 233.

15. Ibid., p. 254.

16. Ibid., p. 323n. Greenway is the second person, after Henry Kissinger, that Huntington cites. The notion that "kin-" sentiments exist between groups within one state and a neighboring state, and that such sentiments can be mobilized

politically, is of course much older. One study focusing on the Balkans, which also used the concept of syndrome, was Myron Weiner, "The Macedonian Syndrome: An Historical Model of International Relations and Political Development," *World Politics* 23, no. 4 (1971): 665–83.

17.   Recent collected works include Peter Schweitzer, ed., *Dividends of Kinship: Meanings and Uses of Social Relatedness* (London: Routledge, 2000); Janet Carsten, ed., *Cultures of Relatedness: New Approaches to the Study of Kinship* (Cambridge: Cambridge University Press, 2000).

18.   David Schneider, *A Critique of the Study of Kinship* (Ann Arbor: University of Michigan Press, 1984). See also Richard Feinberg and Martin Ottenheimer, eds., *The Cultural Analysis of Kinship: The Legacy of David M. Schneider* (Urbana: University of Illinois Press, 2001).

19.   Edward Evans-Pritchard, *The Nuer* (Oxford: Oxford University Press, 1940).

20.   Michael Herzfeld, *The Poetics of Manhood: Contest and Identity in a Cretan Mountain Village* (Princeton, N.J.: Princeton University Press, 1985). Herzfeld has also used Evans-Pritchard's insights elsewhere, perhaps most explicitly in "Segmentation and Politics in the European Nation-State: Making Sense of Political Events," in *Other Histories*, ed. Kirsten Hastrup (London: Routledge, 1992), pp. 62–81.

21.   Thomas Hylland Eriksen, *Ethnicity and Nationalism: Anthropological Perspectives* (London: Pluto Press, 1993), pp. 152–54; Peter Sahlins, *Boundaries: The Making of France and Spain in the Pyrenees* (Berkeley: University of California Press, 1989), pp. 110–12.

22.   The eminent anthropologist Clifford Geertz explored both these aspects of Evans-Pritchard's work in *Works and Lives: The Anthropologist as Author* (Stanford: Stanford University Press, 1988), where he famously dubbed *The Nuer* "that anthropological geometry book" (p. 67).

23.   Evans-Pritchard, *The Nuer*, p. 136.

24.   Ibid., p. 143.

25.   In one alternative metaphor for civilizational solidarity, Huntington calls civilizations armies, in which nations are regiments, and tribes or ethnic groups are platoons (*Clash of Civilizations*, p. 128). The military hierarchy suggests normative obedience to the bugle call of common culture.

26.   Edward Evans-Pritchard, *Kinship and Marriage among the Nuer* (Oxford: Clarendon Press, 1951).

27.   Sharon E. Hutchinson, *Nuer Dilemmas: Coping with Money, War, and the State* (Berkeley: University of California Press, 1996), p. 28.

28.   Ibid., p. 250.

29.   Susan McKinnon, "Domestic Exceptions: Evans-Pritchard and the Creation of Nuer Patrilineality and Equality," *Cultural Anthropology* 15, no. 1 (2000): 35–83; quote is on p. 62.

30. David Schneider, *American Kinship: A Cultural Account* (Chicago: University of Chicago Press, 1980), p. 18.

31. Ibid., p. 70.

32. Kath Weston, *Families We Choose: Lesbians, Gays, Kinship* (New York: Columbia University Press, 1991); John Borneman, "Caring and Being Cared For: Displacing Marriage, Kinship, Gender, and Sexuality," in *The Ethics of Kinship: Ethnographic Inquiries,* ed. James D. Faubion (Lanham, Md.: Rowman and Littlefield, 2001), pp. 29–46.

33. Huntington, *Clash of Civilizations,* p. 290.

34. Gilbert Achcar, "Rasputin Plays at Chess: How the West Blundered into a New Cold War," in *Masters of the Universe? NATO's Balkan Crusade,* ed. Tariq Ali (London: Verso Books, 2000), p. 57.

35. Ger Duijzings, *Religion and the Politics of Identity in Kosovo* (London: Hurst and Company, 1999), p. 207.

36. Ibid., p. 121.

37. Huntington, *Clash of Civilizations,* p. 317.

38. Eugene Hammel, *Alternative Social Structures and Ritual Relations in the Balkans* (Englewood Cliffs, N.J.: Prentice-Hall, 1968).

39. Winston Churchill, *Triumph and Tragedy* (Boston: Houghton Mifflin, 1953), p. 227.

40. Robert Fisk, "The Baby Was Named Kfor: She Lived for Two Days," *The Independent,* June 15, 1999.

41. For an elegant exposition of the link people make between local and national histories, see David E. Sutton, "Local Names, Foreign Claims: Family Inheritance and National Heritage on a Greek Island," *American Ethnologist* 24 (1997): 837–52.

42. See, for example, Kim Richard Nossal, "Throwing Out the Baby with the Bathwater? Huntington's "Kin-Country" Thesis and Australian-Canadian Relations," in *Shaping Nations: Constitutionalism and Society in Australia and Canada,* ed. Linda Cardinal and David Headon (Ottawa: University of Ottawa Press, 2002), pp. 167–81.

43. On international relations, see the contributions in Yosef Lapid and Friedrich Kratochwil, eds., *The Return of Culture and Identity in IR Theory* (Boulder Colo.: Lynne Rienner, 1996). In his widely cited work on social capital in the United States, Robert Putnam notes that social capital was distributed along lines that reveal the endurance of three cultures (traditionalistic, individualistic, and moralistic) identified in the country by the sociologist Daniel Elazar in the 1950s; *Bowling Alone: The Collapse and Revival of American Community* (New York: Simon and Schuster, 2000), p. 346.

44. Schneider, *A Critique of the Study of Kinship,* p. 193.

4. HAUNTED BY THE IMAGINATIONS OF THE PAST

1.   Robert D. Kaplan, *Balkan Ghosts: A Journey through History* (New York: St. Martin's Press, 1996), xxvii.

2.   Ibid., xxxi.

3.   Ibid., xxix.

4.   Maria Todorova, *Imagining the Balkans* (Oxford: Oxford University Press, 1997), 188.

5.   See Kaplan, *Balkan Ghosts,* xxvii and below.

6.   "Fresh Garlands for Ancient Battles," *Congressional Record,* 103d Cong., May 27, 1993, p. S6701.

7.   For instance, the U.S. secretary of state, Warren Christopher, argued that "the hatred between all three groups—the Bosnians and the Serbs and the Croatians—is almost unbelievable. It's almost terrifying, and it's centuries old. That really is a problem from hell." Roger Cohen, *Hearts Grown Brutal: Sagas of Sarajevo* (New York: Random House, 1988), 243. President Clinton suggested that the war could stop only when "people there get tired of fighting each other" (244).

8.   Kaplan, *Balkan Ghosts,* back cover of the 1996 Vintage edition.

9.   Ibid., x.

10.   Ibid., 22.

11.   Ibid. For scholarly accounts of the history of the Bosnian Muslims, see Ivo Banac, *The National Question in Yugoslavia: Origins, History, Politics* (Ithaca, N.Y.: Cornell University Press, 1984); Robert Donia, *Islam under the Double Eagle: The Muslims of Bosnia Hercegovina, 1878–1914,* East European Monographs no. 78 (New York: Columbia University Press, 1981); John V. A. Fine Jr., *The Bosnian Church: A New Interpretation,* East European Monographs no. 10 (Boulder, Colo.: East European Quarterly, 1975; distributed by Columbia University Press); William G. Lockwood, *European Moslems: Economy and Ethnicity in Western Bosnia,* Studies in Anthropology (New York: Academic, 1975). Here, for obvious reasons, I mention only literature published before 1993, when *Balkan Ghosts* was published for the first time. In addition, the following books published since 1993 may be consulted: Francine Friedman, *The Bosnian Muslims: Denial of a Nation* (Boulder, Colo.: Westview Press, 1996); Noel Malcolm, *Bosnia, a Short History* (London: Macmillan, 1994); Mark Pinson, ed., *The Muslims of Bosnia-Herzegovina: Their Historic Development from the Middle Ages to the Dissolution of Yugoslavia,* Harvard Middle Eastern Monographs no. 28 (Cambridge: Harvard University Press, 1993).

12.   Kaplan, *Balkan Ghosts,* 22.

13.   Individuals' abuse of alcohol and drugs may, in a context of violence and impunity, have removed their reticence to commit atrocities against fellow

human beings. From survivors' testimonies, it is well known that Serbian "irregular forces" who raped, tortured, and committed other atrocities were often drunk. But this does not mean that a brew of savage hatred, poverty, and alcohol consumption was the cause of the war or its driving force.

14. Lockwood, *The European Moslems*.

15. Tone Bringa, *Being Muslim the Bosnian Way: Community and Identity in a Central Bosnian Village* (Princeton: Princeton University Press, 1995).

16. In his book *Medjugorje: Religion, Politics, and Violence in Rural Bosnia* (Amsterdam: VU Uitgeverij, 1995), Mart Bax describes a different, antagonistic, and sometimes violent relationship between Catholic (nationalist) Croats and Orthodox (communist) Serbs in a rural community in western Herzegovina.

17. Tone Bringa, "Nationality Categories, National Identification, and Identity Formation in 'Multinational' Bosnia," in *Anthropology of East Europe Review,* special issue: *War among the Yugoslavs,* n.s. 11, nos. 1–2 (spring–fall 1993); Bringa, *Being Muslim the Bosnian Way;* Bringa, "Averted Gaze: Genocide in Bosnia-Herzegovina, 1992–1995," in *Annihilating Difference: The Anthropology of Genocide,* ed. Alexander Laban Hinton (Berkeley: University of California Press, 2002).

18. Bax, *Medjugorje;* Bringa, *Being Muslim the Bosnian Way;* Tone Bringa, review of *Medjugorje: Religion, Politics, and Violence in Rural Bosnia* by Mart Bax, *American Ethnologist* 24, no. 1 (1997); Bringa, "Averted Gaze"; Lockwood, *The European Moslems;* Ivana Macek, *War Within: Everyday Life in Sarajevo under Siege* (Uppsala, Sweden: Uppsala University Publications, 2000); Noel Malcolm, *Bosnia, a Short History* (London: Macmillan, 1994); Chuck Sudetic, *Blood and Vengeance: One Family's Story of the War in Bosnia* (New York: W. W. Norton, 1998); Kemal Kurspahic, *As Long as Sarajevo Exists* (Stony Creek, Conn.: Pamphleteer's Press, 1997); Ivan Lovrenovic, *Bosnia: A Cultural History* (London: Saqii Books, 2001); Donia J. Robert and John V. A. Fine Jr., *Bosnia and Hercegovina: A Tradition Betrayed* (London: Hurst and Company, 1994).

19. See Mark Thompson, *Forging War: The Media in Serbia, Croatia, and Bosnia-Hercegovina* (Luton, U.K.: University of Luton Press, 1999); Kemal Kurspahic, *Primetime Crime: Balkan Media War and Peace* (Washington, D.C.: United States Institute of Peace Press, 2003).

20. See V. P. Gagnon Jr., "Ethnic Nationalism and International Conflict: The Case of Serbia," *International Security* 19, no. 3 (winter 1994–1995): 367–90; Gagnon, "Ethnic Conflict as Demobilizer: The Case of Serbia," Cornell University, Institute for European Studies Working Paper no. 96.1 (1996), www.ithaca.edu/gagnon/articles/demobil, accessed on May 1, 2002. In his book *From Voting to Violence,* Jack Snyder argues in a similar vein that "popular nationalism typically arises during the earliest stages of democratization when elites use nationalist appeals to compete for popular support"; *From Voting to Violence: Democratization and Nationalist Conflict* (New York: W. W. Norton, 2000), 32.

21. The quote is from Noel Malcolm, "Seeing Ghosts," *National Interest* 32 (summer 1993): 84.

22. Ivo Andric, *The Bridge of Drina* (Chicago: University of Chicago Press, 1984).

23. Hukanovic's book was first published in 1993 in Norwegian and Bosnian. The English language edition, however, was not published until 1996 (*The Tenth Circle of Hell* [New York: Basic Books]).

24. Kaplan, *Balkan Ghosts,* xxvii.

25. That year, the situation deteriorated further with the eruption of full-scale war between the Bosnian Croat separatists and the Sarajevo government, who previously had been in an uneasy alliance. The Bosnian army was fighting the Bosnian Serb army to the south, east, and north, and Bosnian Croat forces on the western and central fronts. In central Bosnia, there were pockets within pockets held alternately by the Bosnian government and Croat separatist forces.

26. Rebecca West, *Black Lamb and Grey Falcon: A Journey through Yugoslavia* (1942; reprint, London: Macmillan, 1984).

27. Felicity Rosslyn, "Rebecca West, Gerda, and the Sense of Process," in *Black Lamb and Grey Falcons: Women Travelers in the Balkans,* ed. John B. Allcock and Antonia Young (Bradford, U.K.: Bradford University Press, 1991), 104.

28. Todorova, *Imagining the Balkans,* 188.

29. See Kaplan, *Balkan Ghosts,* 8.

30. Ibid., 7.

31. Ibid.

32. Samuel P. Huntington, *The Clash of Civilizations and the Remaking of World Order* (New York: Simon and Schuster, 1996). In an essay published in *Time* magazine, Slavenka Drakulic succinctly captures the homogenizing and immobilizing effect of the aggressive nationalisms that developed in her native Croatia as it fought a war with its neighbors. She also describes how the violence and nationalist propaganda reduce multifarious identities to one—the nation—a straitjacket that people are sooner or later pushed into; "Overcome by Nationhood," *Time* (January 20, 1992): 27.

33. See Michael T. Kaufman, "The Dangers of Letting a President Read," *New York Times,* May 22, 1999, pp. 16–18; Richard Holbrooke, *To End a War* (New York: Random House, 1998).

34. Kaplan, *Balkan Ghosts,* 1993: x; 1996: xi.

35. Robert D. Kaplan, "Reading Too Much into a Book," *New York Times,* June 13, 1999, pp. 4–7.

36. Malcolm, "Seeing Ghosts," 84. Also see this article for a review of further examples of such stereotypes and imagery in *Balkan Ghosts.*

37. See Malcolm, "Seeing Ghosts."

5. WHY I DISAGREE WITH ROBERT KAPLAN

Portions of this chapter have already appeared in *PoLAR: The Journal of Political and Legal Anthropology* 23, no. 1 (2000): 25–32. Several colleagues scrutinized this chapter and suggested dozens of additional problems with Kaplan's vision that I leave unaddressed. While space constraints forced me to choose among far too many points to critique, I am grateful to Angelique Haugerud, Hugh Gusterson, Rosalind Shaw, the anthropology departments at University of Cape Town and Colby College, and, especially, Pauline Peters for commentary.

1. Robert D. Kaplan, "The Coming Anarchy," *Atlantic Monthly* 273 (February 1994): 44–76. Reprinted in Robert D. Kaplan, *The Coming Anarchy: Shattering the Dreams of the Post Cold War* (New York: Random House, 2000).

2. Kaplan's essay made a particular impact in foreign policy circles, and it joined the list of required university readings across the country. Geoffrey Dabelko reports that the article prompted Vice President Al Gore to direct the CIA "to oversee a systematic investigation of the causes of 'state failure' it described"; Dabelko, "The Environmental Factor," *Wilson Quarterly* (autumn 1999). President Bill Clinton reportedly found the article "'stunning,' remarking that it 'makes you really imagine a future that's like one of those Mel Gibson "Road Warrior" movies'"; Clinton quoted in Robert Kagan, "The Return of Cheap Pessimism: Inside the Limo," *New Republic Online* (April 10, 2000).

3. Paul Richards, *Fighting for the Rain Forest: War, Youth, and Resources in Sierra Leone* (Oxford: James Currey Press; Portsmouth, N.H.: Heinemann, 1996), p. xlv.

4. Mary Catherine Bateson, "It's Just a Game, Really," *New York Times*, August 27, 2000, sec. 4, p. 15, col. 1.

5. See, for example, Carolyn Nordstrom, *A Different Kind of War Story* (Philadelphia: University of Pennsylvania Press, 1997).

6. Peter Uvin, *Aiding Violence: The Development Enterprise in Rwanda* (West Hartford, Conn.: Kumarian Press, 1988); Christopher Taylor, *Sacrifice as Terror: The Rwandan Genocide of 1994* (Oxford: Berg Press, 1999); Alison Des Forges, *"Leave None to Tell the Story": Genocide in Rwanda* (New York: Human Rights Watch; Paris: International Federation of Human Rights, 1999); Philip Gourevitch, *We Wish to Inform You That Tomorrow We Will Be Killed with Our Families: Stories from Rwanda* (New York: Picador, 1998).

7. Uvin, *Aiding Violence.* p. 17.

8. Estimates of the number murdered vary between eight hundred thousand and 1 million.

9. Uvin, *Aiding Violence.*

6. GLOBALIZATION AND THOMAS FRIEDMAN

For helpful comments on an earlier draft, I thank Catherine Besteman, Marc Edelman, Hugh Gusterson, Micaela di Leonardo, Jonathan Marks, Wendy Weisman, and Eric Worby, as well as participants in the fall 2001 Rutgers cultural anthropology discussion group and the October 2001 MIT workshop, "Culture Goes Public." Eric Worby served as discussant for this chapter at the MIT workshop and provided particularly detailed comments, not all of which can be addressed here.

1. Thomas L. Friedman, "Senseless in Seattle," *New York Times*, December 1, 1999.

2. Ibid., p. A23; Thomas L. Friedman, "Senseless in Seattle II," *New York Times*, December 8, 1999, p. A23.

3. Although in the United States the term *liberalism* tends to be equated with the political left and big government, in many other countries *liberalism* refers to free markets, parliamentary democracy, and the political right—hence the wide use outside the United States of the term *neoliberalism* to refer to the economic policies favored by Reagan and Thatcher.

4. Thomas L. Friedman, *The Lexus and the Olive Tree* (New York: Anchor Books, 2000), pp. 104–5.

5. Here, he was writing before the wide media exposure of scandals involving corporations such as Enron, WorldCom, and Tyco.

6. Friedman, "Senseless in Seattle"; Friedman, "Senseless in Seattle II." In the first of these two columns, Friedman termed the Seattle protesters "crazy," "ridiculous," and, as noted in the chapter opening, "a Noah's ark of flat-earth advocates, protectionist trade unions and yuppies looking for their 1960s fix."

7. Friedman, *The Lexus and the Olive Tree*, p. xxi.

8. Mark Rupert created "The Anti–Thomas Friedman Page," found on the Web at www.maxwell.syr.edu/maxpages/faculty/merupert/Anti-Friedman.htm, accessed on May 1, 2004.

9. For thoughtful discussions of alternatives, see George DeMartino, *Global Economy, Global Justice: Theoretical Objections and Policy Alternatives to Neoliberalism* (New York: Routledge, 2000); the final chapter of Joseph E. Stiglitz, *Globalization and Its Discontents* (New York: W. W. Norton, 2001); John Cavanagh, Daphne Wysham, and Marcos Arruda, eds., *Beyond Bretton Woods: Alternatives to the Global Economic Order* (London: Pluto Press, 1994); David C. Korten, *When Corporations Rule the World*, 2d ed. (Bloomfield, Conn.: Kumarian Press; San Francisco: Berrett-Koehler, 2001); Heikki Patomaki, *Democratizing Globalization: The Leverage of the Tobin Tax* (London: Zed Books, 2001).

10. See, for example, Emma Crewe and Elizabeth Harrison, *Whose Development? An Ethnography of Aid* (London: Zed Books, 1998).

11. So observed Eric Worby in his discussant's commentary on an earlier version of this chapter.

12. See Timothy Mitchell, "America's Egypt," in *Power of Development,* ed. Jonathan Crush (London: Routledge, 1995), pp. 129−57.

13. A hundred pages after his Egypt anecdote, Friedman writes that a pure market vision is inadequate because it is "too brutal and politically unsustainable" (*The Lexus and the Olive Tree,* 444). On the other hand, he believes that the paternalism of the welfare state is not economically sustainable. The only way— the "balanced way," as he puts it—to stabilize globalization is the approach of what he terms the integrationist social-safety-netters such as Bill Clinton and Tony Blair (and Friedman himself).

14. See John Bowen, "The Myth of Global Ethnic Conflict," *Journal of Democracy* 7, no. 4 (1996): 1−14; Kwame Anthony Appiah, "African Identities," in *In My Father's House* (New York: Oxford University Press, 1992), pp. 173−80; Leroy Vail, *The Invention of Tribalism in Southern Africa* (Berkeley: University of California Press, 1988); Thomas Spear and Richard Waller, eds., *Being Maasai: Ethnicity and Identity in East Africa* (London: James Currey; Athens, Ohio: Ohio University Press, 1993).

15. Friedman, *The Lexus and the Olive Tree,* pp. 434, 436.

16. See chapter 5 by Catherine Besteman in this volume.

17. For example, anthropologists who have written about the Rwanda genocide include Susan E. Cook, Villia Jefremovas, Charles Mironko, and Christopher Taylor, among others. Historians include Alison Des Forges, David Newbury, Gerard Prunier, Jan Vansina, and Michele Wagner. Political scientists include Rene Lemarchand, Mahmood Mamdani, Catharine Newbury, and Peter Uvin. Interested readers may find the following sources helpful: Alison Des Forges, *"Leave None to Tell the Story": Genocide in Rwanda* (New York: Human Rights Watch; Paris: International Federation of Human Rights, 1999); Susan E. Cook, "Documenting Genocide: Cambodia's Lessons for Rwanda," *Africa Today* 44, no. 2 (1997): 223−27; Philip Gourevitch, *We Wish to Inform You That Tomorrow We Will Be Killed with Our Families: Stories from Rwanda* (New York: Farrar, Straus, and Giroux, 1998); Villia Jefremovas, *Brickyards to Graveyards: From Production to Genocide in Rwanda,* Anthropology of Work Series, ed. June Nash (New York: State University of New York Press, 2002); Rene Lemarchand, "The Apocalypse in Rwanda," *Cultural Survival Quarterly* 18, no. 2−3 (1994): 29−33; Mahmood Mamdani, *When Victims Become Killers: Colonialism, Nativism, and the Genocide in Rwanda* (Princeton, N.J.: Princeton University Press, 2001); Charles Mironko and Peter Uvin, "Western and Local Approaches to Justice in Rwanda," special issue of *Global Governance* 9, no. 2 (April−June 2003), ed. Charles Call and Susan E. Cook; Catharine and David Newbury, "A Catholic Mass in Kigali: Contested Views of the Genocide and Ethnicity in Rwanda," *Canadian Journal of African Studies* 33,

no. 2–3 (1999): 292–328; Samantha Power, *"A Problem from Hell": America and the Age of Genocide* (New York: Basic Books, 2002); Gerard Prunier, *The Rwanda Crisis: History of a Genocide* (New York: Columbia University Press, 1995). See also the special issue of *Africa Today*, "Crisis in Central Africa," 45, no. 1 (January–March 1998), with contributions by Florence Bernault, Catharine Newbury, Thomas Spear, Jan Vansina, and Michele D. Wagner.

18.   For a brilliant evaluation of the morality of neoliberalism and alternatives to it, see George DeMartino, *Global Economy, Global Justice: Theoretical Objections and Policy Alternatives to Neoliberalism* (New York: Routledge, 2000).

19.   See the Adam Smith excerpt and discussion in Marc Edelman and Angelique Haugerud, eds., *Anthropology of Development and Globalization: From Classical Political Economy to Contemporary Neoliberalism* (Malden, Mass.: Blackwell, 2005).

20.   Eric Worby's formulation.

21.   For an overview, see Marc Edelman, "Social Movements: Changing Paradigms and Forms of Politics," *Annual Review of Anthropology* 30 (2001): 285–317.

22.   Angelique Haugerud, *The Culture of Politics in Modern Kenya* (Cambridge: Cambridge University Press, 1995).

23.   "Popular Attitudes to Markets, Selected African Countries, 1999–2000," www.afrobarometer.org/survey2.html, accessed on May 1, 2003.

24.   Joseph E. Stiglitz, *Globalization and Its Discontents* (New York: W. W. Norton, 2002).

25.   Jeffrey Sachs, *Resolving the Debt Crisis of Low-Income Countries*, Brookings Papers on Economic Activity 2002:1 (Washington, D.C.: Brookings Institution).

26.   Figures on global economic inequality in this paragraph are taken from the following sources: David Korten, *When Corporations Rule the World*, 2d ed. (Bloomfield, Conn.: Kumarian Press; San Francisco: Berrett-Koehler, 2001); Philip McMichael, *Development and Social Change: A Global Perspective*, 2d ed. (Thousand Oaks, Calif.: Pine Forge Press, 2000); and United Nations Development Program, *Human Development Report* (New York: United Nations Development Program, 1999).

27.   For example, an Oxfam campaign "exposes the double standards of rich countries' trade barriers"—a free trade agenda that "brings together an unlikely coalition of liberal lobby groups, governments and the World Bank"; Faisal Islam, "Counting the Real Cost of a Cup of Coffee," *Guardian Weekly* 167, no. 26 (January 1, 2003): 17.

28.   See, for example, David Graeber, "The Globalization Movement: Some Points of Clarification," *Items and Issues* (Social Science Research Council, New York) 2, nos. 3–4 (2001): 12–14; and Graeber, "The Globalization Movement and the New Left," in *Implicating Empire: Globalization and Resistance in the Twenty-first Century*, ed. Stanley Aronowitz and Heather Gautney (New York: Basic Books, 2003). See also journalist Naomi Klein's book, *No Logo* (New York: Picador USA, 2002).

29.   The WTO's judicial panels hold hearings and deliberations in secret, and the public usually is not allowed to see legal briefs, supporting evidence, or transcripts from cases, such as the one in which a trade panel ruled it illegal for the United States to require imported shrimp to be caught with nets that allow sea turtles to escape. Critics of WTO secrecy include representatives of groups such as the Sierra Club, the International Forum on Globalization, and Public Citizen's Global Trade Watch, as well as the consumer advocate Ralph Nader.

30.   Friedman, "Senseless in Seattle."

31.   Ibid.

32.   Ibid., p. A23; Friedman, "Senseless in Seattle II," p. A23.

33.   See Edelman, "Social Movements."

34.   See Thomas Friedman, "Evolutionaries," *New York Times*, July 20, 2001.

35.   In this sentence I draw, with thanks, on Eric Worby's conference commentary.

36.   "The WTO under Fire," *The Economist* 368, no. 8342 (September 20–26, 2003): 26–28.

7. ON *THE LEXUS AND THE OLIVE TREE*

Epigraph: This proverb is commonly associated with Abraham Lincoln's talk at a Republican state convention in Bloomington, Indiana, on May 29, 1856. The folklorist Alan Dundes, however, informs us that it is now generally agreed that Lincoln did not coin this statement. Our thanks to Dave Barry, a funny American guy in not-so-funny American times.

1.   Thomas Friedman, *The Lexus and the Olive Tree: Understanding Globalization* (New York: Farrar, Straus, and Giroux, 1999). Friedman is described on the book cover as having won the National Book Award for *From Beirut to Jerusalem*. Before the reader ever gets to the book, the opening page begins with review snippets from major newspapers—the *New York Times Book Review, New York Times, Boston Globe, Minneapolis Star Tribune, Christian Science Monitor,* and *Foreign Affairs*—and the quotes are exuberant: "The best (and most enjoyable) answer yet [to what globalization means]. . . . [Friedman] knows how to cut through the arcana of high tech and high finance with vivid images and compelling analogies. . . . A delightfully readable book. . . . Breathtaking . . . exhilarating . . . a spirited and imaginative exploration of our new order of economic globalization. . . . Friedman gets the economics right . . . a lively mix of anecdote and analysis . . . full of solid reporting. . . . Friedman is eager, provocative, often entertaining . . . insightful."

2.   Thomas Friedman, *Longitudes and Attitudes: Exploring the World after September 11* (New York: Farrar, Straus, and Giroux, 2002).

3.   Incidentally, Woody Allen was wrong: he is definitely *not* the only man ever to have suffered from penis envy.

4.   Which, incidentally, also contributes to ending global warfare: see pp. 195−217.

5.   Franz Boas, *Race, Language, and Culture* (New York: Macmillan, 1955).

6.   www.businessweek.com/smallbiz/content/feb2002/sb20020214_7072.htm, accessed on May 10, 2004.

7.   Juliet Schor, *The Overworked American: The Unexpected Decline of Leisure* (New York: Basic Books, 1991).

8.   Kaiser Commission on Key Facts, "Medicaid and the Uninsured," February 2002, www.kff.org/uninsured/7048.cfm, accessed on May 5, 2004.

9.   See Peter Shorett, "Dogmas of Inevitability: Tracking Symbolic Power in the Global Marketplace," in *Essays in Controlling Processes,* ed. L. Nader, Kroeber Anthropological Society Papers no. 87 (Berkeley: University of California Press, 2002), pp. 219−41.

10.   Mark Green and Gail MacColl, *There He Goes Again: Ronald Reagan's Reign of Error* (New York: Pantheon Books, 1987).

11.   Thomas Frank, review of *The Lexus and the Olive Tree: Understanding Globalization,* by Thomas Friedman, *Harper's* 299, no. 1793 (October 1999): 72.

12.   On private-sector-based programs, see Steve Lerner, *Eco-Pioneers: Practical Visionaries Solving Today's Environmental Problems* (Cambridge: MIT Press, 1997); Harold Willens, *The Trimtab Factor: How Business Executives Can Help Solve the Nuclear Weapons Crisis* (New York: William Morrow, 1984); on strong state intervention, see Allan Chew, *Five-Lab Study Examines Carbon-Reduction Strategies* (Berkeley: Lawrence Berkeley National Laboratory, Environmental Energy Technologies Division, 1998); on nongovernmental organizations, activist movements, citizen resistance, and so on, see Daniel M. Berman and John T. O'Connor, *Who Owns the Sun? People, Politics, and the Struggle for a Solar Economy* (White River Junction, Vt.: Chelsea Green, 1996).

13.   Aldous Huxley, *Brave New World* (New York: Harper and Row, 1932); George Orwell, *1984* (New York: Signet Classic, 1950); on controlling processes, see Laura Nader, "Controlling Processes: Tracing the Dynamic Components of Power," *Current Anthropology* 38, no. 5 (December 1997).

14.   A. L. Kroeber, *Anthropology* (New York: Harcourt, Brace, 1948).

15.   Paul Krugman, review of *The Lexus and the Olive Tree,* by Thomas L. Friedman, *Washington Monthly* 3, no. 6 (June 1999): 49.

16.   Janine Wedel, *Collision and Collusion: The Strange Case of Western Aid to Eastern Europe, 1989−98* (New York: St. Martin's Press, 1998); Janet Abu-Lughod, *Before European Hegemony: The World System,* A.D. *1250−1350* (New York: Oxford University Press, 1989); C. Wright Mills, *The Power Elite* (New York: Oxford University Press, 1957), p. 161; Julia Paley, *Marketing Democracy: Power and Social*

Movements in Post-Dictatorship Chile (Berkeley: University of California Press, 2001), p. 485; Paley, "Toward an Anthropology of Democracy," *Annual Review of Anthropology* 31 (2002): 469–96; Jack Bilmes, "Freedom Not Regulation: An Anthropological Critique of Free Market Ideology," *Research in Law and Economics* 7 (1985): 123–47.

17. Clifford Geertz, *The Interpretation of Cultures* (New York: Basic Books, 1973), p. 57.

8. EXTRASTATE GLOBALIZATION OF THE ILLICIT

Epigraphs: (p. 138) Mark Findlay, *The Globalisation of Crime* (Cambridge: Cambridge University Press, 1999), p. 1; (p. 140) Hendrik Vaal Neto, *O Roque: Romance de um mercado* (Luanda, Angola: Fundação Eshivo, 2001), pp. 20–21, Nordstrom's translation from the Portuguese; (p. 142) Manuel Castells, *End of Millennium* (Oxford: Blackwell, 1998), pp. 166–68; (p. 146) from a discussion with an unnamed person involved in "extralegal" business in Africa, November 2001; (p. 150) Mark Chingono, *The State, Violence, and Development* (Aldershot, U.K.: Avebury, 1996), p. 114; (p. 152) Findlay, *The Globalisation of Crime*, p. 224.

1. The research presented here is based on approximately six years of fieldwork in the last twelve years, carried out predominantly in southern Africa and Europe but also in South Asia. This was made possible by grants from John T. and Catherine C. MacArthur Foundation, the United States Institute of Peace, and the University of Notre Dame, which allowed me to travel extensively internationally in researching globalizing il/licit economies.

2. These terms are loosely defined in the literature; all refer to activities that take place outside formal laws, but they designate different levels of "crime." *Illegal* is the strongest term, referring to breaking actual laws; *illicit* is a broader term that includes both breaking and circumventing laws; and *informal* refers to activities that technically take place outside the law but are not seen as dangerous.

3. Thomas Friedman, *The Lexus and the Olive Tree: Understanding Globalization* (New York: Farrar, Straus, and Giroux, 1999), p. 331.

4. Findlay, *The Globalisation of Crime*, p. 5.

5. Janet MacGaffey, *The Real Economy of Zaire: The Contributions of Smuggling and Other Unofficial Activities to National Wealth* (Philadelphia: University of Pennsylvania Press, 2001), p. 3.

6. George Lopez and David Cortwright, "Making Targets 'Smart' from Sanctions" (paper delivered at the International Studies Association meetings, Minneapolis, March 18–22, 1998); Bureau for International Narcotics and Law Enforcement Affairs, *International Narcotics Control Strategy Report 1996* (Washington, D.C.: Bureau for International Narcotics and Law Enforcements Affairs and U.S. Department of State, 1996).

7.   United Nations Research Institute for Social Development, *States of Disarray: The Social Effects of Globalization* (London: UNRISD, 1995).

8.   Gary Slapper and Steve Tombs, *Corporate Crime* (Essex, U.K.: Longman, 1999).

9.   Suraj B. Gupta, *Black Income in India* (New Delhi: Sage, 1992).

10.   Avner Greif, "Contracting, Enforcement, and Efficiency: Economics beyond the Law," in *Annual World Bank Conference on Development Economics, 1996*, ed. M. Bruno and B. Pleskovic (Washington, D.C.: World Bank, 1996).

11.   John McDowell and Gary Nevis, "The Consequences of Money Laundering and Financial Crime," in *The Fight against Money Laundering*, Economic Perspectives (Washington, D.C.: U.S. Dept. of State, Office of International Information Programs, 2001), pp. 4–6.

12.   For figures on global economies, see the World Bank Website, http://derdata.worldbank.org/data-query, accessed on January 15, 2004. Weapons figures: United Nations Research Institute for Social Development, *States of Disarray*.

13.   John Sevigny, "Mexican, U.S. Officials Discuss Measures to Combat Foreign Smuggling," *Environmental News Network*, www.enn.com/news/2003 -02-07/s.2548.asp, accessed on February 7, 2003; Melanie Gosling, reporter for the *Cape Argus* and specialist in Patagonian tooth fish smuggling, interview by author, October 2001; Detective Viljoen of the Scorpions (an elite South Africa police detective branch), interview by author, May 2002.

14.   Country directors of Hewlett-Packard and IBM, and the Computer Association of South Africa, interviews by author, February 2002.

15.   United Nations Office for Drug Control and Crime Prevention, *Global Report on Crime and Justice* (Oxford: Oxford University Press, 1999); Detective Richard Flynn, Scotland Yard, interview by author, September 2001.

16.   The dangerously criminal, the illicit, and the informally mundane cannot, in actual practice, always or easily be disaggregated. Consider, Castells writes, "everything that receives added value precisely from its prohibition in a given institutional environment: smuggling of everything from everywhere to everywhere, including radioactive material, human organs, and illegal immigrants; prostitution; gambling; loan-sharking; kidnapping; racketeering and extortion; counterfeiting of goods, bank notes, financial documents, credit cards, and identity cards; killers for hire, traffic of sensitive information, technology, or art objects; international sales of stolen goods; or even dumping garbage illegally from one country to another (for example, US garbage smuggled into China in 1996)"; *End of Millennium*, p. 167.

17.   McDowell and Novis, "The Consequences of Money Laundering and Financial Crime," pp. 4–6.

18.   Alexander Aboagye, United Nations Development Program senior economist in Angola, discussions with the author, 1998–2000.

19.   The October 2001 UN report on Angolan conflict diamonds confirmed that a major routing for conflict gems goes through Portugal.

20.   See Stockholm International Peace Research Institute Website (www.sipri .se) and the institute's annual yearbook on armaments and expenditures (*Stockholm International Peace Research Institute Yearbook* [Stockholm, Sweden: SIPRI]).

21.   Quoted in Chingono, *The State, Violence and Development*, p. 114.

22.   Susan Strange, *The Retreat of the State: The Diffusions of Power in the World Economy* (Cambridge: Cambridge University Press, 1996); Castells, *End of Millennium*.

23.   Susan Strange writes, "The fact is that while financial crime has grown enormously . . . it remains, legally and morally, an indeterminate gray area. The dividing line is seldom clear and is nowhere the same between transactions which are widely practiced but ethically questionable and those which are downright criminal. . . . The need to use such secret or covert financial channels is not only a prerogative of organized and economic criminal groups—but also of terrorist and revolutionary groups and indeed of many individuals and economic operators engaged in activities which are not necessarily illicit. Investigations into the biggest financial scandal of the last fifteen years, the bankruptcy of the Bank of Credit and Commerce [I]nternational, showed that BCCI was engaged in 'reserved' or illicit financial services for a very varied group of clients, including Colombian narco-traffickers, Middle-East terrorists and Latin American revolutionary groups, as well as tax evaders, corrupt politicians and several multinational companies"; *The Retreat of the State*, p. 117.

24.   Greif, "Contracting, Enforcement, and Efficiency," pp. 239–65; Ed Ayers, "The Expanding Shadow Economy," *World Watch* 9, no. 4 (1996): 11–23; Carolyn Nordstrom, "Shadows and Sovereigns," *Theory, Culture, and Society* 17, no. 4 (2000): 35–54.

25.   Castells, *End of Millennium*, p. 178.

9. CLASS POLITICS AND SCAVENGER ANTHROPOLOGY
   IN DINESH D'SOUZA'S *VIRTUE OF PROSPERITY*

I am indebted, in multiple senses of the term, to Geeta Patel and Anindyo Roy for suffering my rants and sharpening my critique. Julie Schor generously provided comments on the manuscript. Thanks as well to participants in the workshop convened by Catherine Besteman and Hugh Gusterson at MIT in the summer of 2001 to discuss the possibility of a book such as this.

1.   Dinesh D'Souza, *The Virtue of Prosperity: Finding Values in an Age of Techno-Affluence* (New York: Free Press, 2000).

2.   James Baldwin, *The Fire Next Time* (New York: Dial Press, 1968), 34.

3. Micaela di Leonardo, *The Varieties of Ethnic Experience: Kinship, Class, and Gender among California Italian-Americans* (Ithaca, N.Y.: Cornell University Press, 1984).

4. Beverly Daniel Tatum, *"Why Are All the Black Kids Sitting Together in the Cafeteria?" and Other Conversations about Race* (New York: Basic Books, 1997).

5. Steven Greenhouse, "Americans' International Lead in Hours Worked Grew in 90's, Report Shows," *New York Times on the Web,* September 1, 2001, 1–2, www.nytimes.com/2001/09/01/national/01HOUR.html, accessed on June 1, 2004.

6. Angela Y. Davis, "Incarcerated Women: Transformative Strategies," *Black Renaissance/Renaissance Noire* 1, no. 1 (1996): 21–34; Christian Parenti, *Lockdown America: Police and Prisons in the Age of Crisis* (New York: Verso, 2000); Kathryn Watterson, *Women in Prison: Inside the Concrete Womb,* 2d ed. (Boston: Northeastern University Press, 1996).

7. Kenneth Neubeck and Noel Cazenave, *Welfare Racism: Playing the Race Card against America's Poor* (New York: Routledge, 2001).

8. Karen V. Hansen and Anita Ilta Garey, eds., *Families in the United States: Kinship and Domestic Politics* (Philadelphia: Temple University Press, 1998); Murray A. Straus, Richard J. Gelles, and Suzanne K. Steinmetz, *Behind Closed Doors: Violence in the American Family* (Garden City, N.Y.: Anchor Books, 1981).

9. D'Souza, *The Virtue of Prosperity,* 234; Wayne Ellwood, *The No-Nonsense Guide to Globalization* (Oxford: Between the Lines and New Internationalist, 2001); Barbara Garson, *Money Makes the World Go Around: One Investor Tracks Her Cash through the Global Economy, from Brooklyn to Bangkok and Back* (New York: Penguin, 2002); Harold James, *The End of Globalization: Lessons from the Great Depression* (Cambridge: Harvard University Press, 2001).

10. D'Souza, *The Virtue of Prosperity,* 233.

11. Chuck Collins and Felice Yeskel, with United for a Fair Economy, *Economic Apartheid in America: A Primer on Economic Inequality and Insecurity* (New York: New Press, 2000), 64.

12. But see Kathleen Stewart, "Real American Dreams (Can Be Nightmares)," in *Cultural Studies and Political Theory,* ed. Jodi Dean (Ithaca, N.Y.: Cornell University Press, 2000), 243–44.

13. Marie Michael, "What Is the Poverty Line?" *Dollars and Sense* (January–February 2001): 43; Alice O'Connor, *Poverty Knowledge: Social Science, Social Policy, and the Poor in Twentieth-Century U.S. History* (Princeton, N.J.: Princeton University Press, 2001).

14. Gordon M. Fisher, "The Development and History of the Poverty Thresholds," *Social Security Bulletin* 55, no. 4 (1992): 3–14.

15. P. Sainath, *Everybody Loves a Good Drought: Stories from India's Poorest Districts* (New Delhi: Penguin Books India, 1996).

16. O'Connor, *Poverty Knowledge*.

17. Michael Hudson, ed., *Merchants of Misery: How Corporate America Profits from Poverty* (Monroe, Maine: Common Courage Press, 1996), 148.

18. Charmaine White Face, "It's Time for the United States to Grow Up," *Indian Country Today* (August 22, 2001).

19. Eric Schmitt, "Census Data Show a Sharp Increase in Living Standard," *New York Times on the Web*, August 6, 2001, pp. 1–4, www.nytimes.com/2001/08/06/national/06CENS.html, accessed on June 1, 2004.

20. Collins and Yeskel, *Economic Apartheid in America*, 19.

21. Lendol Calder, *Financing the American Dream: A Cultural History of Consumer Credit* (Princeton: Princeton University Press, 1999).

22. Ibid., 31.

23. Sainath, *Everybody Loves a Good Drought*, 446.

24. Margaret Drabble, *The Peppered Moth* (New York: Harcourt, 2001).

25. Kim Phillips, "Lotteryville, USA," in *Commodify Your Dissent*, ed. Thomas Frank and Matt Weiland (New York: W. W. Norton, 1997).

26. Pico Iyer, *The Global Soul: Jet Lag, Shopping Malls, and the Search for Home* (New York: Vintage, 2000).

27. Barbara Ehrenreich, *Nickel and Dimed: On (Not) Getting By in America* (New York: Metropolitan Books, 2001).

28. Kiran Nagarkar, *Ravan and Eddie* (New Delhi: Penguin India, 1995).

29. Bonnie Thornton Dill, *Across the Boundaries of Race and Class: An Exploration of Work and Family among Black Female Domestic Servants* (New York: Garland, 1994); Judith Rollins, *Between Women: Domestics and Their Employers* (Philadelphia: Temple University Press, 1985).

30. Council of Economic Advisors, *Families and the Labor Market, 1969–1999: Analyzing the Time Crunch* (Washington, D.C.: Government Printing Office, 1999).

31. Ida Susser, "The Construction of Poverty and Homelessness in US Cities," *Annual Review of Anthropology* 25 (1996): 411–35.

32. Mark Maier, "Teaching about Stocks—for Fun and Propaganda," *Dollars and Sense* (March–April 2001): 28–30, 41.

33. Pierre Bourdieu, *Acts of Resistance: Against the Tyranny of the Market* (New York: New Press, 1999), 3.

10. SEX ON THE BRAIN

Thanks to Catherine Besteman, Teresa Lawson, Susan Oyama, Thomas Paxson, Dmitry Portnoy, Miranda von Dornum, and anonymous reviewers for helpful comments on this chapter, and to Hugh Gusterson and Catherine Besteman for inviting our contribution to this volume.

1. Diane Ackerman, *A Natural History of Love* (New York: Random House, 1994); Susan Allport, *A Natural History of Parenting: From Emperor Penguins to Reluctant Ewes, a Naturalist Looks at Parenting in the Animal World and Ours* (New York: Harmony Books, 1997). See also Joanne Ellison Rodgers, *Sex: A Natural History* (New York: Times Books, 2002); and Olivia Judson, *Dr. Tatiana's Sex Advice to All Creation* (New York: Metropolitan Books, 2002).

2. Randy Thornhill and Craig T. Palmer, *A Natural History of Rape: Biological Bases of Sexual Coercion* (Cambridge: MIT Press, 2000).

3. Ibid., p. 6.

4. Susan Brownmiller, *Against Our Will: Men, Women, and Rape* (New York: Simon and Schuster, 1975).

5. Randy Thornhill and Craig T. Palmer, "Why Men Rape," *The Sciences* 40 (2000), 30–36. "The initial print run of 10,000 copies sold out by the first week of February [a week after it was released], and at least another 10,000 copies were ordered"; "Rape Debate," *News for Women in Psychiatry* 19, no. 2 (spring 2001): 6–7. See also Laura Flanders, "Natural Born Rapists," *In These Times*, March 6, 2000, p. 11.

6. Thornhill and Palmer, *A Natural History of Rape*, pp. xii–xiii.

7. Allied critiques—from evolutionary biology, psychology, and anthropology, among other fields—have recently been collected in *Evolution, Gender, and Rape*, ed. Cheryl Brown Travis (Cambridge: MIT Press, 2003).

8. Thornhill and Palmer, *A Natural History of Rape*, p. 12.

9. Other texts in the tradition of evolutionary psychology include Leda Cosmides and John Tooby, "From Evolution to Behavior: Evolutionary Psychology as the Missing Link," in *The Latest on the Best: Essays on Evolution and Optimality*, ed. John Dupré (Cambridge: MIT Press, 1987), pp. 277–306; A. Figueredo and L. McCloskey, "Sex, Money, and Paternity: The Evolutionary Psychology of Domestic Violence," *Ethology and Sociobiology* 14 (1993): 353–79; Jerome Barkow, Leda Cosmides, and John Tooby, eds., *The Adapted Mind: Evolutionary Psychology and the Generation of Culture* (Oxford: Oxford University Press, 1995); Charles Crawford and Dennis Krebs, eds., *Handbook of Evolutionary Psychology: Ideas, Issues, Applications* (Mahwah, N.J.: Lawrence Erlbaum Associates, 1997); David Buss, *Evolutionary Psychology: The New Science of the Mind* (Boston: Allyn and Bacon, 1999).

10. Thornhill and Palmer, *A Natural History of Rape*, p. 17.

11. The germinal text here is Robert Trivers, "Parental Investment and Sexual Selection," in *Sexual Selection and the Descent of Man, 1881–1971*, ed. B. Campbell (London: Heinemann, 1972), pp. 136–79, which builds on the arguments made one hundred years earlier in Charles Darwin, *The Descent of Man and Selection in Relation to Sex* (1871; reprint, Princeton N.J.: Princeton University Press, 1981). Linda Marie Fedigan analyzes how Darwin assumed the very categories—male and female—for which he was seeking an evolutionary genesis; "The Changing

Role of Women in Models of Human Evolution," *Annual Review of Anthropology* 15 (1986): 25–66.

12.   Thornhill and Palmer, *A Natural History of Rape*, p. 40.

13.   Ibid., p. 7.

14.   Ibid., pp. 20–21.

15.   Ibid., p. 16.

16.   Ibid., p. 61.

17.   Ibid., p. 9. There is something odd in the way they lead up to this point: "The challenge in applying an ultimate or evolutionary analysis is not to determine whether an adaptation is a product of selection; it is to determine the nature of the selective pressure that is responsible for the trait. That selective pressure will be apparent in the functional design of the adaptation." If it is apparent, why is it a challenge?

18.   Ibid., p. 3.

19.   Anne Fausto-Sterling, *Myths of Gender: Biological Theories about Women and Men*, rev. ed. (New York: Basic Books, 1992), p. 160.

20.   Thornhill and Palmer, *A Natural History of Rape*, p. 120.

21.   Ibid.

22.   Ibid., p. 2.

23.   Ibid., p. 142.

24.   Ibid., p. 44.

25.   Ibid., p. 2.

26.   Ibid., p. 42. Thornhill and Palmer take for granted a preexisting difference between males and females, as did Darwin in *The Descent of Man and Selection in Relation to Sex*. Thornhill and Palmer's discussion of jealous husbands presumes that men have a sexual right over women; this is what Carole Pateman has called the "sexual contract." Pateman, *The Sexual Contract* (Stanford: Stanford University Press, 1988). Indeed, Thornhill and Palmer's discussions of marriage and husbands appear to be based on a presumption that females are the property of males.

27.   Hamish G. Spencer and Judith C. Masters, "Sexual Selection: Contemporary Debates," in *Keywords in Evolutionary Biology*, ed. Evelyn Fox Keller and Elizabeth A. Lloyd (Cambridge: Harvard University Press, 1992), pp. 294–301; quote is on p. 295.

28.   Thornhill and Palmer, *A Natural History of Rape*, p. 63.

29.   Ibid., p. 64–65. In response to other criticisms of this point, they write: "'We do discuss research on insects called scorpionflies that has identified a clamp on the top of the male's abdomen as an adaptation specifically for rape. This illustrates what an adaptation for rape is, but it does not follow that because scorpionfly males, and males of other non-human species, have an adaptation for rape, that, therefore, men do too"; www.aec.at/festival2000/texte/randy_

thornhill_e.htm, accessed on April 27, 2004. This raises the question of why we "must" look in the male psyche at all. Thornhill and Palmer seem to want to have it both ways.

30.   Thornhill and Palmer, *A Natural History of Rape,* p. 65.

31.   Richard Lewontin, *Biology as Ideology: The Doctrine of DNA* (New York: HarperPerennial, 1991), p. 95.

32.   Thornhill and Palmer, *A Natural History of Rape,* p. 51.

33.   Ibid., pp. 44, 71, 74. This could be scientifically tested, they suggest, by having men "masturbate to audio and video depictions of rapes and of consensual sex acts"; ibid., p. 74. It is unlikely that a proposal to show people videos of fake rapes, while letting them think these are real, would be approved by a university's human subjects committee, which, as Thornhill's employer, the University of New Mexico puts it, seeks to "ensure the safe and ethical conduct of research that ultimately will protect the rights and welfare of human subjects in an atmosphere of mutual trust and scientific integrity in the pursuit of knowledge"; www.unm.edu/~rcs/irb_mission_statement.html, accessed on April 27, 2004. Moreover, from the point of view of experimental design, we could not assume that men watching a video of a fake rape would identify with the rapist; they might identify with the woman's husband, or the woman herself.

34.   Thornhill and Palmer, *A Natural History of Rape,* p. 103.

35.   Ibid., pp. 116–18.

36.   Stephen Jay Gould, *The Structure of Evolutionary Theory* (Cambridge: Harvard University Press, Belknap Press, 2002), p. 1264.

37.   Lewontin, *Biology as Ideology.* See also Donna Haraway, "Animal Sociology and a Natural Economy of the Body Politic: A Political Physiology of Dominance," in *Simians, Cyborgs, and Women: The Reinvention of Nature* (New York: Routledge, 1991), pp. 7–20; Haraway, "The Biological Enterprise: Sex, Mind, and Profit from Human Engineering to Sociobiology," in *Simians, Cyborgs, and Women: The Reinvention of Nature,* pp. 43–68; A. Leah Vickers and Philip Kitcher, "Pop Sociobiology Reborn: The Evolutionary Psychology of Sex and Violence," in *Evolution, Gender, and Rape,* ed. Cheryl Brown Travis (Cambridge: MIT Press, 2003), pp. 139–68; Jerry A. Coyne, "Of Vice and Men: A Case Study in Evolutionary Psychology," in *Evolution, Gender, and Rape,* ed. Cheryl Brown Travis (Cambridge: MIT Press, 2003), pp. 171–89; Elisabeth A. Lloyd, "Violence against Science: Rape and Evolution," in *Evolution, Gender, and Rape,* ed. Cheryl Brown Travis (Cambridge: MIT Press, 2003), pp. 235–61.

38.   Thornhill and Palmer argue that their explanations are not "just-so" stories, because their evolutionary theory "provides criteria for determining whether a given aspect of an organism . . . is an adaptation"; Thornhill and Palmer, *A Natural History of Rape,* pp. 113–14. However, the criteria used by Thornhill and Palmer in the preceding pages—most of which are about how to

infer adaptation and function—are subjective, as we point out throughout this chapter.

39. Ibid., pp. 59–60.

40. Ibid., pp. 64–65.

41. See Heather Paxson, "Rationalizing Sex: Family Planning and the Making of Modern Lovers in Urban Greece," *American Ethnologist* 29, no. 2 (2002): 307–44.

42. We do not try to argue that there have been "rape-free" human societies; this would assume that rape is the same thing everywhere. Though for quite different reasons from Thornhill and Palmer, we also find ourselves unpersuaded by the univeralist arguments made in Peggy Reeves Sanday, *Female Power and Male Dominance: On the Origins of Sexual Inequality* (Cambridge: Cambridge University Press, 1981).

43. Claudia Card, "Rape as a Weapon of War," *Hypatia* 11, no. 4 (1996): 5–18.

44. Susan Gal and Gail Kligman, *The Politics of Gender after Socialism* (Princeton, N J · Princeton University Press, 2000), p. 27.

45. "Sexual Violence as a Weapon of War," part of the United Nations Children's Fund 1996 report *The State of the World's Children, 1996,* www.unicef.org/sowc96pk/sexviol.htm, accessed on April 27, 2004.

46. Marlise Simons, "For the First Time, Court Defines Rape a War Crime," *New York Times,* June 28, 1996.

47. "Sexual Violence as a Weapon of War."

48. Alexandra Stiglmayer, ed., *Mass Rape: The War against Women in Bosnia-Herzegovina,* trans. Marion Faber (Lincoln: University of Nebraska Press, 1994).

49. Veena Das, "Language and Body: Transactions in the Construction of Pain," in *Social Suffering,* ed. Arthur Kleinman, Veena Das, and Margaret Lock (Berkeley: University of California Press, 1997), pp. 67–91; quote is on p. 83.

50. Rwandan President Paul Kagame, quoted in Peter Landesman, "A Woman's Work," *New York Times Magazine* (September 16, 2002).

51. Thornhill and Palmer, *A Natural History of Rape,* p. 17.

52. Ruth Frankenberg, *The Social Construction of Whiteness: White Women, Race Matters* (Minneapolis: University of Minnesota Press, 1993), p. 73.

53. Angela Davis, "Rape, Racism, and the Myth of the Black Rapist," in *Women, Race, and Class* (New York: Vintage, 1981), pp. 172–201.

54. Ibid., p. 175.

55. "The myth of the black rapist . . . [must bear a good portion of the responsibility] for the failure of anti-rape theorists to seek the identity of the enormous numbers of anonymous rapists who remain unreported, untried, and unconvicted"; ibid., p. 199.

56. Peggy Reeves Sanday, *Fraternity Gang Rape: Sex, Brotherhood, and Privilege on Campus* (New York: New York University Press, 1990).

57.   Carol Delaney, "The Meaning of Paternity and the Virgin Birth Debate," *Man* 21, no. 3 (1986): 494–513.

58.   Emily Martin, "The Egg and the Sperm: How Science Has Constructed a Romance Based on Stereotypical Male-Female Roles," *Signs* 16 (1991): 485–501.

59.   See, for example, Beth Gerstein, "Survivorship: Bay Area Rape Crisis Counselors' Narratives of Rape, Sexuality, and Identity" (Ph.D. diss., Department of Anthropology, Stanford University, 1998). See also Cathy Winkler, *One Night: Realities of Rape* (Walnut Creek, Calif.: AltaMira Press, 2002).

60.   Carole S. Vance, "Pleasure and Danger: Toward a Politics of Sexuality," in *Pleasure and Danger: Exploring Female Sexuality,* ed. Carole S. Vance (Boston: Routledge and Kegan Paul, 1984), pp. 1–27.

61.   On male rape, see Richie J. McMullen, *Male Rape: Breaking the Silence on the Last Taboo* (London: GMP Publishers, 1990); Michael Scarce, *Male on Male Rape: The Hidden Toll of Stigma and Shame* (New York: Insight Books, 1997).

62.   Sanday, *Female Power and Male Dominance.* Psychoanalytic theorists might suggest on this evidence that, if there is any sort of analogy in the human male psyche to the "rape clamp" of the male scorpionfly, it would be the phallus, the symbolic complement to the penis that imbues maleness with a sense of authoritative power; however, this would be an ethnocentric view of human nature.

63.   See Emily Martin, "What Is 'Rape?'—Toward a Historical, Ethnographic Approach," in *Evolution, Gender, and Rape*, ed. Cheryl Brown Travis (Cambridge: MIT Press, 2003), pp. 363–81.

64.   Thornhill and Palmer, *A Natural History of Rape*, p. 179.

65.   Howard L. Kaye, *The Social Meaning of Modern Biology* (New Haven: Yale University Press, 1986).

66.   Thornhill and Palmer, *A Natural History of Rape*, p. 112.

67.   Ibid., p. 181.

68.   Barbara Ehrenreich, "How 'Natural' Is Rape?" *Time* 155, no. 4 (January 21, 2000), www.time.com/time/archive/preview/from_redirect/0,10987,1101000131 -38013,00.html, accessed on April 27, 2004.

69.   The State of Texas Commission on Law Enforcement, *Officer Standards and Education Course on Sexual Assault*, chap. 2: "Historical, Legal, and Cultural Background," www.utexas.edu/cee/dec/tcleose/asault/chapter2.html, accessed on April 27, 2004.

70.   Thornhill and Palmer, *A Natural History of Rape*, p. 181.

71.   Michael Ellison, "The Men Can't Help It," *The Guardian* (London), January 25, 2000, Guardian Features Pages, p. 4.

72.   Thornhill and Palmer, *A Natural History of Rape*, p. 84.

73.   Ibid., p. 191.

74.   Ibid., p. 96.

75.   Ibid., p. 93.

76. Ibid., p. 87.

77. Ibid.

78. Ibid., p. 1.

79. Rebecca Campbell, *Emotionally Involved: The Impact of Researching Rape* (New York: Routledge, 2001), p. 115.

80. Thornhill and Palmer, *A Natural History of Rape*, p. 3.

81. Bergen Evans, *The Natural History of Nonsense* (New York: A. A. Knopf, 1946), p. 8.

82. Robert John Russell, William R. Stoeger, and Francisco J. Ayala, eds., *Evolutionary and Molecular Biology: Scientific Perspectives on Divine Action* (Vatican City State: Vatican Observatory Publications, 1998).

83. George Ellis, "The Thinking Underlying the New 'Scientific' World-Views," in *Evolutionary and Molecular Biology: Scientific Perspectives on Divine Action*, ed. Robert John Russell, William R. Stoeger, and Francisco J. Ayala (Vatican City State: Vatican Observatory Publications, 1998), pp. 251–80.

84. Ellis, "Thinking," p. 251.

85. This argument has also been made from a secular point of view by Dorothy Nelkin, "Less Selfish Than Sacred? Genes and the Religious Impulse in Evolutionary Psychology," in *Alas, Poor Darwin: Arguments against Evolutionary Psychology*, ed. H. Rose and S. Rose (New York: Harmony Books, 2000), pp. 17–32.

86. Stephen Jay Gould, "Darwinian Fundamentalism," *New York Review of Books* 44, no. 10 (June 12, 1997): 34–37; Gould, "Evolution: The Pleasures of Pluralism," *New York Review of Books* 44, no. 11 (June 26, 1997): 47–52.

87. M. A. Corey, *The Natural History of Creation: Biblical Evolutionism and the Return of Natural Theology* (Lanham, Md.: University Press of America, 1995); quote is from http://michaelacorey.com/nathist.html, accessed on April 27, 2004.

88. Caryl Rivers and Rosalind Barnett, "A Misguided Effort to Simplify Rape: Male Gene Theory Simply Not Credible," *Boston Globe*, February 20, 2000, p. C2.

89. Ellison, "The Men Can't Help It," p. 4.

90. Daniel Cohen, *A Natural History of Unnatural Things* (New York: McCall, 1971).

11. ANTHROPOLOGY AND *THE BELL CURVE*

Epigraph: Franz Boas, "Recent Anthropology, II," *Science* 98 (1942): 334–36; quote is on 336.

1. R. Herrnstein and C. Murray, *The Bell Curve* (New York: Free Press, 1994).

2. A. Ryan, "Apocalypse Now?" *New York Review of Books* (November 17, 1994): 7.

3. F. Samelson, "On the Uses of History: The Case of *The Bell Curve*," *Journal of the History of the Behavioral Sciences* 33 (1997): 129–33.

4. R. Hofstadter, *Social Darwinism in American Thought* (Philadelphia: University of Pennsylvania Press, 1944).

5. W. G. Sumner, *The Challenge of Facts and Other Essays* (New Haven: Yale University Press, 1914), 57, 90.

6. F. Boas, *The Mind of Primitive Man* (New York: Macmillan, 1911), 17.

7. American eugenics differed from social Darwinism in being rooted in Mendelian genetics and in calling for government interventions, but it shared with social Darwinism the tenet that social inequalities are rooted in natural qualities.

8. P. Bowler, "Social Metaphors in Evolutionary Biology, 1879–1930: The Wider Dimension of Social Darwinism," in *Biology as Society, Society as Biology: Metaphors,* ed. S. Maason et al. (Amsterdam: Kluwer, 1995), 107–26; D. J. Kevles, *In the Name of Eugenics* (Berkeley: University of California Press, 1985).

9. C. S. Coon, *The Origin of Races* (New York: Alfred M. Knopf, 1962), ix–x.

10. H. Garrett and W. C. George, "Findings on Race Cited: White Man Declared 200,000 Years Ahead on Ladder of Evolution," letter to the editor, *New York Times,* October 24, 1962; C. Putnam, *These Are the Guilty,* 1963, pamphlet published and distributed by the National Putnam Letters Committee, Carleton S. Coon Papers, National Anthropological Archives, Washington, D.C.; cf. J. Marks, "Human Biodiversity as a Central Theme of Biological Anthropology: Then and Now," *Kroeber Anthropological Society Papers,* no. 84 (2000): 1–10.

11. A. Jensen, "How Much Can We Boost IQ and Scholastic Achievement?" *Harvard Educational Review* 39 (1969): 1–123.

12. S. J. Gould, *The Mismeasure of Man* (New York: W. W. Norton, 1981).

13. For example, R. R. R. Gates, *Human Ancestry* (Cambridge: Harvard University Press, 1948). To a botanical geneticist, the interbreeding criterion familiarly taught as the "biological species concept" carries less weight, as plants are quite profligate outside recognized species boundaries. Consequently the interfertility of human groups might not be as obvious a marker of unity of humans to a botanist as to a zoologist. On Gates's death, his position on the *Mankind Quarterly* was offered to Carleton Coon, who declined, saying, "I will be very glad to get your monographs and also your magazine, to which I would be happy to subscribe, but I fear that for a professional anthropologist to accept membership on your board would be the kiss of death, here in the so-called land of the free and home of the brave"; Coon to R. Gayre, November 9, 1962, Carleton S. Coon Papers, National Anthropological Archives, Washington, D.C.

14. J. B. S. Haldane, "More on 'Scientific' Racism," *Current Anthropology* 3 (1962): 300.

15. H. Garrett, "The Equalitarian Dogma," *Mankind Quarterly* 1 (1960): 253–57; A. S. Winston, "Science in the Service of the Far Right: Henry E. Garrett, the IAAEE, and the Liberty Lobby," *Journal of Social Issues* 54 (1998): 179–210.

16. J. Comas, "'Scientific'" Racism Again?" *Current Anthropology* 2 (1961): 303–40.

17. B. Škerlj, "The *Mankind Quarterly*," *Man* 60 (1960): 172–73; U. R. Ehrenfels, "Critical Paragraphs Deleted," *Current Anthropology* 3 (1962): 154–55.

18. S. Genoves, "Racism and the *Mankind Quarterly*," *Science* 134 (1961): 1928–32.

19. G. A. Harrison, "The *Mankind Quarterly*," *Man* 61 (1961): 163–64; Roland Littlewood, "*Mankind Quarterly* Again," *Anthropology Today* 11, no. 2 (1995).

20. A. Miller, "Professors of Hate," *Rolling Stone* (October 20, 1994); J. Sedgwick, "Inside the Pioneer Fund," *GQ* (November 1994); C. Lane, "The Tainted Sources of 'The Bell Curve,' " *New York Review of Books* (December 1, 1994): 14–19.

21. J. P. Rushton, *Race, Evolution, and Behavior: A Life-History Approach* (New Brunswick, N.J.: Transaction, 1995).

22. Miller, "Professors of Hate." It strikes me that Rushton's thought, taken at face value, might well have been adopted as a slogan by feminists. Mercifully, it was not.

23. D. P. Barash, review of *Race, Evolution, and Behavior,* by J. Philippe Rushton, *Animal Behaviour* 49 (1995): 1131–33.

24. J. P. Rushton, personal communication.

25. See L. Lieberman, "How 'Caucasoids' Got Such Big Crania and Why They Shrank: From Morton to Rushton," *Current Anthropology* 42 (2001): 69–96.

26. S. Fraser, ed., *The Bell Curve Wars: Race, Intelligence, and the Future of America* (New York: Basic Books, 1995); R. Jacoby and N. Glauberman, *The Bell Curve Debate* (New York: Times Books, 1995); J. L. Kincheloe, S. R. Steinberg, and A. D. Gresson III, eds., *Measured Lies: The Bell Curve Examined* (New York: St. Martin's Press, 1996).

27. D. J. Kevles, "Genetics, Race, and IQ: Historical Reflections from Binet to *The Bell Curve*," *Contention* 5 (1995): 3–18.

28. M. Mead, *Coming of Age in Samoa* (New York: William Morrow, 1928).

29. S. D. Porteus, *The Psychology of a Primitive People* (New York: Longman's, Green, 1931).

30. O. Klineberg, *Race Differences* (New York: Harper and Brothers, 1935).

31. Summarized in O. Klineberg, "Race and Psychology," in *Race, Science, and Society*, ed. L. Kuper (New York: UNESCO and Columbia University Press, 1975), 173–207.

32. S. J. Ceci, *On Intelligence . . . More or Less: A Bioecological Treatise on Intellectual Development* (Englewood Cliffs, N.J.: Prentice Hall, 1990); J. R. Mercer, "Ethnic Differences in IQ Scores: What Do They Mean?" *Hispanic Journal of Behavioral Sciences* 10 (1988): 199–218; quote is from Herrnstein and Murray, *The Bell Curve*, 305.

33. C. S. Fischer, M. Hout, M. S. Jankowski, S. R. Lucas, A. Swidler, and

K. Voss, *Inequality by Design: Cracking the Bell Curve Myth* (Princeton, N.J.: Princeton University Press, 1996), 77.

34. Ibid., 195.

35. Klineberg, "Race and Psychology," 183; B. Singer and C. Ryff, "Racial and Ethnic Inequalities in Health: Environmental, Physiological, and Psychosocial Pathways," in *Intelligence, Genes, and Success: Scientists Respond to* The Bell Curve, ed. B. Devlin, S. E. Fienberg, D. P. Resnick, and K. Roeder (New York: Springer-Verlag, 1997), 89–122.

36. R. J. David and J. W. Collins Jr., "Differing Birth Weights among Infants of U.S.-Born Blacks, African-Born Blacks, and U.S.-Born Whites," *New England Journal of Medicine* 337 (1997): 1209–14.

37. C. Brigham, *A Study of American Intelligence* (Princeton, N.J.: Princeton University Press, 1923), 190.

38. Klineberg, "Race and Psychology."

39. J. Ogbu, "Cultural Amplifiers of Intelligence: IQ and Minority Status in Cross-Cultural Perspective," in *Race and Intelligence: Separating Science from Myth,* ed. J. Fish (Mahwah, N.J.: Lawrence Erlbaum, 2002), 241–78; J. Ogbu and P. Stern, "Caste Status and Intellectual Development" in *Environmental Effects on Cognitive Abilities,* ed. R. J. Sternberg and E. L. Grigorenko (Mahwah, N.J.: Lawrence Erlbaum, 2001), 3–37.

40. R. Lynn, *Dysgenics: Genetic Deterioration in Modern Populations* (Westport, Conn.: Praeger, 1996).

41. E. Sober, "Separating Nature and Nurture," in *Genetics and Criminal Behavior,* ed. D. Wasserman and R. Wachbroit (New York: Cambridge University Press, 2001), 47–78.

42. M. Daniels, B. Devlin, and K. Roeder, "Of Genes and IQ," in *Intelligence, Genes, and Success: Scientists Respond to* The Bell Curve, ed. B. Devlin, S. E. Fienberg, D. P. Resnick, and K. Roeder (New York: Springer-Verlag, 1997), 45–70.

43. J. Hartung, "On the Geneticness of Traits: Beyond $h^2 = V_g / V_p$," *Current Anthropology* 21 (1980): 131–32.

44. R. C. Lewontin, "Race and Intelligence," *Bulletin of the Atomic Scientists* 26, no. 3 (1970): 2–8.

45. N. Block, "How Heritability Misleads about Race," *Cognition* 56 (1995): 99–128.

46. Ibid.

47. Ibid., 118, emphasis in original.

48. B. Devlin, S. E. Fienberg, D. P. Resnick, and K. Roeder, eds., *Intelligence, Genes, and Success: Scientists Respond to* The Bell Curve (New York: Springer-Verlag, 1997); J. Horn, "Selections of Evidence, Misleading Assumptions, and Oversimplifications: The Political Message of *The Bell Curve,*" in *Race and Intelligence: Separating Science from Myth,* ed. J. Fish. (Mahwah, N.J.: Lawrence Erlbaum, 2002).

49. J. R. Flynn, "Massive IQ Gains in Fourteen Nations: What IQ Tests Really Measure," *Psychological Bulletin* 101 (1987): 171–91.

50. A. Anderson, "The Great Japanese IQ Increase," *Nature* 297 (1982): 180–81.

51. D. Wahlsten, "The Malleability of Intelligence Is Not Constrained by Heritability," in *Intelligence, Genes, and Success: Scientists Respond to* The Bell Curve, ed. B. Devlin, S. E. Fienberg, D. P. Resnick, and K. Roeder (New York: Springer-Verlag, 1997), 78.

52. C. Capron and M. Duyme, "Assessment of Effects of Socio-Economic Status on IQ in a Full Cross-Fostered Study," *Nature* 340 (1989): 552–54.

53. C. Jencks and M. Phillips, "America's Next Achievement Test: Closing the Black-White Test Score Gap," *American Prospect* 40 (1998): 48.

54. Fischer et al. note that Herrnstein and Murray's own data do not even fall readily into a bell-shaped curve and had to be extensively transformed (32 ff).

55. Boas, *The Mind of Primitive Man*.

56. Arthur de Gobineau, *The Inequality of Human Races*, trans. Adrian Collins (1854; reprint, New York: Putnam, 1915), 37.

57. J. Marks, "Folk Heredity," in *Race and Intelligence: Separating Science from Myth*, ed. J. Fish (New York: Lawrence Erlbaum, 2002), 95–116.

58. J. J. Jackson Jr., "'In Ways Unacademical': The Reception of Carleton S. Coon's *The Origin of Races*," *Journal of the History of Biology* 34 (2001): 247–85.

59. F. Bacon, *Of the Proficience and Advancement of Learning* (London: Henrie Tomes, 1605).

60. H. F. Weyher, preface to *The Science of Human Diversity: A History of the Pioneer Fund*, by R. Lynn (Lanham, Md.: University Press of America, 2001), pp. ix–lxii.

61. J. P. Rushton, "The Pioneer Fund and the Scientific Study of Human Differences," *Albany Law Review* 65 (2003): 207–61; W. H. Tucker, *The Funding of Scientific Racism: Wickliffe Draper and the Pioneer Fund* (Urbana: University of Illinois Press, 2002); Tucker, "A Closer Look at the Pioneer Fund: Response to Rushton," *Albany Law Review* 66 (2003): 1145–59; P. A. Lombardo, "'The American Breed': Nazi Eugenics and the Origins of the Pioneer Fund," *Albany Law Review* 65 (2002): 743–830; Lombardo, "Pioneer's Big Lie," *Albany Law Review* 66 (2003): 1125–44.

62. V. Sarich and F. Miele, *Race: The Reality of Human Differences* (Boulder, Colo.: Westview, 2004); see also R. Proctor, review of *Race: The Reality of Human Differences*, by Vincent Sarich and Frank Miele, *Nature* 428 (2004).

Suggested Further Reading

The chapters in this book can be grouped with the readings suggested below to build a syllabus for a course about anthropology's engagement with important contemporary issues. The sections below correspond to the outline of the book. We suggest essays or excerpts by each pundit addressed in the preceding chapters so that students can read the original arguments. We also include references to one or two critiques of each pundit's argument. Following these references are suggestions for readings by anthropologists and other social scientists who provide alternative analyses. Using this outline, a semester's course would cover the international system, warfare and conflict, globalization, class, gendered violence, and race.

EXCERPTS FROM HUNTINGTON AND HIS CRITICS

Benthall, Jonathan. "Imagined Civilizations?" *Anthropology Today* 18, no. 6 (2002): 1–2.

Huntington, Samuel. "The Clash of Civilizations?" *Foreign Affairs* 72, no. 3 (1993): 22–49.

———. "The West, Civilizations, and Civilization." In *The Clash of Civilizations: Remaking of World Order*, pp. 301–21. New York: Touchstone, 1996.

Kroeber, A. L. "The Delimitation of Civilization." *Journal of the History of Ideas* 14 (1953): 264–75.

Said, Edward. "The Clash of Definitions: On Samuel Huntington." In *Reflections on Exile and Other Essays*, pp. 569–90. Cambridge: Harvard University Press, 2000.

EXCERPTS FROM KAPLAN AND HIS CRITICS

Kagan, Robert. "The Return of Cheap Pessimism: Inside the Limo." *New Republic Online* (April 10, 2000).

Kaplan, Robert D. *Balkan Ghosts: A Journey through History.* New York: St. Martin's Press, 1996.

———. "The Coming Anarchy." In *The Coming Anarchy: Shattering the Dreams of the Post Cold War,* chap. 1. New York: Random House, 2000.

———. "Was Democracy Just a Moment?" In *The Coming Anarchy: Shattering the Dreams of the Post Cold War,* chap. 2. New York: Random House, 2000.

ALTERNATIVE WORKS ON CONFLICT AND WARFARE

In General

Chomsky, Noam. *Hegemony or Survival: America's Quest for Global Dominance.* New York: Metropolitan Books, 2003.

Gusterson, Hugh. "Nuclear Weapons and the Other in the Western Imagination." *Cultural Anthropology* 14, no. 1 (1999): 111–43.

Johnson, Chalmers. *The Sorrows of Empire: Militarism, Secrecy, and the End of the Republic.* New York: Metropolitan Books, 2004.

Kaldor, Mary. *New and Old Wars: Organized Violence in a Global Era.* Cambridge, U.K.: Polity Press, 1999.

Klare, Michael. *Resource Wars: The New Landscape of Global Conflict.* New York: Metropolitan Books, 2001.

Lifton, Robert Jay. *Superpower Syndrome: America's Apocalyptic Confrontation with the World.* New York: Thunder's Mouth Press, 2003.

Lutz, Catherine. *Homefront: A Military City and the American Twentieth Century.* Boston: Beacon, 2002.

Payne, Richard. "Foreign Policy Begins at Home: Cultural Influences on U.S. Behavior Abroad." In *The Clash of Distant Cultures: Values, Interests, and Force in American Foreign Policy*, pp. 1–34. New York: State University of New York Press, 1995.

Stern, Jessica. *Terror in the Name of God: Why Religious Militants Kill.* New York: Ecco Books, 2003.

In the Balkans

Christie, Deborah. *Bosnia: We Are All Neighbors.* London: Granada TV, 1993. Film.

Duijzings, Ger. "Albanian Dervishes versus Bosnian Ulema: The Revival of Popular Sufism in Kosovo." In *Religion and the Politics of Identity in Kosovo,* pp. 106–31. London: Hurst and Company, 1999.

Malcolm, Noel. *Kosovo: A Short History.* New York: New York University Press, 1998.

Weiner, Myron. "The Macedonian Syndrome: An Historical Model of International Relations and Political Development." *World Politics* 23, no. 4 (1971): 665–83.

In Africa

Besteman, Catherine. "Representing Violence and 'Othering' Somalia." *Cultural Anthropology* 11, no. 1 (1996): 120–33.

Gourevitch, Philip. *We Wish to Inform You That Tomorrow We Will Be Killed with Our Families: Stories from Rwanda.* New York: Farrar, Straus, and Giroux, 1998.

Reno, William. *Warlord Politics and African States.* Boulder, Colo.: Lynne Rienner, 1998.

EXCERPTS FROM FRIEDMAN

Friedman, Thomas L. "Diary: Travels in a World without Walls: September 11, 2001–July 3, 2002." In *Longitudes and Attitudes: Exploring the World after September 11,* pp. 295–379. New York: Farrar, Straus, and Giroux, 2002.

———. "The Groundswell (or the Backlash against the Backlash)." In *The Lexus and the Olive Tree,* pp. 348–64. New York: Anchor Books, 2000.

———. "Prologue: The Super-Story." In *Longitudes and Attitudes: Exploring the World after September 11,* pp. 1–11. New York: Farrar, Straus, and Giroux, 2002.

ALTERNATIVE READINGS ON GLOBALIZATION

de Martino, George. *Global Economy, Global Justice: Theoretical Objections and Policy Alternatives to Neoliberalism.* London: Routledge, 2000.

Edelman, Marc, and Angelique Haugerud, eds. *Anthropology of Development and Globalization: From Classical Political Economy to Contemporary Neoliberalism.* Malden, Mass.: Blackwell Press, 2005.

Farmer, Paul. *Pathologies of Power: Health, Human Rights, and the New War on the Poor.* Berkeley: University of California Press, 2003.

Graeber, David. "The Globalization Movement and the New Left." In *Implicating Empire: Globalization and Resistance in the Twenty-first Century*, ed. Stanley Aronowitz and Heather Gautney. New York: Basic Books, 2003.

———. "The Globalization Movement: Some Points of Clarification." *Items and Issues* (Social Science Research Council, New York) 2, nos. 3–4 (2001): 12–14.

Inda, Jonathan Xavier, and Renato Rosaldo, eds. *The Anthropology of Globalization: A Reader*. Malden, Mass.: Blackwell Publishers, 2002.

Nordstrom, Carolyn. *Shadows of War: Violence, Power, and International Profiteering in the Twenty-first Century*. Berkeley: University of California Press, 2004.

Stiglitz, Joseph E. *Globalization and Its Discontents*. New York: W. W. Norton, 2002.

Wedel, Janine. *Collision and Collusion: The Strange Case of Western Aid to Eastern Europe, 1989–98*. New York: St. Martin's Press, 1998.

EXCERPTS FROM D'SOUZA

D'Souza, Dinesh. "The Lottery of Success: Who Wins, Who Loses." In *The Virtue of Prosperity: Finding Values in an Age of Techno-Affluence*, chap. 4. New York: Free Press, 2000.

———. "Technology and Moral Progress." *Red Herring* (January 15, 2002).

———. "Two Cheers for Colonialism." *Chronicle of Higher Education* (May 10, 2002).

ALTERNATIVE READINGS ON CLASS IN THE UNITED STATES

Bourgois, Philippe. *In Search of Respect: Selling Crack in el Barrio*. Cambridge: Cambridge University Press, 1995.

Dodson, Lisa. *Don't Call Us Out of Name: The Untold Lives of Women and Girls in America*. Boston: Beacon, 1999.

Ehrenreich, Barbara. *Nickel and Dimed: On (Not) Getting By in America*. New York: Metropolitan Books, 2001.

Gilliom, John. *Overseers of the Poor: Surveillance, Resistance, and the Limits of Privacy*. Chicago: University of Chicago Press, 2001.

Henwood, Doug. *After the New Economy*. New York: New Press, 2003.

Hochschild, Arlie, and Barbara Ehrenreich, eds. *Global Woman: Nannies, Maids, and Sex Workers in the New Economy*. New York: Metropolitan Books, 2003.

Lind, Michael. "Are We Still a Middle-Class Nation?" *Atlantic Monthly* (January–February 2004).

Newman, Katherine S. *No Shame in My Game: The Working Poor in the Inner City*. New York: Knopf and the Russell Sage Foundation, 1999.

EXCERPTS FROM THORNHILL AND PALMER

Buss, David M. "Evolutionary Psychology: A New Paradigm for Psychological Science." *Psychological Inquiry* 6 (1995): 1–30.

Thornhill, Randy, and Craig T. Palmer. "Why Men Rape." *The Sciences* 40 (2000): 30–36.

Thornhill, Randy, and Craig T. Palmer. *A Natural History of Rape: Biological Bases of Sexual Coercion,* chaps. 1, 3, 9. Cambridge: MIT Press, 2000.

ALTERNATIVE READINGS ON RAPE

Brownmiller, Susan. *Against Our Will: Men, Women, and Rape.* New York: Simon and Schuster, 1975.

Fausto-Sterling, Anne. "The Five Sexes." *The Sciences* (March–April 1993): 20–24.

Hubbard, Ruth. "Rethinking Women's Biology." In *The Politics of Women's Biology,* pp. 119–29. New Brunswick: Rutgers, 1990.

Lewontin, Richard. "A Tale Told in Textbooks." In *Biology as Ideology: The Doctrine of DNA.* New York: HarperPerennial, 1991.

Lloyd, Elisabeth A. "Violence against Science: Rape and Evolution." In *Evolution, Gender, and Rape,* ed. Cheryl Brown Travis, pp. 235–61. Cambridge: MIT Press, 2003.

Martin, Emily. "What Is 'Rape'?: Toward a Historical, Ethnographic Approach." In *Evolution, Gender, and Rape,* ed. Cheryl Brown Travis, pp. 363–81. Cambridge: MIT Press, 2003.

EXCERPTS FROM MURRAY AND HERRNSTEIN AND THEIR CRITICS

Allen, A., et al. "The Bell Curve: Statement by the NIH-DOE Joint Working Group on the Ethical, Legal, and Social Implications of Human Genome Research." *American Journal of Human Genetics* 59 (1996): 487–88.

Fraser, Steven, ed. *Bell Curve Wars: Intelligence and the Future of America.* New York: Basic Books, 1995.

Murray, C., and R. J. Herrnstein. "Race, Genes, and I.Q.—an Apologia." *New Republic* 211 (October 31, 1994): 27–37.

ALTERNATIVE READINGS ON RACE

American Anthropological Association. *Statement on "Race."* May 17, 1998. www.aaanet.org/stmts/racepp.htm.

Fish, Jefferson M., ed. *Race and Intelligence: Separating Science from Myth.* Mahwah, N.J.: Erlbaum, 2002.

Kenny, M. G. "Toward a Racial Abyss: Eugenics, Wickliffe Draper, and the Origins of the Pioneer Fund." *Journal of the History of the Behavioral Sciences* 38 (2002): 259–83.

Marks, Jonathan. *What It Means to Be 98% Chimpanzee.* Berkeley: University of California Press, 2002.

Montagu, Ashley. *Man's Most Dangerous Myth: The Fallacy of Race.* 6th ed. Walnut Creek, Calif.: AltaMira Press, 1997.

Contributors

CATHERINE BESTEMAN is Associate Professor of Anthropology at Colby College. She is author of *Unraveling Somalia: Race, Violence, and the Legacy of Slavery* (University of Pennsylvania Press, 1999) and editor of *Violence: A Reader* (Palgrave and New York University Press, 2002).

TONE BRINGA is a Senior Researcher at the Chr. Michelsen Institute. With director Debbie Christie, she made the documentary film *Bosnia: We Are All Neighbors* for the Disappearing World Series of Granada Television. She is author of *Being Muslim the Bosnian Way: Identity and Community in a Central Bosnian Village* (Princeton University Press, 1995).

KEITH BROWN holds a Ph.D. in anthropology from the University of Chicago and is Assistant Research Professor at the Thomas J. Watson Institute for International Studies at Brown University. He is author of *The Past in Question: Modern Macedonia and the Uncertainties of Nation* (Princeton University Press, 2003), and a number of other publications focusing on the role of culture in Balkan politics and history.

HUGH GUSTERSON is Associate Professor of Anthropology at MIT. He is author of *Nuclear Rites: A Weapons Laboratory at the End of the Cold War* (University of

California Press, 1996) and *People of the Bomb: Portraits of America's Nuclear Complex* (University of Minnesota Press, 2004). His articles have appeared in numerous academic journals as well as in the *Los Angeles Times,* the *Boston Globe,* the *San Francisco Chronicle,* the *Oakland Tribune, Tikkun, New Scientist,* and *The Sciences.*

ANGELIQUE HAUGERUD is Associate Professor of Anthropology at Rutgers University. She is author of *The Culture of Politics in Modern Kenya* (Cambridge University Press, 1995), coeditor (with M. Priscilla Stone and Peter D. Little) of *Commodities and Globalization: Anthropological Perspectives* (Rowman and Littlefield, 2000), and coeditor (with Marc Edelman) of *Anthropology of Development and Globalization: From Classical Political Economy to Contemporary Neoliberalism* (Blackwell, 2005).

STEFAN HELMREICH is Associate Professor of Anthropology at MIT. His book *Silicon Second Nature: Culturing Artificial Life in a Digital World* (University of California Press, 1998) examines the practices of theoretical biologists at the Santa Fe Institute for the Sciences of Complexity in New Mexico and explores the narratives scientists employ to enliven the evolutionary worlds they simulate in silicon. His latest research, reported in "Trees and Seas of Information: Alien Kinship and the Biopolitics of Gene Transfer in Marine Biology and Biotechnology" (*American Ethnologist* 30, no. 3 [2003]: 341–59), concerns the ways marine biologists are using genomics and biotechnology to reimagine and reframe their scientific portraits of the ocean.

ELLEN HERTZ is Professor of Anthropology at the Institute of Ethnology at Neuchâtel, Switzerland. She works in the area of legal and institutional anthropology and has published on China (*The Trading Crowd: An Ethnography of the Shanghai Stock Market* [Cambridge University Press, 1998]) and on financial workers and the welfare state.

JONATHAN MARKS is a biological anthropologist currently teaching at the University of North Carolina at Charlotte. His primary area of research is molecular anthropology—the application of genetic data to illuminate our place in the natural order—or more broadly, the area of overlap between (scientific) genetic data and (humanistic) self-comprehension. His research has been published in scientific and scholarly journals ranging from *Nature* through the *Journal of Human Evolution* to *History and Philosophy of the Life Sciences;* and he is the coauthor of *Evolutionary Anthropology* (Harcourt, Brace, Jovanovich, 1993) and author of *Human Biodiversity* (Aldine de Gruyter, 1995) and *What It Means to Be 98% Chimpanzee* (University of California Press, 2002), which was awarded the W. W. Howells Prize in Biological Anthropology from the American Anthropological Association.

LAURA NADER is Professor of Anthropology, University of California, Berkeley. Among her published books are *Harmony Ideology: Justice and Control in a Zapotec Mountain Village* (Stanford University Press, 1991); *Naked Science: Anthropological Inquiry into Boundaries, Power, and Knowledge* (Routledge, 1996); and *The Life of the Law: Anthropological Projects* (University of California Press, 2002).

CAROLYN NORDSTROM is Associate Professor of Anthropology, University of Notre Dame. Her academic books include *Shadows of War: Violence, Power, and International Profiteering in the Twenty-first Century* (University of California Press, 2004); *A Different Kind of War Story* (University of Pennsylvania Press, 1997); *Fieldwork under Fire: Contemporary Stories of Violence and Survival* (University of California Press, 1995); and *The Paths to Domination, Resistance, and Terror* (University of California Press, 1992). She has written over three dozen articles on issues of political violence and peace-building, war economics and transnational criminal systems, cultures of globalization, gender and children in war zones, and cultural theory. She serves as associate editor for several journals and book series and is active with a number of international grants and symposia (the John D. and Catherine T. MacArthur Foundation, United States Institute of Peace, and Social Science Research Council).

HEATHER PAXSON has a Ph.D. in anthropology from Stanford University (1998) and is Lecturer in Anthropology at Massachusetts Institute of Technology. She is the author of *Making Modern Mothers: Ethics and Family Planning in Urban Greece* (University of California Press, 2004).

KATH WESTON directs the Women, Gender, and Sexuality program at Harvard University. She is the author of several books, including *Gender in Real Time: Power and Transience in a Visual Age* (Routledge, 2002) and *Long Slow Burn: Sexuality and Social Science* (Routledge, 1998).

Acknowledgments

Some of the essays in this volume were first presented at a roundtable at the American Anthropological Association meetings in 2000. Thank you to everyone who skipped the megasession on Patrick Tierney's *Darkness in El Dorado* to attend our roundtable; the stimulating and supportive feedback we received at the first public presentation of this project let us know we were doing something important and helped us to do it better.

In 2001, MIT's anthropology program kindly funded a two-day workshop that enabled contributors to this volume to meet and discuss one another's papers in detail. This greatly improved the quality of the final book. A number of discussants also attended this workshop and provided invaluable commentary: George Armelegos, John Borneman, Evelynn Hammonds, Michael Herzfeld, Jean Jackson, Anastasia Karakasidou, Debra Martin, Pauline Peters, Anne Pollock, Susan Silbey, Chris Walley, Kay Warren, Jenny White, and Eric Worby.

The MIT grant also enabled us to hire a professional editor to help us bring the essays into closer alignment with one another while making them more accessible to a general audience. We are grateful to MIT for its financial support and to Teresa Lawson for her fine editing skills.

We are also grateful to Bill Beeman and the two anonymous reviewers commissioned by the University of California Press for their thoughtful comments, and to Naomi Schneider and Rob Borofsky, the indefatigable editors of the California Series in Public Anthropology, for their commitment to this project from the first moment they learned of it and for their shrewd advice throughout. Thanks also to Chris Walley, who, at the eleventh hour, dropped everything and stepped in with emergency advice for the treatment of an introduction that was refusing to get better; and thanks to Sandy Brown for making sure the manuscript obeyed the rules. We are also grateful to Charlotte Sheedy for her assistance in negotiating our contract.

Finally, thanks to our spouses, Jorge Acero and Allison Macfarlane, for their patience and support along the long and winding road that finally brought this project to fruition.

Index

paternity reliability: rape and, 196–98; sexual
  selection and, 187
Peru, extrastate economy in, 153
Phillips, M., 223
Pioneer Fund, 213–14, 217, 220, 227
plantation slavery, rape under, 191, 194–96
pornography: illicit trade in, 143–46; rape
  and, 187
Portugal, Angolan diamond smuggling and,
  148–50
poverty: class issues and, 170–79; D'Souza's
  discussion of, 17–23, 155–61, 166–70;
  Friedman's rationalization of, 113–14
poverty line: development of, 162–63; as
  illusion, 167–70
pregnancy, rape and, 192–94, 201–2
prosperity, D'Souza's concept of, 158–61
psychological mechanisms, rape in context
  of, 183–85
Public Citizen's Global Trade Watch, 243n29
public policy: impact of The Bell Curve on,
  206–7; science and, 209–14
pundit, defined, 2
punditry: American influence in, 4, 229n3;
  anthropological research on, 3–6; evolution of, 1–6
Putnam, Carleton, 212
Putnam, Robert, 235n43

race: D'Souza's disregard of, 156–61, 169;
  intelligence and, 21–22, 215–27; Kaplan's
  overgeneralizations concerning, 87–101;
  parenting skills and, 223; pundits' discussion of, 17–23; rape and, 194–96, 253n55;
  Rwanda genocide and, 94–95; social Darwinism and eugenics and, 211–14; Somalia crisis and, 95–97
Rainforest Action Network, 118
rape: natural history context of, 182–85; in
  nonhumans, 185–87; pundits' discussion
  of, 18–23; Thornhill/Palmer history of,
  180–205; victims of, 200–202; as war
  crime, 191–94
Ravan and Eddie, 175
Reagan, Ronald, 129–30, 133–36
realism: in Friedman's globalization ideology,
  107–20; in Kaplan's work, 98–99
religion: Bosnian crisis and, 67–68; rape and,
  203–5

Revolutionary United Front (Sierra Leone), 93
Richards, Paul, 87, 93
Rivers, Caryl, 204–5
Rolling Stone, 213
Rosaldo, Renato, 31, 231n13
Rosslyn, Felicity, 78
Rubin, Robert, 107
Rupert, Mark, 107
Rushton, J. Phillipe, 213–14, 227
Russia, extrastate economy in, 153
Rwanda: anthropological research on geno-
  cide in, 94–95, 112, 239n8, 241n17; eco-
  nomic inequalities in, 98; Friedman's dis-
  cussion of, 111–12, 134–35; mass rape in,
  20, 194, 200
Ryan, Alan, 208–9

Sachs, Jeffrey, 116
Said, Edward: Huntington critiqued by, 30–
  31; on multiculturalism, 35; on punditry, 3
Sanday, Peggy Reeves, 196–98, 253n42, 254n62
Sarich, V., 227
Savimbi, Jonas, 147
Schmitt, Eric, 164–65
Schneider, David, 45–46, 51–52
Schumpeter, Joseph, 136–37
Science magazine, 213
scientific research: distortion of, in Yugoslavia, 74–75; Huntington's misuse of,
  38–40; intelligence testing and, 216–17;
  misuse of, in The Bell Curve, 207–9; on
  rape, 181–82, 202–4
segmentation, anthropological concept of,
  48–49
segregationism, eugenics and, 212–14
Semai culture, study of, 32
"Senseless in Seattle," 102, 109–10, 118–20,
  240n6
September 11 attacks, view of Islamic culture
  and, 36–38
Serbia, Kaplan's discussion of, 65–80
sex, anthropological research about, 196–98
sex and pornography industry, as illicit economy, 143–46
sexual contract, rape and, 251n26
sexual selection, rape and, 182–85
Sierra Club, 243n29
Sierra Leone: anthropological research in, 93;
  illicit economy in, 149–50

simplistic reasoning, Friedman's use of,
132–33
slaves, rape of, 191, 194–96
social capital, kinship and, 59, 235n43
social Darwinism: eugenics and, 209–14,
256n7; intelligence and, 21–22; post–cold
war era, 10; rape in context of, 183–85,
250n11
socioeconomic status, intelligence testing
and, 216–19
Somalia, anthropological research on, 95–97
Soros, George, 136
South Africa: arms smuggling in, 150–51;
intelligence testing in, 220; Kaplan's discussion of, 92
Spearman, Charles, 215
Spencer, Hamish, 187
Spengler, Oswald, 44
Sri Lanka, 118
State of Texas Commission on Law Enforce-
ment, 200
statistical evidence. D'Souza's use of, 155–
61; heritability and, 222–23; misuse of, in
The Bell Curve, 208–9
Stiglitz, James, 116
Stockholm International Peace Research
Institute, 151, 247n20
Strange, Susan, 152–53, 247n23
"strategic hamlet" policy, 11–12; Huntington
as architect of, 24
structural violence, Friedman's discussion of,
113
Summers, Lawrence, 107
Sumner, William Graham, 209
Sunni Islam, Kosovo conflict and, 55

Taylor, Christopher, 94–95
Tenth Circle of Hell, The, 76
Terkel, Studs, 156
Terman, Lewis, 215
terrorism, impact on punditry of, 5–6
Third World cultures: class issues in, 170–79;
Friedman's contempt for, 124–29; Hunt-
ington on migration from, 27; Hunting-
ton's view of, 26–27; illicit economies in,
140–42, 152–53; Kaplan's view of, 83–
101; pundits' view of, 7–9
Thornhill, Randy, 9, 17–23, 180–205
Thrivers, Robert, 250n11

Tito, Josip, 73, 193
Todorova, Maria, 61, 78
Toynbee, Arnold, 44
tradition, Friedman's view of, 110–11
transnational companies, illicit economies
and, 152–53
travel journalism: anthropological research
and, 87–92; Friedman's work as, 107–10,
122–27
Trobriand Islanders, 196–97
Truth and Reconciliation Commission, 150
Tucker, W. H., 227
Tudjman, Franjo, 74–75
Turkey, Kaplan's discussion of, 91
Tutsi refugee crisis, 94–95
Tylor, Edward, 210

United States: Africa as threat to, 99–101;
extrastate economy in, 153
United Steelworkers of America, 118
universities, pundits at, 3–4
upward mobility, D'Souza's discussion of,
167–70
Uvin, Peter, 94–95, 98

Varieties of Ethnic Experience, 157–58
Victoria's Secret, 118
violence: Balkans and, 61–63, 71, 74–77;
cultural weakness linked to, 91–92
Virtue of Prosperity, The, 17–18, 154–79

Wahlsten, Douglas, 223
Wallerstein, Immanuel, 44
Wall Street Journal Europe, 81–82
Washington Week in Review, 106
wealth: democracy threatened by, 130–31;
D'Souza's discussion of, 17–23, 154–79;
globalization and, 116–17
Wedel, Janine, 135
Weiner, Myron, 234n16
Welfare Racism, 159–60
West, Rebecca, 76–80
Western culture: historical changes in, 32–33;
Huntington on superiority of, 11, 28–29,
40–41; intelligence testing and, 215–17,
224–27; Kaplan on disintegration of, 99–
101; Kaplan's view of, 86–101; militarism
in, 39–40; multiculturalism and, 34–36
Weston, Kath, 18, 51, 154–79

Text: 10/14 Palatino
Display: Univers Consensed Light 47; Bauer Bodoni
Compositor: BookMatters, Berkeley
Indexer: Diana Witt